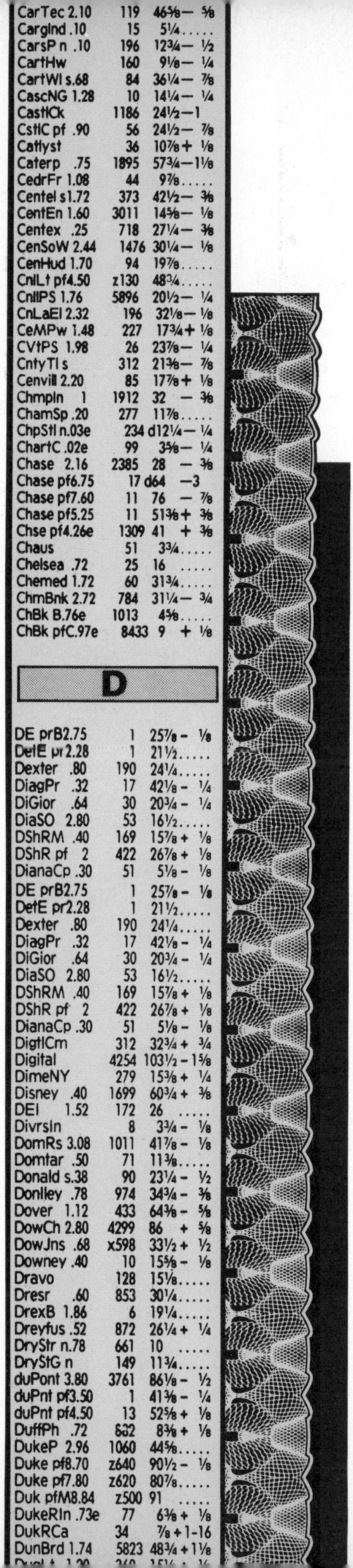
CarTec 2.10 119 46⅝— ⅝
CargInd .10 15 5¼.....
CarsP n .10 196 12¾— ½
CartHw 160 9⅛— ¼
CartWl s.68 84 36¼— ⅞
CascNG 1.28 10 14¼— ¼
CastlCk 1186 24½—1
CstlC pf .90 56 24½— ⅞
Catlyst 36 10⅞+ ⅛
Caterp .75 1895 57¾—1⅛
CedrFr 1.08 44 9⅞.....
Centel s1.72 373 42½— ⅜
CentEn 1.60 3011 14⅝— ⅛
Centex .25 718 27¼— ⅜
CenSoW 2.44 1476 30¼— ⅛
CenHud 1.70 94 19⅞.....
CnlLt pf4.50 z130 48¾.....
CnlIPS 1.76 5896 20½— ¼
CnLaEl 2.32 196 32⅛— ⅛
CeMPw 1.48 227 17¾+ ⅛
CVtPS 1.98 26 23⅞— ¼
CntyTl s 312 21⅜— ⅞
Cenvill 2.20 85 17⅞+ ⅛
Chmpln 1 1912 32 — ⅜
ChamSp .20 277 11⅞.....
ChpStl n.03e 234 d12¼— ¼
ChartC .02e 99 3⅝— ¼
Chase 2.16 2385 28 — ⅜
Chase pf6.75 17 d64 —3
Chase pf7.60 11 76 — ⅞
Chase pf5.25 11 51⅜+ ⅜
Chse pf4.26e 1309 41 + ⅜
Chaus 51 3¾.....
Chelsea .72 25 16 .....
Chemed 1.72 60 31¾.....
ChmBnk 2.72 784 31¼— ¾
ChBk B.76e 1013 4⅝.....
ChBk pfC.97e 8433 9 + ⅛
D
DE prB2.75 1 25⅞ - ⅛
DetE pr2.28 1 21½.....
Dexter .80 190 24¼.....
DiagPr .32 17 42⅛ - ¼
DiGior .64 30 20¾ - ¼
DiaSO 2.80 53 16½.....
DShRM .40 169 15⅞ + ⅛
DShR pf 2 422 26⅞ + ⅛
DianaCp .30 51 5⅛ - ⅛
DE prB2.75 1 25⅞ - ⅛
DetE pr2.28 1 21½.....
Dexter .80 190 24¼.....
DiagPr .32 17 42⅛ - ¼
DiGior .64 30 20¾ - ¼
DiaSO 2.80 53 16½.....
DShRM .40 169 15⅞ + ⅛
DShR pf 2 422 26⅞ + ⅛
DianaCp .30 51 5⅛ - ⅛
DigtlCm 312 32¾ + ¾
Digital 4254 103½ - 1⅝
DimeNY 279 15⅜ + ¼
Disney .40 1699 60¾ + ⅜
DEI 1.52 172 26 .....
Divrsln 8 3¾ - ⅛
DomRs 3.08 1011 41⅞ - ⅛
Domtar .50 71 11⅜.....
Donald s.38 90 23¼ - ½
Donlley .78 974 34¾ - ⅜
Dover 1.12 433 64⅜ - ⅝
DowCh 2.80 4299 86 + ⅝
DowJns .68 x598 33½ + ½
Downey .40 10 15⅝ - ⅛
Dravo 128 15⅛.....
Dresr .60 853 30¼.....
DrexB 1.86 6 19¼.....
Dreyfus .52 872 26¼ + ¼
DryStr n.78 661 10 .....
DryStG n 149 11¾.....
duPont 3.80 3761 86⅛ - ½
duPnt pf3.50 1 41⅜ - ¼
duPnt pf4.50 13 52⅝ + ⅛
DuffPh .72 632 8⅜ + ⅛
DukeP 2.96 1060 44⅝.....
Duke pf8.70 z640 90½ - ⅛
Duke pf7.80 z620 80⅞.....
Duk pfM8.84 z500 91 .....
DukeRln .73e 77 6⅜ + ⅛
DukRCa 34 ⅞ + 1-16
DunBrd 1.74 5823 48¾ + 1⅛

What Investing Is All About

4th Edition

John Barnes

Registered Investment Advisor
Securities & Exchange Commission

HM55DB
PUBLISHED BY
SOUTH-WESTERN PUBLISHING CO.
CINCINNATI WEST CHICAGO, IL CARROLLTON, TX LIVERMORE, CA

Barnes, John,
    What investing is all about / John Barnes. -- 4th ed.
        p.   cm.
    Includes index.
    ISBN 0-538-70091-2
    1. Investments--Handbooks, manuals, etc.   I. Title.
HG4527.B24   1990
332.6'78--dc20

                                        88-62190
                                        CIP

CONTENTS

PREFACE

The revisions and additions required in this fourth edition of *What Investing Is All About* are so numerous that only a few of them can be mentioned here.

In the past few years, one of the big changes in the investment scene has been the deregulation of the thrift industry by the Depository Institutions Deregulation Committee. Increasingly, the difference between banks and savings and loan institutions is becoming so blurred that the general public has difficulty distinguishing one from the other.

Stocks and mutual funds had a tremendous rise in market value and popularity from 1982 to 1987. When the stock market crashed on October 19, 1987, many investors became unhappy with their losses. However, they also became wiser in their ability to evaluate their investments and more sensible in their anticipation of future stock performance. Chapter 2 on common stock and Chapter 4 on mutual funds recognize this long bull market and its subsequent fall.

In approximately the same time frame, commercial real estate values also suffered, especially in highly leveraged limited partnerships. As a consequence, Chapter 5 on real estate had to be revised accordingly.

In the third edition, estate planning was mainly concerned with the avoidance of paying burdensome estate taxes upon death of a testator. Today the individual exemption applied against the combined federal estate and gift tax is $600,000—ten times as much as the comparable tax only a few years ago. Because of this generous amount, the Internal Revenue Service has calculated that only 3 percent of the American people will have to pay an estate tax when a testator dies.

As with previous editions, I have not attempted to tell the reader what to buy or what not to buy. I have tried to give fundamental information so that when the reader walks into an investment firm, he or she can have the feeling of familiarity and confidence that only knowledge can bring. Investments should be made on the basis of facts, not on rumors or hunches. Unfortunately, however, too many people are forced to use the latter method because they have never been exposed to practical information on investments in high school or college.

Since most books on investing are too technical for the general reader, I have attempted to write this text in easy-to-understand language. The principles of sound, long-term investing need not be difficult to understand.

Finally, it has been said that in the United States—the wealthiest nation on earth—only one person in ten retires on anything more than Social Security and perhaps a pension. The fourth edition of *What Investing Is All About* endeavors to change this percentage by giving information that should encourage more people to achieve financial independence.

John Barnes

CHAPTER 1
OUTLINE

I. **MONEY PROBLEMS AND THEIR SOLUTIONS**
   A. Not Enough Money
   B. Too Much Money
   C. The Risk of Inflation
   D. The Risk of Deflation
   E. Dying Too Soon
   F. Living Too Long

II. **THE FOUR-CORNERSTONE PHILOSOPHY**
   A. A Cash Reserve for Everyday Needs and Small Emergencies
   B. An Adequate Life Insurance Program
   C. A Systematic Savings Program Adhered to During Working Years
   D. A Lump-Sum Investment of Excess Dollars in a Sound Ownership

III. **INVESTING AS A CREDITOR**
   A. Putting Money in Depository Institutions
   B. Putting Money in U.S. Government Bonds
   C. Putting Money in Municipal or Corporate Bonds
   D. Putting Money in a Mortgage on Real Estate

IV. **INVESTING AS AN OWNER**
   A. Proprietorship
   B. Partnership
   C. Corporation

1
UNDERSTANDING THE PROBLEM OF INVESTING

Why should you be concerned about investments? After all, you're healthy and you have the rest of your life before you. You may feel there is plenty of time to think about investing when you are past middle age. Unfortunately, that's how too many people feel, which is why they reach retirement years only to discover they don't have adequate financial resources to enable them to live comfortably. They find out too late that property at work has to take the place of a man or woman at work. It's never too soon to think about investing because, by careful planning now, you can ensure your financial security in the future.

When contemplating investment options, many people feel that there are literally dozens of places to put their money to work. This is not true. There are only eight places to put a dollar to work. Six of these places are in *fixed dollars*, and the person investing in them is acting as a creditor. The other two places are in *fluctuating dollars*, and the person investing in them is acting as an owner.

Fixed dollars do not increase or decrease in number. They earn interest only. People who place their money in fixed dollars will have more dollars someday only if they save the interest that is earned. Fluctuating dollars may increase or decrease in number. When money is put into fluctuating dollars, there is no guarantee of the return of the dollars themselves or the amount of income they will earn. People invest in fluctuating dollars for the opportunity to make a profit.

In this chapter, we will first look at common money problems and how to solve them. Then we will explore the reasons why sound investments are appropriate and look at an investment philosophy that works for most people. You will discover strengths and weaknesses in your own financial position, and together we will lay the groundwork for understanding your investment options. The final decisions will be up to you, depending on your personal preferences and based, for the most part, on how much risk you are willing to take.

MONEY PROBLEMS AND THEIR SOLUTIONS

As people go through life, they are faced with (or so it seems) endless money problems. Actually there are only six money problems: (1) not enough money, (2) too much money, (3) the risk of inflation, (4) the risk of deflation, (5) dying too soon, and (6) living too long. Each of these problems is discussed below.

NOT ENOUGH MONEY

"You can stop right there," you might say. "That's my problem. I know where my money goes." And so you do. Every month all of us write checks to pay for rent or mortgage, food, clothing, transportation, utilities, education, and perhaps a doctor's or a dentist's bill, etc. Withholding taxes and Social Security contributions are deducted from our paychecks. There never seems to be anything left.

It is also true that since human beings were created, food, clothing, and shelter have been the basic necessities of life. In the Stone Age, when people lived in caves, they had a roof over their heads. But they still had to clothe themselves, hunt to feed themselves, and cook the meat when they came back. Today, to these three basic necessities we have to add transportation. For in this era, who can get along without a car, or if not a car, bus fare? Besides transportation, we have to add one more necessity—utilities—because without gas, light, and water it is almost impossible to live today.

The problem of not having enough money is where most of us stumble in our desire to be financially independent. What should be done about it, then? You must learn to pay yourself first. If you sit down each month and pay all the obligations we have talked about and tell yourself, "I will save what is left," there is never anything left. This is the wrong way to do it. Instead, you should decide for yourself how much you can comfortably save and then deduct this amount each month from your paycheck—or from your profit if you are self-employed. This way you will get yours first, and then the rest of the people will get theirs.

If you have to make someone wait 30 or 60 days to be paid, let him or her wait. It is surprising how soon your budget will adjust itself to your savings program. Within six months you will realize the difference this method makes.

TOO MUCH MONEY

What exactly is meant by the problem of having too much money? Does anyone ever have this problem? We guess not. But if a person has a few hundred dollars, or a few thousand dollars, or a hundred thousand dollars of excess money and doesn't know where or how to invest it properly, then that person has too much money. She or he needs to know what to do with it.

THE RISK OF INFLATION

Buying securities or real estate involves risk, but risk by no means is confined solely to investments. No matter what you do with your excess dollars, they are subject to a possible loss. Many people mistakenly feel they have a risk-proof situation when they save dollars, particularly if they put them in robbery-proof vaults of a bank or a savings and loan association (S&L) with their accounts insured by an agency of the federal government. The risk they have overlooked is a very real one. That risk is **inflation**, or the loss of the purchasing power of those dollars.

In the 1920s, a day's pay was $5, but $2.50 bought an excellent pair of shoes. Today a college graduate can expect to earn a beginning salary of $200 a day, and $100 buys an excellent pair of shoes. In the 1920s, you could buy all you could eat for $1 a day. Today it costs twice that much—and even more in some parts of the country—for a cup of coffee and a sweet roll at a restaurant.

In 1967, a dollar was worth a dollar in purchasing power. Today it is worth 26 cents, which means that you had better have three times as much money than you had in 1967. Going back even further in time, the 1940 dollar is worth 15 cents today. If you were earning $6,000 annually in 1940, you had better have an income of over $36,000 today to have the same purchasing power you had in 1940.

This is inflation. Those who save dollars run the risk of inflation, with the probability that when they retire their dollars will not buy what they hoped they would. Then what happens? They have to lower their standard of living to fit their retirement income.

It should also be realized that inflation is not peculiar to any one nation or any one time. Inflation is universal. It has been going on since the dawn of history. There is not, nor has there ever been, a single currency anywhere that has not suffered from inflation.

What can you do about inflation? Only one thing: Put your long-term excess dollars in a sound ownership which can increase in value with time. Then, even though it costs you more each month to live because of rising prices, you will have more dollars with which to maintain or even improve your standard of living. This way you will be protected.

If you are not self-employed, there are just two kinds of ownership available to you as an average investor: (1) real estate, and (2) the common stocks of publicly held corporations. Your role as an owner will be discussed later in this chapter.

THE RISK OF DEFLATION

The problem of deflation is not heard of much these days. We haven't had a serious **deflation**, which is a prolonged period of falling prices, in the past 50 years. And the last deflationary period was relatively short-lived. People don't seem to be concerned about deflation anymore. Nevertheless, deflation could be a money problem. When prices of almost everything you buy are going down and your investments are declining in value also, fixed dollars would look

pretty good to you. This is because you would have the same number of dollars, and with the new low prices they would buy a lot more.

DYING TOO SOON

A young head of the family who hasn't had the time to save enough to provide a spouse and dependent children with food, clothing, and shelter can die too soon. If this person dies too soon, the survivors could be left with debts instead of dollars, and possibly a huge mortgage on a home. But if this person had realized the importance of an adequate life insurance program, he or she could have left the family a free and clear home, plus money in the bank.

LIVING TOO LONG

Perhaps the most tragic of all money problems is that of living too long. Nothing is more pitiful than a penniless old person. It is much better to be well-to-do grandparents bearing gifts for grandchildren than to be forced to take handouts from relatives just to be able to live. Money comes from only two sources: (1) a person at work and (2) property at work. If you are so old that you can no longer work, you had better have an income from property to take your place.

THE FOUR-CORNERSTONE PHILOSOPHY

The six money problems that have been discussed can be solved by adopting a four-cornerstone philosophy: (1) a cash reserve for everyday needs and small emergencies, (2) an adequate life insurance program, (3) a systematic savings program adhered to during working years, and (4) a lump-sum investment of excess dollars in sound ownership. Each of these cornerstones is discussed below.

A CASH RESERVE FOR EVERYDAY NEEDS AND SMALL EMERGENCIES

Everybody has to have cash in order to pay monthly bills. Unfortunately, 90 percent of everything you earn has to be paid out to others just to meet the necessities of life, plus a few luxuries of course. Even though you want to become financially successful someday, you should also smell the roses as you go.

How much should be in a small cash reserve? There are a lot of arguments over this question. Some financial counselors suggest a total of six months' earnings, and many urge a year's income. There is only one thing wrong with these suggestions—you may never start investing at all. Cash in a bank or S&L account, or even in government bonds purchased through a payroll deduction plan, consists of *put-and-take dollars*. You put them in and take them out. It is very difficult to save anything this way because the money is too easily available.

Your excess dollars are sought after so avidly that it is a wonder any money is saved this way at all. Advertising on television and radio, in magazines, and in newspapers is constantly urging you to spend your money. For the most part, such advertising lures you to spend on the small and large luxuries that perhaps you cannot afford. It's difficult to resist these cleverly contrived advertisements, which are conjured up by the best advertising brains available. It's too easy to be urged to buy a new television set when you don't need one, or to take a trip to Hawaii when a vacation in nearby states may be just as enjoyable and far less expensive.

No, keeping too much in put-and-take dollars is not wise. So we have to modify the suggestion that you should not invest until you have six months' or a year's income in the bank as a cash reserve. If you have been living from paycheck to paycheck until now, earnings for two months would be enough. Look back over the last five years and ask yourself if you have ever had a small emergency that required you to have more than this amount available. Probably not. Remember, we are talking about life's *small* emergencies, not a big one that would put you into a financial bind no matter how well you prepared for it in advance.

You also need a cash reserve because you should not have to touch your investment if a small problem presents itself. Investments fluctuate in value, and it might well be that you would need money at a time when your investments are worth less than what you paid for them. Then you would lose part of your savings, and of course you wouldn't want that to happen.

AN ADEQUATE LIFE INSURANCE PROGRAM

When no significant savings have been accumulated, there is only one way a young head of a family can create an estate which he or she has not had the time to save for. This is through the purchase of life insurance. By the stroke of a pen and the payment of a single premium, a sizable sum of money can be created if death should occur. Admittedly, the mathematical chance of that happening when a person is young is remote, but it does happen—usually as the result of an accident. But even so, no one should expose a spouse and dependent children to this risk. If the head of a family should die before that person's time, the family will still need the necessities of life. Nothing will have changed. Where there was a breadwinner at work, suddenly there must be property at work to take that person's place.

How much life insurance? This depends upon the breadwinner's salary, the amount of home mortgage, and the size of the family. Certainly, it should be enough to pay off the mortgage and include $100,000 in addition if the family is small, say a surviving spouse and two small children. The insurance should be straight protection, preferably renewable term insurance, for this is the only way the annual premium can be kept within the family's pocketbook. Such a policy is inexpensive because it provides no cash buildup if the insured should live. Furthermore, Social Security would provide a monthly income until the children are out of school.

However, there is an alternative to purchasing term insurance. One can buy a universal life policy, which builds up a high cash value and which is rapidly replacing the former ordinary life insurance. A **universal**

life policy is an insurance policy that provides a high cash surrender value. This policy is bought instead of term insurance because (1) the breadwinner can afford it, and (2) the policy owner wants something for himself or herself in the form of a cash surrender value.

The *cash value* of a universal life policy, as compared with its cash surrender value, builds up rapidly for two reasons. First, a high interest rate is assumed because the insurance companies are investing the premium money at higher rates of return than they did formerly. Second, the cost of the insurance is spread over 15 or 20 years rather than being deducted during the first year. This allows much more money to go to work for the insured—and at a higher rate of return. At the end of 15 or 20 years (the number of years chosen can vary), the cash surrender value and the cash value are the same and are equal to the amount of the premiums that have been paid. (A word of caution: Much less insurance can be purchased this way because of the higher premium.)

A SYSTEMATIC SAVINGS PROGRAM ADHERED TO DURING WORKING YEARS

A regular savings program should be maintained, if at all possible, through good years and bad; therefore, the monthly amount saved should be small. Ideally, your systematic savings should not amount to more than 8 percent of gross income. But if you can save more and it increases your bank account, you can always invest later. It would be better to save $50 a month and keep it up than to save $100 a month only to stop later because you tried to save too much.

There are a lot of places to put these systematically saved dollars. You can continue to save through fixed dollars if investments scare you to death. Six places to put

your systematically saved money will be discussed in the next section of this chapter.

On the other hand, if you are of a more adventurous bent, you need to know the various accumulation plans for fluctuating dollars that are available to you. These can be much more rewarding with time and can make you more financially independent than you previously imagined. A modest investment program in fluctuating dollars observed faithfully over a period of 30 years can be worth over $150,000, as we shall see in Chapter 4 when discussing dollar cost averaging. Such a program should not be lightly dismissed from your thinking even though you might decide, after seriously reviewing your situation, that it is not for you.

A LUMP-SUM INVESTMENT OF EXCESS DOLLARS IN A SOUND OWNERSHIP

As mentioned earlier, if you are not self-employed, there are only two ownerships available to you: real estate and common stocks. If you could examine the portfolios of wealthy, successful individuals, you would find that the major part of their wealth is invested in one or both of these places. If it is good for them, it should be good for you too.

Because of high taxes and inflation, it is no longer possible to build a sizable estate by saving only fixed dollars, whether they are in savings accounts, bonds, or the cash value buildup of permanent life insurance. It is doubtful that you could find someone who has accumulated $100,000 or more by this method. If a retired person or couple has an estate of this size in cash, it was probably originally acquired by investing in a sound ownership that greatly increased in value over a long period of time. It is true that a few younger people do have that much cash to invest, but where did it come from? Possibly from an inheritance or from the death benefit of life insurance.

INVESTING AS A CREDITOR

If you wish to have your systematically saved dollars work for you, there are two roles you can play. You can be either a creditor or an owner. Your role as a creditor is discussed here, and your role as an owner will be discussed in the section on investing as an owner.

As a *creditor*, you lend someone your money in exchange for two guarantees: (1) that you will receive interest on your money and (2) that the principal will be returned to you dollar for dollar. To obtain these two guarantees, you can lend your money by putting it in any of six different places: (1) banks, (2) savings and loan associations, (3) credit unions, (4) government bonds, (5) municipal or corporate bonds, and (6) mortgages on real estate. The first three places—banks, S&Ls, and credit unions—are types of depository institutions and are discussed in the next section. A **depository institution** is an institution that accepts money from the public and pays interest on that deposit. Bonds will be discussed in Chapter 3 and mortgages in Chapter 5.

PUTTING MONEY IN DEPOSITORY INSTITUTIONS

Although each of these depository institutions—banks, S&Ls, and credit unions—originally served a different function and had a different clientele, banks and S&Ls have come closer together in organization and function, and credit unions have greatly expanded their services. Still, S&Ls today are the major source of *home mortgage money*, while banks loan more to businesses. This is why S&Ls will usually pay one-half of 1 percent more on their accounts than banks. The S&Ls are making more money on home mortgage loans, which are long-term loans, while the banks are making less money on loans to businesses, which are short-term loans. The general public is increasingly making little distinction between these two institutions.

When you put your money in any of these three depository institutions, you are investing as a creditor. You are letting the institution use your money with the promise to pay you a specified rate of interest and to return your original principal at a later date.

Effects of the Depository Institutions Deregulation and Monetary Control Act of 1980

This act served to eliminate many of the traditional differences among *thrift institutions* (S&Ls and credit unions) and expanded their lending powers. It permitted interest-bearing checking accounts to be offered by all of the affected institutions and made all of them maintain reserves based on their deposit balances. It increased the amount of deposit insurance on accounts up to $100,000, and one of its major provisions provided for the systematic elimination of interest rate ceilings in all three depository institutions.

Effective in the spring of 1986, each depository institution was free to determine how much interest it would pay on every type of account it offered. Now it can also set the rules governing minimum deposits, minimum balances to maintain in these accounts, and the service charges that can be levied against the accounts each month. *Before* this deregulation act of 1980, each institution was limited by law to a specified interest rate. For example, a regular passbook account at a bank would earn 5.25 percent. The same type of account at a S&L would earn 5.50 percent. S&Ls were allowed by law to pay ¼ of 1 percent *more* than the banks. This was the government's way of encouraging home mortgage lending, in which the S&Ls specialized. Under these conditions, it was fairly simple to decide where to deposit your money. You always knew that all the banks paid the same interest rate, and all the S&Ls paid a little bit more.

Conditions are not that way today. As we have stated, now it is wise to be aware that rates and terms on depository accounts vary from institution to institution, and it's best to shop around in order to determine the best place to deposit your money.

Chartering and Regulation of Depository Institutions

Banks, S&Ls, and credit unions can be chartered by either state or federal authorities. A state-chartered organization is subject to the regulations of the specific state in which it is located. A federally chartered organization is regulated by an appropriate agency of the federal government. The Federal Reserve Bank is the federal agency that regulates banks, and the Federal Home Loan Bank is the federal agency that regulates S&Ls. These agencies also have regulatory power over any state depository institution that is insured by an agency of the federal government.

Establishment of Credit Unions

A credit union can be established by any homogeneous group, but usually this group consists of the employees of a private firm or a government agency. Deposits are often made through a payroll deduction plan as a convenient means of saving money. Other employees become members because they need to borrow money. Thus, a credit union becomes a two-way street, with employees who want to save money loaning it to their fellow employees who need to borrow.

Credit unions mostly pay a slightly higher rate of interest to their depositors than that obtained from other fixed-dollar methods of saving because they are non-profit institutions. Officers of the company or agency frequently supervise the credit union without pay, with the only cost being office expenses. (Note: At the time of this writing, the federal government is investigating the tax-free status of credit unions,

claiming that the credit unions make money like any other depository institution.)

Insurance of Depository Institution Accounts

During the Great Depression of the early 1930s, thousands of banks failed and billions of dollars in bank accounts were wiped out. Many lost their entire life savings. Now all federally chartered banks, S&Ls, and credit unions are required to insure their depositors against loss through a specified agency. Bank deposits are insured by the Federal Deposit Insurance Corporation (FDIC). S&L deposits are insured by the Federal Savings and Loan Insurance Corporation (FSLIC). Credit unions are insured by the National Credit Union Share Insurance Fund (NCUSIF).

State-chartered organizations also have the option of carrying deposit insurance appropriate to their institutions. Every depository institution must meet the requirements of the insurer and is subject to examination and regulation by said insurer. The premium the institutions pay for this insurance is currently $\frac{1}{12}$ of 1 percent of its deposits. Each depository institution prominently displays the emblem of the insurer so that a depositor can easily determine that his or her account is insured.

The current insurance limit for all three institutions is $100,000 per account. This means that a couple with no children could have $100,000 in a joint account, and each spouse could have $100,000 in an individual account. By this method, the couple could have accounts insured for a total of $300,000 in the same depository institution.

It should be understood that the purpose of federal insurance is to protect depositors and to build confidence among the general public in the American banking system. Obviously, if all the depository institutions in the country failed, there certainly would not be enough money in the insurance funds to pay the depositors. But common sense dictates that a situation like this is highly unlikely to happen.

Types of Accounts in Depository Institutions

There are three basic types of accounts in depository institutions: (1) demand deposit accounts, (2) regular savings accounts, and (3) certificates of deposit.

Demand Deposit Account. A **demand deposit account** is usually the first account an average person opens in a depository institution. From this type of account, you may withdraw your funds on demand at any time. The most common type of demand deposit is the *checking account*. By federal requirement, funds in a checking account must be made available in a maximum time of 14 days after your notice of intention to withdraw them. But even in this type of account, the financial institution has the right to withhold any funds that have not been collected. For example, assume that you deposit a check drawn on an out-of-town bank. It takes your bank several days to collect and turn that check into cash. Until it is able to do this, your bank has the right to refuse your request to withdraw.

Most people put money into a checking account because it is a convenient way to make payments to others. But it is not the type of account in which to accumulate your emergency reserve fund or place your systematic savings. Don't put that money into a demand deposit account because it can be taken out too easily.

Regular Savings Account. A **regular savings account** is not a demand deposit from which you can withdraw money at any time. Most people view a savings account that way because, normally, you can walk into your depository institution and make a withdrawal at will. But this is not always the case. There is a legal distinction between a demand deposit account and a savings account. The depository institution—whether it be a bank, an S&L, or a credit union—has the legal right to require a 30-day written notice before allowing you to withdraw from your savings account. Most people are not

aware of this because the restriction is so seldom imposed. The requirement exists to give depository institutions time to liquidate assets if too many depositors are demanding their money at the same time. If you have a regular savings account, take a look in the front of your passbook. You will find a statement to the effect that your depository institution has the right to demand a 30-day written notice of your intention to withdraw.

Traditionally, regular savings accounts were known as **passbook accounts** because the depositor was issued a passbook to show that he or she had made a deposit. Any time the depositor wanted to make an addition to or a withdrawal from the account, the passbook had to be presented for updating. This type of savings account is still offered and used by many people. However, most institutions offer an alternative. Instead of opening a regular savings account, you may open a *statement account*. The basic difference between the two is one of convenience. Rather than being issued a passbook, the depositor is given a plastic card which is used for all transactions. Deposits and withdrawals may be made at a teller window during regular business hours if that choice is preferred. These transactions may also be made at *automated teller machines (ATMs)* conveniently located on the street in front of a bank, in shopping malls, in grocery stores, and even at some service stations. Because of the widespread use of ATMs, federal legislation was passed to protect the consumer from fraudulent use of what is known as *electronic funds transfer*, of which ATMs are a part.

Certificate of Deposit. A **certificate of deposit (CD)**, when issued by a depository institution, has a set maturity date. The shortest term available is 14 days and the longest term is usually five years, although some institutions offer a term of ten years. Because the money is not available for withdrawal during the term specified, the interest rate is higher than on a regular savings account. Also, the interest rate is higher the longer the depositor stretches out the term. Each depository institution chooses the various maturity dates it is willing to offer, sets the interest rate for each term, sets the minimum balance requirement, and decides if any additions can be made to the account during its term.

A CD may have a fixed interest rate for the term chosen or a variable interest rate based on some economic indicator, such as the U.S. *Consumer Price Index*, which is chosen by the issuer.

Some CDs may be automatically renewable at the end of the term, while others are not. The automatic renewal feature can be a convenience, but if you don't want this feature, be sure to choose a depository institution that will send you a written notice about ten days before maturity of the CD so that you will know it in advance. Usually you have from seven to ten days after the maturity date to make any changes in your deposit. If you choose a CD without the automatic renewal feature, your deposits will normally be paid the regular savings rate for the time it remains on deposit after it matures.

When you open a CD with a bank, an S&L, or a credit union, you are entering into a legally binding contract. You are promising to leave your money on deposit for a specified period of time, and the institution is promising to pay you a stated amount of interest on your dollars. If you decide that you need or want this money prior to the maturity date, the institution has no legal obligation to give it to you. Some organizations actually state on the face of the certificate that they will not release the funds prior to maturity. Most financial institutions, however, will release your funds on request subject to a significant interest penalty for early withdrawal. This is actually a legal requirement on the part of the depository institution. At the time of this writing, the current penalty is as follows:

Maturity Period	Penalty
Under 90 days	All of the interest earned
2 to 12 months	90 days' interest
1 year or more	180 days' interest

The interest penalty is based on the interest rate your account has been earning. It is possible to make an early withdrawal and receive less than you deposited. For example, assume you deposit $1,000 in a one-year CD at an interest rate of 6 percent. Two months later you decide that you need the money. The penalty would be three months' interest. Thus, you would lose that amount from your original principal of $1,000.

You also may make a partial withdrawal. If you do, the interest penalty is not assessed against the full amount of the CD but is assessed only against the amount you withdraw. For example, assume you open a six-month CD for $5,000. Before the maturity date is up, you withdraw $1,000. The 90 days' interest penalty is charged on the $1,000. The balance of the money remains in the CD under the original contract.

There is a special class of CD for those who invest $100,000 or more. It is called a **jumbo certificate of deposit**. The interest rate on a jumbo CD can be negotiated between you and the institution. The jumbo CD is used mostly by businesses and government agencies when they make their fixed-term deposits.

PUTTING MONEY IN U.S. GOVERNMENT BONDS

U.S. government bonds are issued by the federal government and sold to the public as one means of financing the public debt, which is currently over one trillion dollars. This public debt consists of *marketable debt* and *nonmarketable debt*. Because the value of the marketable debt fluctuates when bonds are bought and sold, we will consider that type of debt in a later chapter. In this chapter we will discuss the federal government's **nonmarketable debt**, which is issued in the form of EE bonds and HH bonds.

EE Bonds

Commonly known as savings bonds, **EE bonds** are bought by millions of Americans. Billions of dollars are saved this way. These bonds are not "put-and-take" dollars because they cannot be redeemed for the first six months. They should be a part of the investor's long-term dollars. People like to buy these bonds because they are as safe as the U.S. Treasury (as safe as a church, as the old saying goes), and indeed they are.

For many years, EE bonds earned a fixed interest rate. But because interest rates some years ago became more volatile, the government changed to a variable interest rate. The rate is 85 percent of the yield on five-year Treasury notes, calculated every six months. A **Treasury note** is a short-term obligation of the U.S. government of from one to seven years, as opposed to a **Treasury bond**, which is issued up to 30 years. There is no limit as to how high the interest rate on an EE bond may rise, but there is a guaranteed floor below which it may not fall. Currently this guaranteed floor is 6 percent. However, the rate of 6 percent cannot be earned until the owner holds the bonds for five years.

Government EE bonds can be bought at bond teller windows in banks and S&Ls. They are also frequently purchased through a payroll savings plan where the saver works or by a bond-a-month plan at a depository institution. EE bonds are bought at a 50 percent discount and mature at their face value. For example, an EE bond for $50 costs $25 when purchased and matures for the face amount of $50. The face amount can be bought in denominations of $50, $75, $100, $200, $500, $1,000, and $10,000.

EE bonds may be owned by adults or minors. There are several ways to hold title to them. You can own one individually or jointly with one or more other persons. If the ownership is a joint one, either co-owner has the right to redeem the bonds.

Those who purchase EE bonds sometimes make the mistake of thinking the bonds would be excellent collateral for a loan. Actually, EE bonds cannot be transferred, sold to someone else, or used as security for a loan. This nonnegotiable feature is a disadvantage to consider before buying EE bonds.

The accrued interest on EE bonds may be either tax deferred or tax exempt. The interest is *tax deferred* until the bonds mature or are cashed. At that time, all of the accrued interest must be reported by the taxpayer in the tax year in which the interest is realized. The interest is *tax exempt* if the bonds are not cashed during the lifetime of the purchaser. However, this does not relieve the bondholder's beneficiaries from paying the tax if they should redeem the bonds. The bonds are also tax exempt if the boldholder exchanges them for current income government HH bonds (see the next section).

EE bonds may be retained an additional ten years beyond their original maturity date. No action need be taken by the bondholder to accomplish this. The bonds are automatically renewed and continue to earn a compounded return at the same interest rate.

HH Bonds

U.S. government **HH bonds** cannot be bought directly. The only way they can be acquired is by exchanging EE bonds for them. A bondholder makes the exchange because that person no longer wants to compound the return on the amount invested in the EE bonds. For example, if the bondholder bought the EE bonds for retirement and is now retired, that person can exchange them for HH bonds and receive a check twice a year from Washington, D.C., at the same interest rate that he or she was receiving on the EE bonds, with the added advantage of not having to pay an income tax on the accrued interest in the EE bonds.

HH bonds are sold at their face value, not at a discount like the EE bonds. They are issued in denominations of $500, $1,000, $5,000, and $10,000. The interest on HH bonds is subject to federal income tax, but not to state or local income taxes.

PUTTING MONEY IN MUNICIPAL OR CORPORATE BONDS

Municipal bonds are issued by a state or local government. They are purchased mainly because they are federally tax exempt. The issuer of municipal bonds uses the money from the sale of the bonds to run the government or to build a highway or a bridge. The issuer of corporate bonds uses the money in his or her business. Both municipal bonds and corporate bonds fluctuate in value. They are mentioned here because they are an investment for you as a creditor. They are discussed in more detail later in Chapter 3.

PUTTING MONEY IN A MORTGAGE ON REAL ESTATE

When putting money in a mortgage on real estate, you act as an individual mortgagee by lending money in the form of a mortgage on the property. As an investor, you are making a loan in much the same way that banks and S&Ls lend their money so people can buy homes. The mortgage is a lien on the property that is being used as collateral for the loan. If the borrower does not make the mortgage payments, you as the lender have the right to foreclose on the property. The process of foreclosure involves a legally prescribed procedure of having the property sold to pay the mortgage debt.

Although you are giving up the guarantee of the return of your principal and interest when you put money in a mortgage on real estate, you do have the collateral of the real estate as your security. You must be aware that you would lose some of your money if the property cannot be sold for the amount that is owed you.

An individual might invest in a mortgage loan for one of several reasons. If the interest rate available through other investments is too low, mortgages might offer a higher rate of return. If the market interest rate is falling, this might be a way to lock in a higher rate for a definite period of time. Or perhaps you are trying to sell your home, and the traditional home lenders are quoting an interest rate that is beyond the financial capability of your prospective buyer. You may find that the only way you can make the sale is by taking back a mortgage yourself. This method was called *creative financing* back in the days of very high interest rates during the early 1980s.

You should not think lightly of becoming a mortgage lender. But if you're thinking of becoming one, it might be a good idea to check with a professional loan officer who could tell you how to limit your risk.

INVESTING AS AN OWNER

When you invest as an *owner*, you buy something with your money—a business, real estate, or stocks and bonds—and hold title to your investment. You invest as an owner for two reasons: (1) you want to have the opportunity to earn more on your money than you would earn as a creditor, and (2) you want to have the opportunity for a profit. Since you are expecting a greater return than you would receive as a creditor, you should realize that you are giving up the guarantees you have as a creditor. When you invest as an owner, there is no guarantee that your money will earn interest or that it will be returned to you.

Of the two basic incentives for being an owner, the opportunity for profit is the greater. As an owner, you share fully in the profits. If the business or real estate you own does well, you will have an excellent income. Also, if the price of the business or real estate you own goes up, you can later sell for a profit. Conversely, however, there could be no income and/or the value of your investment could decline drastically, or worse, become worthless. This is what is meant by a fluctuating-dollar investment.

The various kinds of ownership investments will be covered in detail in later chapters of the text. Here we will examine the three basic forms of business ownership—proprietorship, partnership, and corporation—to familiarize you with their similarities and differences.

PROPRIETORSHIP

A **proprietorship** is a business owned by one person. It is entirely dependent upon the credit, skill, knowledge, integrity, personality, and leadership of that one person. It is the most common form of business ownership and the simplest to establish.

A proprietor will have to meet some legal requirements, depending upon the type of business being opened, whether or not employees are being hired, and the requirements of state and local ordinances. But the amount of "red tape" is minimal compared with that required for other forms of ownership.

If you should decide to become a proprietor, you must be prepared for hard work, long hours, and risks. For many people, these hardships are outweighed by the advantages of being one's own boss. A proprietor is a person with confidence in himself or herself. This person knows that any risk of loss is a personal risk, and any errors made cannot be blamed on someone else. However, the rewards for success don't have to be shared with anyone else. This is one of the main attractions of becoming a business proprietor.

A proprietor pays taxes on the profits of his or her business as if it were income earned from any other source. Conversely, if the business incurs losses, these are also reported on the proprietor's personal income tax return. This is only fair because the proprietor has unlimited liability for the debts of the business. If the business is unable to pay its bills, the personal assets of the owner can be attached by the creditors of the business.

In the event of the proprietor's death, the business is dissolved unless the heirs of the deceased decide to carry on the business. When there is no competent person to carry on, the only solution for inexperienced heirs is to put the business on the auction block. This usually results in a severe loss for as much as 50 percent or more of the value of the business. To eliminate the risk of this loss, the simplest solution is for the proprietor to take out enough additional personal life insurance.

For example, assume that the proprietor values the business at $50,000 and anticipates that the inventory, fixtures, and goodwill could be sold for no more than $20,000 in the event of death. The proprietor simply takes out a life insurance policy for $30,000. Then the heirs would receive $20,000 from the business sold at auction, plus $30,000 from the insurance. Thus, the heirs would receive $50,000 as though the business were sold for its full value.

There is another solution to the problem of succession in a proprietorship. If the proprietor has experienced key employees, that person can enter into a buy-and-sell agreement similar to a partnership agreement. The buy-and-sell agreement is described on page 14.

PARTNERSHIP

A **partnership** is an association of two or more persons to carry on a business as co-owners for a profit. For some reason, the partners involved feel they have a better chance of running a successful business by pooling their efforts than by going it alone. The reason may be that each of the partners is skilled in a different area. Perhaps one partner is an expert at television repair but knows nothing about running a business. The other partner may be an experienced manager. So the two join forces to open a television repair business.

Another reason for forming a partnership could be a financial one. If a person has a special talent or process for producing a product but not enough capital to start a business, that individual could combine forces with another person who is willing to contribute capital to the venture in return for a share of the profits.

Articles of Partnership

A contract called **articles of partnership** is entered into when a partnership is formed. As with any other contract, the agreement contains many details and assigns various responsibilities among the partners involved. Because of this, the contract should never be verbal but should always be reduced to writing. In addition to the date the partnership was formed, the identity of the partners, and the purpose of the partnership, the articles of partnership should include the following information:

1. Name and duration of the partnership.
2. Amount of capital contributed by each partner.
3. Amount of profits to be retained by the business.
4. Location of the business.
5. Name of the partner who controls the partnership funds.
6. Duties and limitations of each partner.
7. Location of partnership records.
8. Number of times and the amounts each partner is entitled to withdraw from the partnership's funds.
9. Relative shares of each partner in the profits, losses, and assets of the business.
10. The basis of remuneration for each partner (whether it is a drawing account or a salary).
11. Procedure for termination of or withdrawal from the partnership.

This may sound like a lot of needless information, but it is the only way that all of the partners can be protected. Misunderstandings can be prevented if everything is put in writing and is clearly understood at the outset.

Even in Benjamin Franklin's day it was considered the height of folly for prudent businesspeople to form a partnership without a written agreement. Here is what Ben Franklin had to say on the matter:

Partnerships often finish in quarrels but I was happy in this, that mine were all carried on and ended amicably; owing, I think, a good deal to the precautions of having very explicitly settled in our Articles of Partnership everything to be done by, or expected from,

each partner, so there was nothing to dispute, which precaution I would therefore recommend to all who enter into partnership.[1]

General Partners and Limited Partners

A partnership may have general partners and limited partners. Every partnership must have at least one general partner. A **general partner** is active in the business and is fully responsible for its debts, even to the extent of his or her personal wealth. A **limited partner** is neither active in the business nor liable for its obligations. The limited partner is a silent partner. As such, a limited partner cannot lose any more money than he or she invested in the partnership.

Powers of Partners in Conducting the Business

Every partner is an agent of the partnership. This means that the acts of any one of the partners bind the other partners and the business itself, as long as these acts are within the scope of the business.

Importance of a Buy-and-Sell Agreement

The partnership relationship is a personal one. If a partner should die, by law the partnership is immediately dissolved. The only way the business can be continued is by written agreement before the event of the death, and even then it will become a new firm. Sometimes this is taken care of in the wills of the individual partners, but the best way is for the partners to enter into a buy-and-sell agreement drawn by an attorney.

In a **buy-and-sell agreement**, each partner agrees to sell his or her interest in the partnership and the other partner or partners agree to purchase such interest at the price and under the terms and conditions set forth in the agreement. This is fine as long as the surviving partner or partners possess the cash. Too often the surviving partners do not. At this point, then, lack of cash with which to buy out the deceased partner's interest becomes the partnership's biggest money problem.

The simplest way to solve this is by means of life insurance. For instance, if there are only two partners, each of whom has a 50 percent interest, each takes out a life insurance policy on the life of the other partner equal to a one-half interest in the firm. If one of the partners should die, the insurance company pays the death benefit to the surviving partner. In turn, the surviving partner pays this sum to the deceased partner's heirs, who, by the terms of the buy-and-sell agreement, are required to accept the amount offered. The surviving partner then owns the entire firm and carries on as a proprietor.

CORPORATION

A **corporation** is an artificial being created by law and endowed with the rights, duties, and powers of a person. The owners, or stockholders, of a corporation may change from time to time, but the corporation continues to exist. Being artificial and intangible and a mere creature of the law, a corporation possesses only those properties that its charter confers on it.

Creation of a Corporation

A corporation is formed by a group of individuals who apply to a state authority for approval of a *charter*. In most states, the authority is the secretary of state. The charter is the birth certificate of the corporation. The usual information required in the *articles of incorporation*, which is the application for a charter, consists of the following:

1. The exact name of the corporation.
2. The details of the type of business to be conducted.
3. The location of the business.
4. The names, addresses, and occupations of the incorporators.
5. The number of shares and the par value, or stated value, of the common stock.

Structure of a Corporation

The stockholders of a corporation are the owners of the business. Annually, they elect a *board of directors* whose function is to set broad management policy. The board of directors also elects the corporate officers who manage the business. The number and titles of the specific officers of a corporation are set by statute or by the corporation's bylaws. Most commonly, these officers include a president, one or more vicepresidents, a secretary, and a treasurer.

If the directors don't like the way the officers are running the business, they can remove them and appoint new ones. If the stockholders don't like the way the directors are doing their job, they can elect new directors at the next annual meeting. Figure 1-1 shows an organization chart of a typical corporation.

Advantages of Corporations

A corporation has several advantages over a proprietorship and a partnership. The most important of these advantages are briefly explained below.

Potential Perpetual Life. Because of the nature of a corporation, it continues its separate legal existence independently of the death, retirement, or change in composition

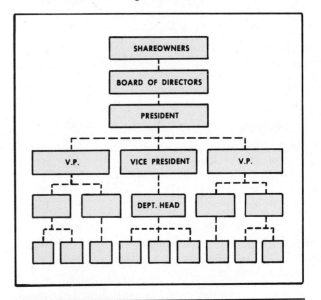

FIGURE 1-1 An Organization Chart

This is a typical organization chart showing lines of responsibility and authority in a corporation.

of its stockholders, directors, and officers. It does not cease to exist unless it is dissolved.

Limited Liability of Stockholders.

The stockholders of a corporation, like limited partners in a partnership, have limited liability. That is, an individual stockholder can lose only the amount that person has invested in the corporation. For example, if you buy 100 shares of common stock of a corporation, you can lose only the amount you paid for those shares.

Large Operation.

Because a corporation is a separate legal entity and has potential perpetual life, it can engage in much larger transactions than either a proprietorship or a partnership. A corporation can do this in two different ways: (1) by borrowing money, or (2) by issuing more stock with the approval of the existing stockholders.

Ease in Transferring Ownership.

Stockholders of large corporations that are publicly owned don't have to find someone to buy their stock if they want to sell. They simply sell their shares through a stockbroker, either in the auction market if the stock is listed on one of the stock exchanges, or in the negotiated market if the stock is sold over the counter. The seller of a stock never knows who bought it, nor does the buyer know from whom the stock was purchased. Furthermore, neither of them cares.

Rights of Stockholders

As owners of the corporation, stockholders have certain rights. These rights are established by the corporation's bylaws, by state statutes, and by the stock certificates the stockholders receive. The rights of stockholders are discussed below.

Right to a Stock Certificate.

A stock certificate is evidence of ownership of the corporation. Every stockholder is entitled to have such a certificate issued in his or her name, showing the number of shares owned. When the stockholder sells the stocks, the stock certificate is surrendered and a new certificate is issued in the name of the new owner.

Right to Vote at Stockholders' Meetings.

As a partial owner of a corporation, each stockholder has the right to vote at stockholders' meetings, which are normally held once a year. Each share of common stock entitles the holder to one vote.

If a stockholder cannot attend the annual meeting, that person may vote by proxy. When the stockholder is sent a notification of the annual meeting, a **proxy statement** is included. This is a form that when signed and mailed back to the corporation gives someone else the right to cast the stockholder's vote at the annual meeting. Most people who hold stock of large corporations go along with management's recommendations when voting by proxy. Many other stockholders, especially if they own only a few shares, don't even bother to vote because they consider their vote a mere formality. Figure 1-2 shows an example of a proxy statement.

Other Rights.

Stockholders have certain *preemptive rights* that are basic to stock ownership. These are the following:

1. The right to hold and transfer stock certificates.
2. The right to receive corporate reports such as semiannual and annual financial statements.
3. The right to receive dividends if and when they are declared by the board of directors.
4. The right to participate in new stock offerings. The company will notify the stockholder how many shares that person is entitled to buy. This is usually based on the number of shares currently owned—for instance, one right for each ten shares held. These rights have a value; if the stockholder doesn't want to exercise them to buy more shares, they may be sold to someone who does want to exercise his or her rights.
5. The right to share in the assets of the corporation in the event it is dissolved.

FIGURE 1-2 A Proxy Statement (Front and Back)

THE SHARES COVERED BY THIS PROXY WILL BE VOTED AS SPECIFIED. IF NO SPECIFICATION IS MADE. THE PROXY WILL BE VOTED **IN FAVOR** OF THE FOREGOING PROPOSALS.

Dated: , 199..

....
Signature

633 20-53-19622-6   98
GARY V DENNY &
ALICE C DENNY JT TEN
1910 LADYELLEN DRIVE
CINCINNATI, OH 45230

....
Signature

Signatures of stockholders should correspond exactly with the names shown on the proxy card. Attorneys, trustees, executors, administrators, guardians and others signing in a representative capacity should designate their full titles.

PLEASE FILL IN, DATE, SIGN AND RETURN THIS PROXY IN THE ACCOMPANYING ENVELOPE.

HUMANA INC.

PROXY SOLICITED BY THE BOARD OF DIRECTORS FOR ANNUAL MEETING OF STOCKHOLDERS
TO BE HELD JANUARY 13, 199-

The undersigned hereby appoints David A. Jones, Wendell Cherry and Carl F. Pollard, and each of them, his attorneys and agents, with full power of substitution to vote as Proxy for the undersigned, as herein stated, at the annual meeting of stockholders of Humana Inc. to be held in the Regency Center Ballroom of the Hyatt Regency Hotel, Louisville, Kentucky, on Thursday, the 13th day of January 199-, at 10:00 A.M. (E.S.T.), and at any adjournments thereof, according to the number of votes the undersigned would be entitled to vote if personally present on the proposals set forth below and in accordance with their discretion on any other matters which may properly come before the meeting or any adjournment thereof.

The Board of Directors recommends a vote **FOR** each of the following proposals:

1. **FOR** ☐ the election of H. J. Boone, Jr., W. Cherry, M. E. Gellert, J. D. Grissom, D. A. Jones, A. T. Knoppers, J. W. Landrum, C. F. Pollard, D. C. Scott, C. L. Weisberg and W. T. Young as Directors except as indicated below, or **WITHHOLD AUTHORITY** ☐ to vote for all nominees in such election. **INSTRUCTION:** To withhold authority to vote for any individual nominee write the nominee's name in the space provided herein:

....

2. **FOR** ☐ **AGAINST** ☐ **ABSTAIN** ☐ from voting on amendment to the Thrift Plan to increase the maximum Company contribution allowed.

3. **FOR** ☐ **AGAINST** ☐ **ABSTAIN** ☐ from voting on appointment of the Company's auditors.

Types of Corporations

There are many classifications of corporations. We shall examine only three of them: (1) close corporations, (2) open corporations, and (3) Subchapter S corporations.

Close Corporations. If the stock of a corporation is not available for purchase by the general public, it is a **close corporation**. Most corporations begin their lives as close corporations. This is because they are small to begin with and because the stockholders, directors, and officers are all the same people and own 100 percent of the stock. Family-held corporations and corporations formed by conversion of proprietorships or partnerships are typical of the closely held type.

If one of the stockholders dies, a close corporation has the same cash problem as does a proprietorship or a partnership. The close corporation's cash problem is solved by stock retirement plans. These plans are similar to buy-and-sell agreements of partnerships in that the deceased stockholder's interest is purchased by the remaining stockholders, usually financed by means of life insurance.

Open Corporations. When a closely held corporation needs or wants to expand beyond the capacities of its original founders to raise capital, it "goes public" and becomes an **open corporation**. It first consults with an underwriting firm, which advises the corporation on the amount of capital it will require and the price at which its stock can be successfully sold to the public in order to raise the capital. The owners themselves often include part of their shares in this initial public offering, thereby becoming wealthy because they have succeeded in establishing a successful business. A new underwriting requires the approval of the Securities and Exchange Commission (SEC) to protect the public from promotional stock schemes that could have very little intrinsic value.

All of the largest corporations in the United States went public many years ago. Figure 1-3 shows that as of 1985 the nation had more than 47 million stockholders.

Subchapter S Corporations. A **Subchapter S corporation** has all the advantages of operating in the corporate form but is treated more as a partnership for federal income tax purposes. To qualify for Subchapter S treatment, a corporation must meet the following conditions:

1. It must be a domestic corporation.
2. It must not have more than 35 stockholders.
3. Its stockholders must be individuals, not institutions.
4. It must have only one class of stock.
5. It must not have a nonresident alien as a stockholder.
6. All of its stockholders must elect to have the corporation treated as a Subchapter S corporation on a form prescribed by the Internal Revenue Service.

If all the above conditions are met, the Subchapter S corporation will not pay any federal income taxes (with some minor exceptions) but will pass along the pro rata share of its net income to each individual stockholder, who reports this information on his or her individual income tax return.

Prior to passage of the Tax Reform Act of 1986, the normal way to open an incorporated business was to use the close corporation or the open corporation. The 1986 act created an environment for those who are incorporating a new business to elect Subchapter S treatment as the normal way to do business. This is because for the first time in history, the highest personal income tax rate (28 percent) is less than the highest corporate tax rate (34 percent) (see the next section). In addition, changes in the taxation of corporate business sales will impose a double tax on many regular corporations but not on Subchapter S corporations. From now on, because of these changes, there would have to be compelling reasons for new corporations not to elect the Subchapter S treatment.

Taxation of a Corporation

As a separate legal entity, a corporation is taxed on its profits. The amount of taxes a corporation pays on its profits is computed as follows:

Taxable Income	Rate	Amount of Tax
0–$50,000	15%	$ 7,500
$50,000–$75,000	25%	6,250
$75,000–$100,000	34%	8,500
Total		$22,250
Over $100,000	34%	

In addition, a 5 percent surtax is imposed on corporate taxable income between $100,000 and $335,000. The effect of this surtax is to tax every extra dollar of earnings in the $100,000 to $335,000 range at 39 percent (34 percent plus 5 percent = 39 percent). Thus, a corporation with taxable income of $335,000 will pay $22,250 on $100,000 plus $91,650 on $235,000, or a

FIGURE 1-3 Geographic Distribution of Stockholders of Publicly Held Corporations

State	Shareowners (thousands)						
	1965	1970	1975	1980	1981	1983	1985
Alabama	172	318	286	319	339	424	483
Alaska	9	18	27	88	77	114	160
Arizona	179	292	285	364	382	513	575
Arkansas	94	172	159	178	200	246	311
California	2,540	3,833	3,152	3,525	4,016	5,367	6,006
Colorado	240	367	337	407	445	598	695
Connecticut	505	798	582	560	611	835	946
Delaware	79	140	131	87	89	122	142
Dist. of Columbia	121	148	94	131	137	193	211
Florida	704	1,232	1,263	1,272	1,366	2,056	2,343
Georgia	243	463	428	570	606	804	1,000
Hawaii	39	74	58	175	174	234	256
Idaho	43	53	62	98	101	136	158
Illinois	1,308	1,956	1,523	1,866	1,924	2,468	2,565
Indiana	382	568	516	674	682	751	856
Iowa	202	471	274	357	361	427	442
Kansas	221	313	287	260	305	352	400
Kentucky	161	296	277	325	324	392	462
Louisiana	149	220	179	397	440	568	633
Maine	123	214	170	123	127	165	188
Maryland	424	715	560	602	644	879	936
Massachusetts	805	1,214	839	941	991	1,292	1,477
Michigan	946	1,403	1,157	1,349	1,385	1,672	1,786
Minnesota	260	476	370	514	544	681	794
Mississippi	92	181	130	169	179	220	251
Missouri	501	728	558	587	616	796	939
Montana	61	98	79	74	85	107	112
Nebraska	99	211	178	193	207	255	286
Nevada	42	62	66	109	118	156	168
New Hampshire	101	182	159	112	124	167	203
New Jersey	1,086	1,345	1,036	1,176	1,228	1,675	1,905
New Mexico	60	104	90	133	154	183	221
New York	2,407	3,103	2,055	3,177	3,357	4,695	4,954
North Carolina	322	611	573	639	660	822	963
North Dakota	30	33	22	65	71	93	117
Ohio	865	1,335	1,205	1,466	1,513	1,884	1,939
Oklahoma	181	337	320	285	345	452	515
Oregon	200	283	263	314	331	389	441
Pennsylvania	1,408	1,849	1,479	1,521	1,615	2,071	2,139
Rhode Island	122	173	211	130	138	188	206
South Carolina	117	206	214	282	296	361	406
South Dakota	40	54	39	69	70	91	103
Tennessee	201	369	342	428	460	614	665
Texas	744	1,383	1,295	1,720	1,898	2,606	3,061
Utah	78	150	115	176	185	246	276
Vermont	72	144	108	57	62	86	92
Virginia	422	694	636	678	739	987	1,204
Washington	262	447	382	571	620	805	847
West Virginia	100	167	142	209	209	251	257
Wisconsin	360	558	454	619	640	779	851
Wyoming	41	51	39	59	70	92	94
U.S. Terr. & Poss.	14	13					
U.S. Citizens			[64	[N/A	[N/A	[N/A	[N/A
Living Abroad	143	225					
Total	20,120	30,850	25,270	30,200	32,260	42,360	47,040

N/A-Not Available

Source: *The New York Stock Exchange Fact Book, 1988.* New York Stock Exchange, Inc., Eleven Wall Street, New York, NY 10005.

total of $113,900—which in effect is 34 percent on $335,000.

Also, if the board of directors declares a dividend, the stockholders have to report it on their individual income tax returns. This results in *double taxation* of corporate profits. There is considerable agitation in Congress to abolish this, but so far nothing has been done about it.

SUMMARY

As people go through life, they are faced with six money problems. The best way to solve them is by adopting the four-cornerstone philosophy discussed in this chapter. No matter what is done with excess dollars, a risk is incurred. Most people don't realize this. If they did, more of them would seriously consider investments. The risk for those who put their money in fixed-dollar investments is loss due to inflation. When inflation takes place—and history shows that it always will—their dollars will buy less than they could at the time they were saved. This loss of purchasing power is a real one.

You should realize that there are two basic ways in which excess dollars can be put to work. As a creditor, the saver is assured that the money loaned will be returned. As an owner, the investor takes the risk of a partial or complete loss. People assume the risk of ownership because a sound investment offers opportunities for profit.

When investing in American industry, you should understand the three basic forms of business ownership. You should realize that when you purchase the stock of an open corporation, you will have virtually nothing to say about how the corporation is managed. However, you should also appreciate the fact that you can fire that management any time you choose by the simple expedient of selling your stock and putting your money elsewhere.

ENDNOTE

1. H. P. Gravengaard, *Partnerships and Life Insurance* (Cincinnati: The National Underwriter Company, 1977), 36.

1

REVIEW QUESTIONS
SHORT ESSAY

Name _____

Date _____ Points _____

Directions: Answer the following questions according to your instructor's directions.

1. Distinguish between fixed dollars and fluctuating dollars. Why would you choose an investment in each?

   _____

   _____

   _____

   _____

   _____

   _____

   _____

2. Identify the six money problems that people may face as they go through life.

   a. _____

   b. _____

   c. _____

   d. _____

   e. _____

   f. _____

3. What is the first step you should take to solve the problem of not having enough money?

   _____

   _____

   _____

4. Explain the risk of inflation.

   _____

   _____

5. Why is the Deregulation and Monetary Control Act of 1980 important to depository institutions?

_____

_____

_____

_____

6. Why is life insurance important for a young family?

_____

_____

_____

_____

7. When does a person have the problem of having too much money?

_____

_____

_____

8. What is meant by living too long?

_____

_____

_____

9. What is the legal distinction between demand deposit accounts, savings accounts, and certificates of deposit?

_____

_____

_____

10. Briefly explain the four-cornerstone philosophy.

_____

_____

_____

1

REVIEW QUESTIONS
MULTIPLE CHOICE

Name _____

Date _____ Points _____

Directions: For each of the following, select the best answer and place the letter that represents it in the Answers column.

ANSWERS

1. You can do something about inflation by
   a. putting your money in an insured savings account.
   b. trusting to luck.
   c. putting your long-term excess dollars into a sound ownership.
   d. saving dollars so that some day they will be worth more.   _____

2. You should have extra cash for emergencies because
   a. you may have to cash an investment at the wrong time.
   b. it is always a good idea to have a little extra money around.
   c. a big emergency is always just around the corner.
   d. most people feel more comfortable with a large bank account.   _____

3. Federal insurance programs insure each type of depository institution account for
   a. $10,000.
   b. $15,000.
   c. $25,000.
   d. $100,000.   _____

4. Interest rates on depository institution accounts are set by
   a. the U.S. Congress.
   b. each individual institution.
   c. the Securities and Exchange Commission.
   d. state banking authorities.   _____

5. A penalty imposed by law against early withdrawal of certificates of deposit is that
   a. no interest is paid on the account.
   b. you must wait 90 days before any interest is paid.
   c. no passbook interest is paid from the time of deposit.
   d. you lose interest depending on the term of the deposit.   _____

6. Which of the following accounts is available on demand by the depositor?
   a. certificate of deposit.
   b. savings account.
   c. checking account.
   d. all of the above.   _____

7. Which type of bond cannot be purchased with cash?
   a. HH.
   b. EE.
   c. municipal.
   d. corporate.   _____

8. The simplest form of business ownership is the
   a. close corporation.
   b. open corporation.
   c. proprietorship.
   d. partnership.   _____

9.   You become an owner rather than a creditor because you want to
   a.   have a guaranteed income.
   b.   have an opportunity for profit.
   c.   avoid the risk of bad debts.
   d.   be assured of receiving dividends.   _____

10.   If proprietors go bankrupt, they stand to lose
   a.   only the amount they invested in the business.
   b.   the amount that they invested, plus what they borrowed.
   c.   the amounts invested and borrowed and their personal wealth,
        which is subject to creditors' claims.
   d.   only what they agreed to pay for in writing.   _____

11.   A corporation with $335,000 in taxable income pays, in effect, the
     following percentage in taxes:
   a.   45 percent.
   b.   32 percent.
   c.   40 percent.
   d.   34 percent.   _____

12.   A corporation has an advantage over a proprietorship or a
     partnership in that a corporation
   a.   has potential perpetual life.
   b.   ceases to exist on the death of a stockholder.
   c.   is limited in the scope of its operation.
   d.   is not a separate legal entity.   _____

13.   If a proprietor cannot enter into a buy-and-sell agreement with
     employees, the best way to solve the succession problem is for the
   a.   heirs to sell the business at auction when the proprietor dies.
   b.   proprietor to insure his or her life for the value of the business.
   c.   heirs to carry on the business even if they are inexperienced.
   d.   proprietor to take out additional life insurance to cover the
        anticipated shrinkage of the business.   _____

14.   Which of the following businesses has to pay federal income taxes
     on its profits?
   a.   proprietorship.
   b.   partnership.
   c.   corporation.
   d.   Subchapter S corporation.   _____

15.   Which of the following is an important provision in a buy-and-sell
     agreement?
   a.   it must be financed by means of life insurance.
   b.   the surviving partner must buy out the deceased partner's
        interest.
   c.   arrangements for financing are usually left to chance.
   d.   the deceased partner's heirs may or may not accept the value
        stated in the buy-and-sell agreement.   _____

<table>
<tr><td>

1

REVIEW QUESTIONS
TRUE-FALSE

</td><td>

Name _____

Date _____ Points _____

</td></tr>
</table>

Directions: Circle T or F to indicate whether each statement is true or false.

ANSWERS

1. A regular savings program should be maintained through good years and bad.   T   F

2. A person who puts money into fixed dollars plays the role of a creditor.   T   F

3. Banks and credit unions are depository institutions.   T   F

4. The interest rate paid on a savings account is set by the depository institution.   T   F

5. Banks are the chief source of mortgage money in the United States.   T   F

6. Savers should consult with several depository institutions before opening an account.   T   F

7. Depository institutions are protected from an unusually large demand for cash.   T   F

8. A credit union may be established by a homogeneous group.   T   F

9. EE bonds are purchased at a discount.   T   F

10. HH bonds can be bought by anyone.   T   F

11. Municipal bonds finance state and local projects.   T   F

12. A partnership is an agreement between two or more persons to place their money, labor, and skill into a business.   T   F

13. A buy-and-sell agreement is seldom funded by means of life insurance.   T   F

14. A corporation is artificial, intangible, and a mere creature of the law.   T   F

15. The board of directors of a corporation elects the officers who run the corporation.   T   F

16. The stockholders of a corporation have limited liability.   T   F

17. The voting right is not important in a small corporation.   T   F

18. Credit unions do not provide insurance on deposits.   T   F

19. Legislation in 1980 eliminated many of the differences among
    depository institutions.   T   F

20. A stockholder has the right to examine corporate records.   T   F

21. Corporations are required to pay annual dividends to their
    stockholders.   T   F

22. A limited partner cannot have personal assets attached by the
    creditors of the partnership.   T   F

23. It is not necessary to enter into articles of partnership if you know
    and trust your partner.   T   F

24. The amount of risk one is willing to assume governs one's
    investment choices.   T   F

25. Interest rates on savings accounts in S&Ls are always higher than
    they are on savings accounts in banks.   T   F

1	Name ————————————————
PROJECT	Date ————— Points —————

Mary and Tom Baldwin, both age 30, are married and have one son, age 5. Mary and Tom both work, and their combined salaries amount to $50,000. Several years ago they bought a home, and they have an equity in it of $12,000. They have saved $25,000 and have decided to open a dry cleaning business. They have concluded that it will take all of their effort to make the business successful, so both are quitting their jobs.

You are to help them in their plans by answering the following questions. (Use the space below and on the back of this page if necessary.)

1. Which of the three forms of business ownership should they use?
2. How will they report their profit at the end of the year if the business is successful?
3. If the business should fail, are they liable for any outstanding debts, even though they are business and not personal debts?
4. How can Mary and Tom best protect themselves against the loss of the business if one of them should die? State the reasons for your decision.

CHAPTER 2
OUTLINE

I. **COMMON STOCK**
   A. Reasons for Buying Common Stock
   B. Basic Types of Common Stock
   C. Fluctuations in Common Stock
   D. Short-Term and Long-Term Trading
   E. Understanding Stock Quotations
   F. Yardsticks in Evaluating Common Stock
   G. Calculating the Dividend Return on Common Stock
   H. Other Classifications of Common Stock
   I. Stock Splits and Stock Dividends
   J. Stock Warrants and Stock Rights

II. **RULES FOR SOUND INVESTING IN COMMON STOCK**
   A. Before You Invest
   B. After You Invest

III. **PREFERRED STOCK**
   A. Preferences Enjoyed by Preferred Stock
   B. Features of Preferred Stock
   C. Reasons for Buying Preferred Stock

2

FUNDAMENTALS OF COMMON AND PREFERRED STOCK

When you invest in American industry, you may invest in three different ways. You may buy common stock, preferred stock, or bonds. Common stock and preferred stock are discussed in this chapter. Bonds will be discussed in Chapter 3.

When you buy common stock, you become a part owner of the business, thereby taking a businessperson's risk. If the business prospers, the stock will go up in value and the quarterly dividends will be good. Then you will have made a wise investment. If the stock doesn't go up and the dividends are just fair, then you will have made a mediocre investment. If the stock goes down, stays down, and the dividends are zero, then you will have made a poor investment. Or, if you are really unfortunate, you could lose your entire investment if the business is declared bankrupt. In the event that the business is dissolved, the bondholders are paid first; the preferred stockholders are paid second; and the common stockholders divide what is left.

COMMON STOCK

Common stock is often referred to as an equity security. **Equity** is simply another word for ownership. The market value for that equity is whatever you could sell the stock for on a given day.

When it is first issued, a common stock may have a **par value** (or a stated value). Par value has nothing to do with what a stock is really worth. A stock that has a par value of $5 can be worth $200 or it can be worth nothing. Par value is a bookkeeping item on the balance sheet of the corporation. It is the hypothetical amount that the company owes the common stockholders in the event the corporation should be dissolved.

Who issues common stock? Generally corporations organized for profit make their shares available to the individual investor. At the same time, not all corporations organized for the primary purpose of making money do this. As we saw in Chapter 1, most small corporations do not make their shares

available to the public because they are closely held companies. On the other hand, more than a million people own stock of the International Business Machines Corporation. In terms of total value, more than 40 percent of all common stock bought and sold by both individual and institutional investors is publicly traded on the New York Stock Exchange.

REASONS FOR BUYING COMMON STOCK

People usually buy common stock for two basic reasons: (1) the dividend and (2) the possible appreciation in price. Of the two motives the possible appreciation in price is the stronger.

Although the problem of inflation was emphasized in Chapter 1, it bears repeating here, for it is a serious problem. We cannot let it become as bad as it was in Germany between World War I and World War II, when a person's insurance death benefit was worth so little in purchasing power that it just paid for the wreath that the bereaved family hung on the door![1]

In his book *What's Wrong with Your Life Insurance*, Norman Dacey also says:

> Germany had printing-press inflation. France, on the other hand, had a controlled inflation; since World War I, the franc has shrunk to 1/84th of its former value. We are having controlled inflation in this country. Let us consider what it will mean to us if we have the same degree of inflation the French have had. The price of the average medium-priced car will climb to $250,000. One hundred dollars will buy enough meat for a meal for two adults—or one large dog. If you leave your wife $100,000 worth of life insurance, it will provide her with room and board for one year.[2]

Whether Mr. Dacey was being serious or simply facetious in demonstrating a point is really not germane to the question. The fact is that inflation is a problem, and the past performance of the stock market demonstrates that buying stocks is one way to protect the purchasing power of one's dollars from inflation's serious inroads.

BASIC TYPES OF COMMON STOCK

Now that you know who issues common stocks and understand the reasons for buying them, let us examine the two basic kinds of stock associated with the stock market: (1) blue-chip stocks and (2) growth stocks.

Blue-Chip Stocks

When does a corporation have such a top-drawer classification as to have its common stock called "blue chip"? A corporation's stock is considered to be a **blue-chip stock** when the company has met four rigid standards:

1. The corporation must be a leader in a major industry. Such an industry could be food, automobiles, or health care. There can be several leaders within an industry, and all can qualify. In the food industry, General Mills would be one leader; Procter & Gamble, another; and Kellogg Co., still another.
2. The corporation must have a proven record of earnings during good times and bad. Naturally, the earnings will be higher in some years than in others. Nevertheless, management must have turned in a consistent record of being able to make a profit year after year.
3. The corporation must have had an unbroken dividend record over a period of years—say 25 years—during which a cash dividend has been paid every year regardless of market conditions or the general level of business. It is surprising how many firms listed on the New York Stock Exchange can meet at least this one standard. Information provided by the New York Stock Exchange shows that 69 firms have had a continuous cash dividend record every year since the nineteenth century.
4. The corporation must have definite prospects of being able to continue this stellar past performance. During the latter stages of a long rise in stock prices, blue-chip stocks tend to fall out of favor with the investor because speculative fever takes over and investors back growth stocks more heavily. Similarly, when the market has taken a beating, the proven record of these blue-chip corporations comes into the right perspective and they again come into favor.

Growth Stocks

A better-than-average increase in the market price of a stock in a relatively short period of time is the chief characteristic of a **growth stock**. But it is very difficult to determine this until after the growth has taken place, hindsight being very easy, particularly in the marketplace. Investing only after as much information as possible has been obtained is essential at all times, but never more so than when attempting to choose a growth company. The following characteristics must be present for a corporation to be considered a growth company:

1. The corporation's earnings should be compounding at an unusually high rate. Ten percent is not enough, as this can be obtained from among the better blue chips. Twenty percent and more should be the rate of increase. Franklin Resources, which operates a group of investment companies with $33 billion in assets, is a growth corporation. Its revenues were $36.7 million in 1984, $63.3 million in 1985, $143.1 million in 1986, and $206.5 million in 1987.

2. The firm must be a leader in the right industry at the right time. Here is the true problem: you, the investor, must have the luck, the intuition, or the ability to choose that particular industry that is going to have unusual growth in the immediate future.

3. Net income per share should go up by approximately the same percentage as earnings. (See Chapter 7.) This is almost automatic if earnings are going up drastically. Nevertheless, net income per share must be watched. For Franklin Resources, net income per share was 23 cents in 1984, 51 cents in 1985, $1.99 in 1986, and $3.93 in 1987.

4. Adequate working capital is essential and should be generated from within if possible. In other words, the working capital should be increasing from retained earnings and not from borrowed capital or from the issuance of new common stock. The ability to pay bills promptly is exceptionally important in a young company, where a top line of credit with a banking syndicate may not be available. Not enough money with which to meet current obligations and to finance expansion is one of the chief causes of lack of growth for many small businesses.

FLUCTUATIONS IN COMMON STOCK

Have you ever wondered why common stocks fluctuate so much? There is no pat answer. No one can assess the mass psychology of thousands of investors and determine why they sell and why they buy. It is astonishing how much the common stock of a corporation can fluctuate in the short span of one year.

Tables 2-1 and 2-2 demonstrate such fluctuations. As a practical matter, few in-

TABLE 2-1   Effects of Price Fluctuation (One-Year Percentage Gain)

| | *Percentage GAIN if Investor Bought at Year's Low and Sold at Year's High* | | | | |
Corporation	*1982*	*1983*	*1984*	*1985*	*1986*
Boeing	113.7	51.0	67.0	46.0	46.0
Coca-Cola	81.0	26.4	34.0	49.0	74.0
Exxon	37.0	38.0	26.0	25.0	53.0
General Motors	88.9	42.0	34.0	32.0	34.0
General Electric	80.0	30.0	23.0	32.0	33.0

Source: Based on data from Standard & Poor's *Corporation Records,* 1986. Standard & Poor's Corporation, 345 Hudson St., New York, NY 10014.

TABLE 2-2	Effects of Price Fluctuation, (One-Year Percentage Loss)				
	Percentage LOSS if Investor Bought at Year's Low and Sold at Year's High				
Corporation	1982	1983	1984	1985	1986
Boeing	57.7	33.0	40.0	31.0	31.0
Coca-Cola	44.0	20.0	25.0	32.0	42.0
Exxon	22.0	36.1	20.0	30.0	33.0
General Motors	47.0	30.0	26.0	24.0	25.0
General Electric	44.0	23.0	19.0	23.0	25.0

Source: Based on data from Standard & Poor's *Corporation Records,* 1987. Standard & Poor's Corporation, 345 Hudson St., New York, NY 10014.

vestors would have enjoyed the gains or suffered the losses indicated because they would not have bought and sold at the absolute extremes (year's low and year's high). Note also that the stocks shown are blue-chip stocks. These stocks have established a reputation for consistent returns or earnings.

Why will a blue-chip stock advance in one year from a low of 51 to a high of 112 and the following year drop back to a low of 53 when its earnings remain the same, its balance sheet is similar, and its prospects for continued high volume of sales are excellent? The answer is simply that there is one factor that should not be expected of a common stock, and that is price stability. As the famous financier J. Pierpont Morgan once said when asked what the stock market was going to do that year, "It's going to fluctuate!"

One of the fundamental facts about the stock market is that it is an *auction market.* This means that it is subject to the law of supply and demand and to the whims, emotions, desires, and fears of millions of people. These emotions are more likely to be triggered by rumors, tips, and greed than by sober evaluation of the facts.

SHORT-TERM AND LONG-TERM TRADING

The effects shown in Tables 2-1 and 2-2 could make short-term trading appear very profitable. As a matter of fact, few people, even professionals, make money in the stock market by buying and selling frequently during the course of a year. Short-term trading is tempting and seemingly possesses enormous profit potential. However, it is much better to buy stocks on the facts and hold them over a period of time than to indulge in short-term trading.

You might well wonder why conservative people invest in common stocks at all. Well, despite the eccentric and often irrational way prices fluctuate in the short term, the record shows that over longer periods stock prices tend to rise in value and reflect the solid growth of the American economy.

Table 2-3 indicates the probable results of successful long-term investing during the period 1894–1985 (a total of 91 years). Notice that a person who held stock for just a year would have won only 58 percent of the time in the 91 one-year periods. A person who held stock for five years would have gained just 60 percent of the time, which is not much of an improvement over the one-year periods. A person who held for ten years would have gained 84 percent of the time. And a person who owned stocks during any of the 62 thirty-year periods involved could not have lost.

In a few more years we will be in the twenty-first century. The changes that will take place in the American economy, mainly because of technology, the myriad of new products available, and growth in the **gross national product (GNP)**—which is the sum of all the goods and services sold in the United States in one year—will be astonishing and vigorous indeed. There is nothing

TABLE 2-3 Probable Results of Successful Long-Term Investing
(Based on the Period 1894–1985)

Number of Years Stock Was Held	Number of Periods Involved	Percentage Chance of Gain	Percentage Chance of Loss
1	91	58	41
5	87	60	31
10	82	84	15
20	72	94	6
30	62	100	0

nebulous about the long-term growth of American industry. The record is there, and no one doubts its future long-term expansion.

Bull Market

When the broad trend of the market is up and the market has continued on this upward trend for some time, a **bull market** exists. Most of the economic indicators—such as the GNP, the number of people employed, corporate profits and earnings, personal income, total savings, and the availability of credit—are favorable during a bull market. A general optimism prevails under these conditions. The volume of shares traded on the stock exchange is high and has a *broad base*, meaning that most of the stocks listed are participating in the rise. The number of stocks reaching new highs for the year is impressive and the number reaching new lows is small. A bull market will last for several years. Normally the rise is not spectacular but steady. There are, of course, fluctuations during which market averages will decline.

It would be good to know when a bull market is coming to a close. That would be the time to sell and, by having your money in a cash position, wait out the subsequent down market. Then, when the market *bottoms out* (a gradual leveling of market prices after a long, steep decline), you could again invest at much lower prices. Unfortunately, even professional traders have a hard time doing this.

Bear Market

When the market is going down rather abruptly over a period of many months, a **bear market** exists. Usually, future business conditions and the international scene appear unfavorable. Unfortunately, the general market quite often anticipates this future condition by as much as six months and starts going down before the individual investor is aware of what is happening. Profits and earnings are still reported as good, and everyone is optimistic. Nevertheless, the future is not bright. It is the inability to foresee future bad times that prevents people from having the insight to know that a bear market is forming and that it is time to sell and wait for improved market conditions.

While the topping out of a bull market is very difficult to determine, even for professionals, the bottoming out of a bear market is more obvious. Market averages usually will fall 20 to 35 percent. Many individual issues will fall more. Investors who stay with a bear market suffer appreciable losses—at least on paper. The point at which the general market hits bottom will not be immediately apparent. If the market does not decline further over a period of several months in spite of continued bad news about general business conditions, it might be reasonable to conclude that the bear market is over.

UNDERSTANDING STOCK QUOTATIONS

How can you determine the price of a stock of a given corporation? After you buy the stock, how can you continue to follow its price fluctuations? The prices of all the stocks traded on the New York Stock Exchange and the American Stock Exchange are quoted every day in the daily newspapers (see Figure 2-1). Notice that stock prices are quoted in eighths of a dollar, such as 17⅛. A surprising amount of information is given on

FIGURE 2-1 New York Stock Exchange—Composite Transactions

NEW YORK STOCK EXCHANGE

COMPOSITE TRANSACTIONS

DOW JONES STOCK AVERAGES

1988 High	1988 Low		Open	High	Low	Close	Chg.
2,110.08	1,879.14	30 Indus	1,946.29	1,967.67	1,938.16	1,962.53	+21.05
904.12	737.57	20 Trans	784.80	798.39	782.11	794.95	+10.90
190.02	167.08	15 Utilities.......	168.09	169.39	167.56	169.16	+ 1.19
785.28	700.70	65 Stocks	720.60	729.40	717.84	727.29	+ 7.99

VOLUME—Indus: 12,823,600 Trans: 3,221,500 Util: 2,105,800 Stocks: 18,150,900

STANDARD & POOR'S AVERAGES

1988 High	1988 Low		High	Low	Close	Chg.
316.49	278.41	400 Industrials	293.50	290.74	293.49	+ 2.75
221.70	187.37	20 Transportation..........	191.11	187.71	191.05	+ 3.29
113.27	101.21	40 Utilities	103.66	102.22	103.66	+ 1.44
24.04	21.51	40 Financials	22.42	22.05	22.42	+ 0.37
271.55	242.63	500 Index	253.51	250.83	253.51	+ 2.68
258.09	232.45	100 Stocks	241.55	239.33	241.55	+ 2.03

NEW YORK STOCK EXCHANGE INDEXES

1988 High	1988 Low		High	Low	Close	Chg.
153.20	136.72	Composite	143.53	142.28	143.53	+ 1.32
187.02	163.02	Industrials	173.71	171.37	173.71	+ 1.49
140.34	118.10	Transportation	123.89	122.68	123.89	+ 1.62
73.97	67.74	Utilities	68.75	68.15	68.75	+ 0.67
128.24	115.75	Finance	120.29	119.05	120.29	+ 1.42

WHAT THE MARKET DID

	Tue.	Mon.	Fri.	Thur.	Wed.	Wk.Ago
Volume*	139,900	102,640	120,600	165,160	209,420	133,850
Issues	1,960	1,942	1,960	1,979	1,988	1,979
Advances	948	424	841	640	283	521
Declines	509	1,078	605	843	1,288	985
Unchanged	503	470	514	496	417	473
New Highs	10	5	9	5	9	11
New Lows	14	22	13	24	21	12

* NYSE Only: Thousands of Shares

NYSE LEADERS

Stock	Sales	Close	Chg.
NoeastUtl	23,814,200	19⅝	unch
KansPwLt	4,614,100	24	unch
Boeing	2,213,300	53⅞	+2⅛
Citicor s	1,410,700	22½	+ ¾
Varity	1,362,700	3¼	+ ¼
DominRes	1,333,800	41⅞	+ ⅜
Texaco	1,264,500	45⅞	− ¼
MayDSt	1,161,200	29⅜	unch
FedNatMt	1,108,300	37	+1½
Anheusr	1,085,300	30⅛	+ ½
DetEdison	1,051,900	13⅛	+ ⅜
AT&T	1,035,000	26½	+ ⅛
Chrysler	993,700	20⅞	− ½
GenElct	935,700	40⅛	+ ½
IBM	900,900	109¼	+ ½

WILSHIRE INDEX

The Wilshire Associates' 5000 Equity Index, the market value of 5000 NYSE, American and OTC issues, was $2,528.-146 billion Tuesday, up $21.210 billion on Monday.

ODD LOTS

Transactions for May 23: purchases of 186,932 shares; sales of 551,222 shares including 99,363 shares sold short.

TECH INDEX

Hambrecht & Quist Technology Growth Index closed at 538.68 Tuesday, up 0.45 percent from 536.26 Monday.

52 Week High	52 Week Low	Stock	Div	PE	Sales Hds	Last	Net Chg
20½	17⅞	Duq pf	2.00		z250	19	
24⅜	19	Duq prK	2.10		8	20¼	− ⅛
26⅞	14¾	DynAm	.20	10	51	20¾	+ ¼
25⅝	9	Dyncrp	.31	29	87	18⅝	+ ⅛
		E					
14	7¾	ECC	.20	8	6	7¾	
29	6¼	EMC s		6	151	6⅞	− ⅛
45⅛	27	EGG	.60	16	308	32¼	+ ⅞
12	7½	EQK G	1.16	30	94	11⅝	
14⅜	11	EQK Rt	1.66	156	1	14	− ¼
15½	6½	ERC		8	41	9⅜	
40⅞	23	E Syst	.50	14	1359	27	+ ⅜
47⅜	19⅜	EagleP	1.12	7	60	28¾	+ ⅝
29½	19	EastGF	1.30	11	88	24⅛	
33¾	21⅛	EastUtl	2.40	7	55	23⅛	+ ¼
70⅝	39¾	EKodk s	1.80	11	6550	41⅛	+ ½
107¾	55½	Eaton	2.00	10	365	77	+ ⅜
19⅜	10¾	Echlin	.62	19	857	16¼	+ ¼
33¾	18½	Ecolab	.62	5	639	23⅞	+ ⅜
40¼	21⅞	EdisBr	1.80		77	77	
21	11⅝	EDO	.28	14	82	14	+ ⅛
32⅜	14¼	Edward	.68	9	115	15⅜	− ⅛
4¼	1⅝	EKCO		40	395	2	− ¼
13¾	5¼	Elcor	.22	35	2	6⅝	− ⅛
24¾	13⅞	Eldon s	.24	21	9	24½	+ ¼
4¾	2⅛	ElecAs		60	24	3	− ⅛
2⅝	1	Elscint			30	1⅛	− ⅛
10	5¼	Emrld	1.20	5	109	8⅛	+ ⅛
42⅜	26¾	EmrsE s	1.00	13	2342	29⅛	+ ⅛
8	2⅛	EmRad			382	3¼	+ ⅛

52 Week High	52 Week Low	Stock	Div	PE	Sales Hds	Last	Net Chg
69	28	GaGulf	1.20	6	891	53¾	+ 1½
48¾	22¾	GaPac	1.20	8	1120	37¾	+ ⅜
26⅞	22¾	GaPw pf	2.50		3	25¼	+ ⅛
26⅛	22	GaPw pf	2.43		55	24⅝	
25½	19⅞	GaPw pf	2.30		19	23½	+ ¼
26⅞	23¾	GaPw pf	2.47		59	25¼	+ ⅜
24½	19¾	GaPw pf	2.09e		1000	23⅛	− ⅜
29¼	25¼	GaPw pf	3.00		9	27¾	− ⅛
26¾	21¾	GaPw pr	2.56		5	25⅞	
26¾	21	GaPw pf	2.52		3	25	+ ⅛
28½	23¼	GaPw pf	2.75		2	27¼	+ ½
81	68	GaPw pr	7.80		z1340	75¼	− 1¼
80	69	GaPw pr	7.72		z70	74	− ½
63	22½	GerbPd	1.32	39	844	41¾	+ 1⅜
24⅛	12⅛	GerbSc s	.12	17	991	18	+ ¼
12⅛	5⅝	GerFd	1.55e		44	6⅝	
25	12¼	Getty s	.20	12	41	15¾	
26⅛	13¼	GIANT		16	273	18¾	+ ⅛
10½	3¼	GibrFn			96	3½	
49	17⅝	Gillete	.86	17	3383	37⅛	+ 1
30⅝	15¾	Glaxo n	.45e	17	2780	17⅛	+ ⅝
19⅞	8½	GleasC		40	69	13¼	+ ¼
32½	16⅞	Glenfed	1.00	4	311	20¼	+ ¼
10¾	9¼	GlbGvt n	.08e		682	10	
11	8	GGInc	1.02e		8	9¾	
4½	1⅛	vjGlbM			63	1¼	+ ⅛
10¾	2¼	vjGlM pf			7	2½	− ⅛
10½	8⅞	GlobYld	1.08		888	10	+ ⅛
15¼	7⅝	GldNug		3	281	13¾	− ¼
1½	1/64	GldN wt			781	3/32	− 1/32
43¾	20½	GldWF	.24	6	2055	24⅛	+ 1⅛
7¾	2¾	Gldme n			118	3¼	+ ½

52 Week High	52 Week Low	Stock	Div	PE	Sales Hds	Last	Net Chg
79	37¾	IrvBnk	2.42		3528	62⅞	+ ½
12⅝	6¼	Italy n	.29e		14	6⅞	
		J					
24⅞	12	JP Ind		11	14	16⅞	
33	11¾	JWP s		10	203	19⅛	+ ⅜
14½	6¾	Jackpot	.20a	14	168	12⅝	+ ⅝
38⅛	18½	JRiver	.40	9	680	22	+ ⅜
58½	37½	JRvr pf	3.37		15	41¾	− ¼
52½	29¼	JRvr pf	3.50		1	43	+ ½
15	5⅞	Jamswy	.08	11	83	8½	− ¼
42½	23	JeffPl	1.28	13	418	30¾	+ ⅝
13¾	5	Jepson		7	78	6⅝	− ⅛
87¾	72¾	JerC pf	8.12		z350	79	
23⅝	19¼	JerC pf	2.18		19	22¼	+ ⅛
105⅝	55	JohnJn	2.00	14	3907	73¼	+ 1⅜
40	20½	JohnCn	1.10	12	277	30½	− ⅜
24½	12⅛	Johnlnd		7	4	15⅝	− ⅛
14⅜	6⅛	JhnCRt	.70	32	58	6¾	− ¼
47	3/32	JhCR wt			5	3/32	
30½	17¾	Jorgen	1.00	31	7	26⅛	− ¼
24¾	15⅛	Jostens	.56	7	346	17⅛	− ⅜
		K					
19⅝	8½	KDI	.30	6	45	11⅛	
27¾	13¼	KLM	.75e		359	17¾	+ ¼
48¾	21⅝	K mart	1.32	10	3253	32¾	+ ⅞
19⅝	11½	KN Eng	1.08	19	74	16¼	− ¼
23¼	7¾	Kaisrtc	.15j		1825	17⅝	− ¼
11½	6⅛	KanbEn	2.40	13	169	7½	

52 Week High	52 Week Low	Stock	Div	PE	Sales Hds	Last	Net Chg
74¼	48	Merck wi			149	49⅞	+ ⅝
11¾	4½	MercSL	.40b	16	24	7¼	+ ⅛
43¼	23	Merdth	.64	13	345	26⅝	+ ¼
41½	19½	MerLyn	1.00	7	1539	22⅞	+ ¼
17⅞	9⅛	MesaLP	2.00	29	505	12¾	+ ⅛
15¼	9	MesLP pf	1.50		970	11¾	− ⅛
2	1 1/16	MesaOf	.31e		x927	1⅜	+ ⅛
45¾	33	MesaR	1.11e		x103	36¾	+ ⅛
2⅝	1	Mesab			16	1¾	+ ⅛
13⅝	7¾	MetrFn	.44	5	32	8⅜	− ⅛
14¼	3	MaxFd	.15e		481	5¾	
25¼	17¾	MchER	1.44	13	22	23⅞	+ ¼
8	3⅞	Micklby	.06	4	6	5⅜	
11¾	7¾	MidSUt		6	7108	9½	− ⅛
21¼	15	MWE	1.52	10	110	19	+ ⅛
46½	27⅛	Millipre	.32	20	101	36	− ¾
15¼	8½	MitnR	.44	15	5	14	
83½	45	MMM	2.12	14	3748	58½	+ 1
27¾	19½	MinnPL	1.72	11	249	24⅛	+ ¼
5⅝	2¼	Mitel			757	2¼	
55	32	Mobil	2.40	12	3376	44¼	− ⅛
36	12¼	Mohsc s	.28	18	554	35⅝	
85	38½	MonCa		8	129	39¾	
24½	11⅞	Monrch	.80	123	5	19¾	− ¼
100¼	57	Monsan	3.00	11	2386	77	+ 1
37¼	29½	MonPw	2.68	12	573	33¼	
19	7¾	Monted			50	11¾	+ ¼
21¾	17¼	MonSt	1.94e		15	18¾	
8⅝	5½	MONY	.72	12	79	7⅜	+ ¼
26⅝	16½	Moore	.76	15	196	24¼	− ⅛
53⅝	27	Morgan	1.50	50	5220	34⅝	+ ⅞
80½	71½	Morgn pf	5.00e		1	72⅝	

Source: Reprinted from the *San Francisco Chronicle* (1988). All Rights Reserved.

one line: the high and low price for 52 weeks; the name of the stock; its annual dividend; its price-earnings ratio; sales in hundreds; the last price for the day; and the net change from the day before.

Stock Key

Once in a while you will find a letter following the dividend listed in a stock quotation. An explanation of the various letter designations can be found in the "stock key" at the very end of the stock listings for that day. For example, if you want to know what the letter "b" stands for, look at the stock key and you will find that it means "annual rate plus stock dividends." Figure 2-2 shows a reprint of the stock key. An explanation of how to read daily quotations is given in Figure 2-3.

The NASDAQ National Market

Common stock is not limited to stock that is traded on organized security exchanges such as the New York Stock Ex-

---

FIGURE 2-2   Stock Key

STOCK KEY

Sales figures are unofficial. s —stock split or stock dividend amounting to 25 percent or more in the past 52 weeks. Dividend begins with the date of split or stock dividend. n—new issue in past 52 weeks. g—dividend or earnings in Canadian money. Stock trades in U.S. dollars. No yield or PE shown unless stated in U.S. money. Unless otherwise noted, rates of dividends are annual disbursements based on last quarterly or semiannual declaration. Special or extra dividends or payments not designated as regular are identified as follows:

a—also extra or extras. b—annual rate plus stock dividend. c—liquidating dividend. e—declared or paid in preceding 12 months. i—declared or paid after stock dividend or split up. j—paid this year, dividend omitted, deferred or no action taken at last dividend meeting. k—declared or paid this year, an accumulative issue with dividends in arrears. r—declared or paid in preceding 12 months plus stock dividend. t—paid in stock in preceding 12 months, estimated cash value on ex-dividend or ex-distribution date.

x—ex-dividend or ex-rights. y—ex-dividend and sales in full. z—sales in full.

cld—called. wd—when distributed. wi—when issued. ww—with warrants. xw—without warrants. xdis—ex-distribution.

vj—in bankruptcy or receivership or being reorganized under bankruptcy act, or securities assumed by such companies.

---

change. In terms of number of corporations, not value of stocks, much more stock is traded over the counter than is bought and sold on the security exchanges. (Chapter 6 discusses security exchanges and the over-the-counter market.)

In the NASDAQ National Market, where the over-the-counter stocks are listed, the price at which an investor can buy a stock is quoted, with the net change from the day before. Figure 2-4 shows over-the-counter quotations from the NASDAQ National Market system.

YARDSTICKS IN EVALUATING COMMON STOCK

What yardsticks should be used in evaluating common stocks? There are enough books on this subject to fill a large library. As an investor, you should have knowledge of the most commonly used yardsticks. These are (1) the corporation's balance sheet, (2) the corporation's income statement, (3) the corporation's price-earnings ratio, (4) industry data, (5) stock market averages, and (6) the number of shares traded daily. Because the balance sheet and the income statement are the two most important yardsticks in evaluating a corporation's common stock, these financial statements will be discussed in great detail in Chapter 7. In this chapter we will examine the other four mentioned above.

Price-Earnings Ratio

Investors frequently use the **price-earnings ratio** in determining the value of a stock. This ratio is calculated by dividing the current market price of a share by its earnings for the previous year. For example, if the current market price is $80 per share and the earnings for the previous year were $4, the price-earnings ratio would be 20, or 20 to 1. The price-earnings ratio is probably one of the most widely used yardsticks for evaluating whether a stock is reasonably priced.

For stocks in general, a price-earnings ratio of 10 to 1 is considered low. On the other

FIGURE 2-3 How to Read Stock Quotations

1. The abbreviated name of the company issuing the stock is given—in this case, Anheuser Busch.
2. Stocks are common unless "pf" follows the name, indicating a preferred stock.
3. Columns show the highest and lowest prices paid for a stock on the exchange during the past 52 weeks—for Ashland Oil, 71¾ and 46½.
4. Numbers following names show the rate of annual dividend—for Atlantic Richfield, $4.00. The amount may be changed but is an estimation based on the last quarterly or semiannual payments. Letters following the dividend numbers indicate other information about the dividend.
5. The "e" indicates that in addition to the annual dividend rate shown ($0.25 for Avalon), an extra dividend was paid. Other symbols used are explained in a table appearing in each newspaper.
6. This column shows the number of shares reported traded for the day, expressed in hundreds—for Bank of America, 363,800. This number does not include stocks bought and sold in odd-lot quantities, that is, in quantities less than 100 shares for most stocks.
7. The highest price paid for Baxter during the trading session was 23¼.
8. Net change for Bear Stevens from the previous day is indicated by "+⅜" in the Net Change column.

52 Week High	52 Week Low	Stock	Div	PE	Sales Hds	Last	Net Chg
34⅜	18½	Angelic	.72	15	404	27	
14⅞	9⅝	AnglRl n	1.52	43	72	10¾	
40⅛	25¾	Anheus	.60	16	2720	31⅞	− ⅜
17⅜	6¾	Anthm		25	130	12½	− ⅛
14⅞	7¾	Anthony	.44b	8	122	12⅝	+ ¼
29⅞	20½	Aon Cp s	1.28	11	382	25⅜	
12½	6⅝	Apache	.28		401	8½	− ⅛
8⅜	2¾	ApcP un	.70		661	2⅞	− ⅛
97	72	ApPw pf	8.12		z2500	84	
36	17¼	ApplBk		8	202	32⅜	+ 1½
20⅞	8½	ApplM s		18	361	16⅞	− ⅛
27¾	17½	ArchDn	.10b	12	6989	22½	− ⅛
38¾	17	ArcoCh	.40e		1250	32¾	− 1
39	16¾	Aristec	.80	12	4359	33	+ ½
20⅞	8⅛	ArkBst	.36	16	263	13¾	− ⅛
26½	15⅝	Arkla	1.08	16	1423	20	− ¼
59	34½	Arkla pf	3.00		629	42	
14¾	7⅛	Armco		10	3912	12⅛	− ⅜
25½	18¼	Armc pf	2.10		1	23¾	+ ¼
46	37¾	Armc pf	4.50		5	42⅞	
47⅜	22½	ArmWI	.90	13	902	40½	− 1½
30½	13	Armtek	.48	13	704	28⅞	− ⅜
12⅛	4⅞	ArowE			389	7⅞	+ ⅛
21½	12	ArowE pf	1.94		57	15¼	
33	11	Artra			119	20⅜	− ⅜
39¾	14¾	Arvin	.68	10	608	23¼	
34¼	15	Asarco	.20e	4	1359	23⅜	− ⅛
71¾	46½	AshlOil	1.80	12	1654	70¾	+ ⅝
12	3⅝	AsiaPc			89	6½	+ ⅛
13	5	AtalSos	.40e	10	2	8½	+ ⅛
23⅛	9⅞	Athlone	1.60		21	13⅝	
37¼	28¾	AtlEnrg	2.68a	8	475	33¾	+ ½
99⅛	58¾	AtlRich	4.00	14	3923	90¾	+ ⅜
235¾	155½	AtlRc pr	2.80		7	215¾	+ 1¾
53	21¾	AtlasCp		23	26	36	+ ¼
8	3	AudVd		20	1371	5¼	− ¾
28⅝	10⅝	Augat	.40	23	152	14¾	
29½	10	Ausimt	.60	16	367	26⅞	− ⅜
54½	32¼	AutoDt	.44	23	1834	44⅜	− ¼
8	4⅛	Avalon	.20e		66	4¾	
25¼	14⅝	AVMC s	.28	12	18	24⅜	
29¼	15⅛	Avery	.42	28	470	25	+ ⅜
39¼	18½	Avnet	.50	26	274	27¼	− ½
38⅝	19¼	Avon	2.00	11	x1322	25½	+ ⅛
35⅝	16	Aydin		6	32	24¼	
		B					
32⅝	23½	BCE g	2.44		621	31⅞	+ ⅛
20¼	13⅜	BET n	.77e	13	19	17	− ⅜
9⅞	3¼	BMC		9	434	7¼	
32⅜	23½	BRE	2.40	13	24	29½	+ ⅛
19⅝	14½	BRT	2.48	7	87	18⅛	
42¼	20	Bairnco	.80	12	66	33⅛	− ⅜
27⅜	11⅛	BakrHu	.46		3611	19⅜	
67	38⅝	BkrH pf	3.50		334	51	+ ¼
28	17	Baldor	.48	25	56	26⅞	
48½	27¼	Ball	.96	12	198	33⅜	+ ⅛
27¾	10½	BallyMf	.20	11	1547	17½	− ⅛
21½	9¾	BaltBcp	.50	9	640	16¼	− ¼
34	19	BaltGE	1.90	9	1869	31⅞	
62	50	Balt pfB	4.50		z100	51	− 1½
27⅜	16⅛	BncOne	.92b	11	1026	24⅜	− ⅛
4¼	1⅛	BanTx n			64	1½	
69	42	Bandag	.80	16	406	64	− 3
38	17⅞	BkBost	1.08	249	357	24⅞	+ ⅛
52¾	47½	BkB pfA	3.46e		31	48	− ½
37¼	20¼	BkNE	1.24	12	285	28	− ⅛
45⅞	24½	BkNY	1.80	11	695	32¾	− 1⅛
13¼	6⅝	BnkAm			3638	10½	− ⅛
35	24½	BkA pf	3.42e		49	31½	+ ¼
58	42	BkA pf	6.00e		1	52½	− ¼
9⅞	6⅛	BkA pf	2.88		217	7⅜	+ ¼
700	600	BkA pfD			1	700	
55¼	26¼	BankTr	1.86	600	1142	32	+ ½
27¾	13⅜	Banner			99	15½	
42½	29	Barclay	1.88e		47	31¾	− ¼
49⅝	25	Bard	.48	20	667	42¾	− ¼
40¼	26¼	BarnGp	1.20	13	85	36½	− ⅜
41¾	27⅛	Barnet s	.92	10	1760	33½	+ ⅞
19¾	9¼	BaryWr	.60	14	365	14½	+ ⅛
8⅜	¾	viBASIX			67	⅞	
29⅞	12¾	BatlMt s	.10	22	988	16⅛	− ⅛
48⅞	30¾	Bausch	1.00	16	1363	44¼	− ⅜
29¼	15½	Baxter	.50	20	5028	23¼	+ ⅜
50⅞	45¼	Bax pfA	3.53e		1	46	− ¼
93	61	Bax pfB	3.50		41	75¼	− ½
24⅛	13⅞	BayFin	.05i		42	14⅝	− ½
30¼	19¾	BayStG	1.52	9	26	22¾	− ⅛
21½	8	BearSt	.50	10	1740	14¼	+ ⅜

hand, a growth stock with a price-earnings ratio of 50 to 1, while considered high, is not necessarily excessive.

When the 30 stocks used in determining the Dow Jones industrial average (discussed in the following pages) are considered, an average price-earnings ratio of all the 30 stocks is low at 10 to 1 and high at 20 to 1. When these stocks are selling at a price-earnings ratio of 10 to 1, it is one indication that a bear market is drawing to a close. When they are selling at a price-earnings

FIGURE 2-4 Quotations for Over-the-Counter Markets

NASDAQ NATIONAL MARKET

MOST ACTIVE

	Volume	Bid	Asked	Chg
Acadln	2,157,500	1 3/8		−1/16
Sovran	1,574,000	33		− 1/4
MCI	1,415,800	13 1/2		+ 1/4
TlcmA s	1,377,600	22 3/4		+ 1/2
CoatSl	1,347,800	4 3/4		+ 3/4
AppleC s	1,274,600	38 7/8		+ 7/8
Intel s	905,200	29 5/8		+ 3/8
MedcC s	772,500	15 5/8		+1
FarGp s	670,100	58 7/8		+ 1/4
USWNV	655,400	15 1/4		+1

MARKET PROFILE

Most act.	Sovran 33 + 1/8
NASDAQ sales	109,730,600
NASDAQ composite	365.16 + 1.90
NMS composite	157.74 + 0.86
Advanced	1,087
Declined	934
Unchanged	2,633
Total issues	4,654
New highs	78
New lows	71

Source: Reprinted from the *San Francisco Chronicle* (1988). All Rights Reserved.

ratio of 20 to 1, it is one indication that a bull market is topping out.

Industry Data

Several sources provide industrial data, and every major industry today has its own trade publication giving the latest developments concerning its particular segment of the economy. Examples of such publications are *Automotive News, Iron Age,* and *Food Industries*. Government data available from the Commerce Department, the Federal Reserve Board, the Labor Department, and other agencies give vital information about the status of the national economy. The most frequently referred to financial publications are *The Wall Street Journal, Barron's Financial Weekly,* and *Commercial and Financial Chronicle*.

Stock Market Averages

The oldest and best-known stock market average—the one that is still the most widely watched—is the **Dow Jones industrial average (DJIA)**. The DJIA is an index consisting of 30 industrial stocks that are considered by Dow Jones to be sufficiently representative of what the market is doing as a whole.

This index dates from 1884, when Charles Henry Dow added together the trading prices of 11 industrial stocks and divided the total by 11. Over the years, the composite stocks have changed so that today they are 30 in number, with only two left of the original 11. These two are the General Electric Company and the American Tobacco Company (now called American Brands). Today—to compensate for the numerous stock splits that have taken place in these stocks over the years—instead of dividing by 30, a divisor of 0.754 is used.[3]

When the stock market crashed in 1929, the DJIA plummeted from 381.17 to a low of 41.22 in 1932. By 1946 it was back up to 163.12. It then continued rising over the next 20 years to an intraday high of 1,000 early in 1966—only to fall back to near disaster, below 650, in May 1970. Again it recovered, only to fall badly again in October 1974, when it dropped below 600. But once more, as the stock market has a habit of doing, the DJIA came back in 1976 to go over the magical mark of 1,000, only to decline again to 776.92 on August 12, 1982. On that date the stock market started its most spectacular rise in history. From a DJIA of 776.92 on August 12, 1982, it rose to a high of 2,722.42 on August 25, 1987. From this high point, the market lost almost 1,000 points in two months, culminating in a 508-point crash on Black Monday, October 19, 1987, when 608 million shares were traded in a single day.

Figure 2-5 lists the performance of 30 well-known stocks over a 59-year period from 1928 to 1986. This analysis assumes an initial investment of $10,000 in each case, with all dividends taken in cash. Note that the performance of the top 13 companies was truly remarkable, for the original investment in each case was worth more than $200,000 at the end of the period. The leader, Coca-Cola, was worth more than $1 million at the end of 1986.

In addition to the DJIA, Dow Jones publishes a separate average for 20 transportation stocks, 15 utilities, 65 common stocks, and 40 bonds.

Other widely watched stock market averages are (1) Standard and Poor's Index of 500 Common Stocks, (2) the New York Stock Exchange Index of the average price of all stocks listed on its exchange, and (3) the American Stock Exchange Index.

Volume of Daily Trading

The number of shares traded every day on the stock exchanges and the over-the-counter market is another indicator of how the stock market is performing. A volume of 125 million shares indicates a slow day, meaning that investors are watchful and are standing on the sideline. On the other hand, a volume of 200 million or more shares indicates a big day. It usually means that investors, particularly large institutional investors such as mutual funds, pension funds, and insurance companies, are optimistic and are buying.

CALCULATING THE DIVIDEND RETURN ON COMMON STOCK

If you paid $20 for a stock today and the corporation's board of directors declared a dividend of 25 cents every quarter during the first year and thereafter, you would have an annual dividend of $1. The dividend return would be calculated as follows:

$$\frac{\$1.00}{\$20.00} = .05 \text{ or } 5\%$$

Let's assume, however, that you bought the stock for $20 several years ago and that it currently sells for $40 and pays a dividend of $2 a year. In this case, you should calculate the dividend return in relation to the current market price, not the original cost price. Thus, your current dividend return is still 5 percent, ($2/$40), not 10 percent ($2/$20), which is the way some investors would calculate it.

FIGURE 2-5 Common Stock Investing Does Require Skill

Stock	Original Investment Mar. 1, 1928	Value* Dec. 31, 1986
Coca-Cola	$10,000	$1,057,243
Hershey Foods	10,000	710,461
Exxon	10,000	459,368
Eastman Kodak	10,000	423,288
Procter & Gamble	10,000	374,053
Goodyear Tire & Rubber	10,000	365,749
General Electric	10,000	334,950
International Paper	10,000	293,252
Sears Roebuck	10,000	263,284
Westinghouse Electric	10,000	227,733
American Brands	10,000	227,051
Chevron Corp.	10,000	216,626
Firestone	10,000	205,188
DuPont	10,000	167,874
United Technologies	10,000	160,470
Texaco	10,000	150,793
Union Carbide	10,000	149,756
Aluminum Company of America	10,000	119,800
Chrysler Corp.	10,000	79,156
General Motors	10,000	73,010
Woolworth	10,000	44,290
Allied Corp.	10,000	43,430
International Telephone & Telegraph	10,000	25,440
American Can	10,000	23,369
Navistar International**	10,000	19,343
American Telephone & Telegraph	10,000	18,834
U.S. Steel	10,000	14,183
Bethlehem Steel	10,000	14,149
Singer Manufacturing	10,000	9,191
International Nickel	10,000	6,639

*It was assumed that the full $10,000 was invested in each stock and that fractional shares were purchased where required to use up the full amount. No brokerage charges were included in the cost. Adjustments were made for all stock splits and stock dividends. No adjustments for cash distributions have been taken into consideration.

**Formerly International Harvester.

Source: *The Pioneer Story*, Pioneer Fund, Inc., 60 State St., Boston, MA 02109.

Suppose, however, that the stock for which you paid $20 several years ago currently sells for $40 but still pays a dividend of only $1. In this case, your current dividend return is only 2.5 percent ($1/$40). If you need income, you should sell the stock at $40 and put your money into a savings account or into another stock that is paying 5 percent on its current market value. By doing this you would double your income; that is, the $40 would pay you $2, not $1.

OTHER CLASSIFICATIONS OF COMMON STOCK

Some common stocks are classified as either defensive stocks or cyclical stocks. Others are described as special situation stocks, voting trust certificates, or American depository receipts. All of these are described below.

Defensive and Cyclical Stocks

People always have to eat and will always need gas, light, and water, regardless of the times. Therefore, food and utility stocks are not likely to suffer too badly during a recession. **Defensive stocks** are those issued by businesses whose products or services are consumable necessities and are consequently always in demand.

Cyclical stocks are just the opposite. By the nature of their business, cyclical stocks are adversely affected by a decline in general business activity. Building can always wait; therefore, stocks of the construction industry are considered cyclical. In other words, their prices will rise and fall as the business cycle goes up or down.

Special Situation Stocks

When something unusual happens to increase the value of a common stock, it becomes a **special situation stock.** Examples of such unusual events are the discovery of oil on land owned by a railroad, the introduction of a popular new product developed by a company's own research department, or the effective reorganization of a company with new management.

Voting Trust Certificates

Occasionally a corporation gets into trouble. If it has borrowed money from a bank, the bank may become concerned and insist on being repaid. If the bank is not repaid, it may temporarily take over voting control of the company. **Voting trust certificates** are evidence that the common stockholders have placed their stock in the hands of a trustee, usually a bank, for a certain period of time. The trustee has the right to vote their stock for them at the annual stockholders' meeting. When the time has expired, the stock is returned to the owners. Stockholders have the right to agree or not to agree to changes proposed by management by casting their vote, usually one vote for each share owned.

American Depository Receipts

U.S. investors in European corporations are issued **American depository receipts (ADRs)** instead of stock certificates as evidence of ownership. There is a technical problem in connection with ownership of shares in European corporations because such shares are generally *bearer instruments*. In other words, whoever possesses the certificates may cash them. They are not registered in the name of the owner on the books of the company as they are in this country.

In order to obtain any dividends that are declared, U.S. investors arrange for a foreign bank to collect and convert them from the foreign currency into U.S. dollars. On U.S. stock exchanges, instead of trading directly in shares of European companies, the usual practice is to trade in ADRs for such shares.

STOCK SPLITS AND STOCK DIVIDENDS

A corporation sometimes splits its stock to bring the market price within a range that is attractive to investors, thus enabling the stock to be more widely held. In a **stock split**, the common stock outstanding is divided into additional units, such as two for one or three for one. Let us say that a stock is split two for one, and that before the split you owned 100 shares worth $50 a share. After the split you will own 200 shares worth $25 a share. Obviously, you have gained nothing from this transaction, since 100 shares of stock at $50 a share and 200 shares at $25 a share are both worth $5,000. But corporations have found that investors will more readily purchase a stock selling for $25 a share than one selling for $50 a share because they can buy twice as many shares for the same amount of money.

Stock splits should never be confused with **stock dividends**, which are a distribution of profits in the form of stock rather than cash. A corporation distributes stock dividends when it wants to give its stockholders credit for profits earned but at the same time retain the cash in the business. Using the above example, let us say that you own 100 shares worth $50 a share and the company declares a 100 percent stock dividend. This means that you now own 200 shares worth $50 a share. Obviously, your shares have doubled in number as well as in value.

It is important to note that neither stock splits nor stock dividends are reported to the Internal Revenue Service as income. Your total cost remains the same. If you sell the shares later at a profit, your cost in the above example is still $5,000.

STOCK WARRANTS AND STOCK RIGHTS

Stock warrants, or stock subscription warrants, are not to be confused with stock rights. A **stock warrant** is a certificate that gives its holder the option to purchase the common stock of a corporation at a stated price, which is almost always at a lower price than the current market value of the stock. A stock warrant is usually issued along with the offering of a bond. The stock warrant adds speculative appeal to the bond offering and therefore makes the bonds more attractive to the buying public. Figure 2-6 shows a stock subscription warrant of the San Diego Gas and Electric Company.

A **stock right** is the preemptive right of existing stockholders to participate in *new* stock offerings of the corporation. A stock right gives the common stockholder the right to purchase a certain number of shares of the new stock offering—for example, the right to buy one share for every ten shares already held. Stock rights have a small value. If the stockholder does not wish to exercise his or her stock rights, they may be sold through a stockbrokerage firm.

RULES FOR SOUND INVESTING IN COMMON STOCK

After you have learned something about the stock market, you cannot do as the man did in the famous quotation by Stephen Leacock: "So he flung himself upon his horse and rode madly off in all directions." Here are before-and-after rules to follow that will give you a better-than-average chance for success.

BEFORE YOU INVEST

1. Commit only a percentage of your excess funds in the market. Remember the number one cornerstone presented in Chapter 1—you should maintain a cash reserve for any unforeseen emergency. Many experienced stockbrokers and investment counselors recommend investing no more than 50 percent of one's excess money in the market. This may be too little or too much, depending on your circumstances. The percentage of excess funds you hold back is up to you, but don't invest all of them.

2. Buy on facts, not rumors or hunches. No matter what your objective may be, do not invest until you have the facts. Anyone who buys and sells thousands of dollars' worth of securities on the basis of a two-minute telephone conversation with a stockbroker deserves to lose. Even though you have faith in your broker, you should still find out all you can about a company and its management before you invest. If your broker insists on handling your investments on the basis of quick telephone calls, you should shift your account to someone else.

3. Set your sights high. Try for a 100 percent increase in one year. You probably won't get it, but you certainly won't if the stock doesn't have a ghost of a chance of doing that well. If you do only half as well as 100 percent, you will still double your money in two years. And if you do only a fourth as well as 100 percent, you will double your money in four years.

FIGURE 2-6 Stock Subscription Warrant

SUBSCRIPTION WARRANT FOR COMMON STOCK OF
SAN DIEGO GAS & ELECTRIC COMPANY
The registered owner named hereon, or assigns, is entitled to subscribe for shares of Common Stock upon the terms and conditions specified in the Prospectus relating thereto.

THESE RIGHTS EXPIRE AND BECOME VOID AT 3:30 P.M., EASTERN DAYLIGHT SAVING TIME, ON OCTOBER 10, 19__

WARRANT FOR / RIGHTS

NINE RIGHTS AND FULL SUBSCRIPTION PRICE ARE REQUIRED TO SUBSCRIBE FOR EACH SHARE OF COMMON STOCK
Subscription Price per Share: $31.00

ISSUED SEPTEMBER 18, 19__, BY:
SAN DIEGO GAS & ELECTRIC COMPANY

WARRANT NO.

IT IS NECESSARY TO FILL OUT AND SIGN ONE OF THE FORMS ON THE OTHER SIDE OF THIS WARRANT

ISSUING AGENT

This warrant is transferable and may be divided or combined at the office of either of the following Subscription Agents:

THE FIRST NATIONAL TRUST AND SAVINGS BANK OF SAN DIEGO
Corporate Trust Dept., 1007 Fifth Avenue, San Diego 2, CA 92410

THE CHASE MANHATTAN BANK
Corporate Agency Dept., 80 Pine Street, New York, NY 10005

THIS WARRANT WILL BE VOID AND VALUELESS AFTER 3:30 P.M., EASTERN DAYLIGHT SAVING TIME, OCTOBER 10, 19__

FORM 1 — To subscribe for full shares use this form: Your signature will authorize the Subscription Agent to buy eight or less additional rights needed for your subscription or to sell any excess rights represented by this warrant.

Number of full shares
Subscribed for _____ Shares

Total cost of shares
Subscribed for _____ $ _____
(Payment of this amount must accompany subscription)

Signature of
Subscriber _____

THESE RIGHTS EXPIRE AND BECOME VOID AT 3:30 P.M., EASTERN DAYLIGHT SAVING TIME, ON OCTOBER 10, 19__

FORM 2 — To sell through a bank or broker or transfer rights use this form: For value received the rights represented by this warrant are assigned to:
(Please print name, address and number of rights)

Signature of
Registered Owner _____

Signature
Guaranteed by _____

FULL INSTRUCTIONS FOR USE OF FORMS APPEAR IN THE LETTER ACCOMPANYING THIS WARRANT.

SUBSCRIPTION AGENTS

THE FIRST NATIONAL TRUST AND SAVINGS BANK OF SAN DIEGO
1007 Fifth Avenue
San Diego, CA 92410

THE CHASE MANHATTAN BANK
Corporate Agency Dept.
80 Pine Street
New York, NY 10005

THIS WARRANT MAY BE USED TO SUBSCRIBE FOR COMMON STOCK OR MAY BE TRANSFERRED IN THE SAME MANNER AND WITH THE SAME EFFECT AS ANY NEGOTIABLE INSTRUMENT.

DO NOT FILL IN SPACE BELOW — RESERVED FOR AGENT'S PURPOSES			
CLERK	RTS. BOUGHT	AMOUNT DUE $	WARRANTS SUBMITTED
TKT. NO.	RTS. SOLD	PROCEEDS $	NO. OF PIECES
DATE		PRICE	NO. OF RIGHTS
			TOTAL RIGHTS

Address for mailing certificates if other than imprinted on face of warrant.

Source: *Financial Handbook* (New York: The Ronald Press), 13–27.

---

4. *No speculative investment is a safe investment.* If you are deliberately speculating, you should stand ready to lose everything. Therefore, speculation in the marketplace should be reserved for those who have time on their side. If they lose, they have the time to save and invest again.

5. *Avoid short-term trading.* Short-term trading is only for the professional investor. Amateurs who trade in and out when a stock moves a few points are just kidding themselves. If you own a seat on the New York Stock Exchange with millions at your disposal and you have spent a lifetime studying the market, perhaps you can make money in day-by-day short-term trading. Otherwise, forget it.

6. *Long-term trading is a must.* The days are gone when you could just buy blue-chip stocks and put them away in a safe-

deposit box, hoping that 30 or 40 years later—or so the theory goes—you could take them out and find that you had become wealthy. Our economy has become far too complex for this. It has been estimated that more than 70 percent of the products that will be sold 20 years from now are not yet on the drawing boards, much less produced. To use an extreme example, in the early part of this century, those who stayed with the horse-and-buggy industry came to realize to their sorrow that they should have shifted to the automobile industry.

7. *Invest in stocks for growth, not dividends, if you are employed and are not close to retirement.* If you want growth, stay away from stocks that pay high dividends. Companies that pay out most of their net profits to their stockholders in the form of dividends have very little left in retained earnings for expansion. A rule of thumb is that the higher the dividend yield, the lower the chance for market appreciation.

8. *Invest in blue-chip stocks when you need income, not growth.* You will get a lot of argument over this rule because once in a while you can buy a blue-chip stock that will double in price in a couple of years. For example, many years ago you could have bought General Electric stock, which doubled in price, yet it definitely meets all four standards of a blue-chip stock. (This company has paid a dividend every year since 1899.) But, for the most part, corporations whose stock is in the blue-chip category no longer face the prospect of dynamic growth. They have established reputations, and their management is not likely to be aggressive. They seem to adhere to the philosophy "When you have it made, why upset the applecart?"

9. *Look at a stock's potential, not its high price.* Many people wouldn't think of buying International Business Machines stock because of its high price. Yet IBM has proved to be a wonderful growth stock over the years, although most investors have stayed away from it since the price rose above $100 per share. Remember, there is no such thing as a too highly priced stock in terms of dollars if its potential for growth is extremely good.

10. *Buy a stock only when it is going up in price, never at any other time.* No matter how sold you may be on a company and its growth potential, never buy a stock that is just holding its own or decreasing in price. Remember that risk in the stock market is all on the down side. Wait until the stock starts to rise in price, and even then don't be in too big a hurry to buy it. You should deliberately miss a part of the profit to be sure that the stock is really moving up. Some profit is better than none.

AFTER YOU INVEST

11. *Supervise your investments continuously.* Don't count on your broker to supervise your investments for you. Brokers are primarily interested in customers who are trading (buying and selling), for such customers are the biggest source of brokers' commissions. Individual investors should make it a point to constantly monitor the stock market and be aware of how their stocks are faring.

12. *Diversify your holdings.* "Don't put all your eggs in one basket" is a rule we all have heard since childhood. But how much diversification should you have? Four or five different stocks are enough. You should not spread yourself so thin that it becomes impossible for you to manage your portfolio intelligently. The sheer weight of numbers alone will not protect you from a loss.

13. *Dollar cost average only when a stock is going up, never when it is going down.* Many stockbrokers advise dollar cost averaging, or doubling up on a stock when the price goes down in order to reduce the average cost. For example, if in the past you purchased 100 shares of a stock at $40 per share and it is now selling at $30 per share, your broker might suggest that you dollar cost average and buy another 100 shares. This suggestion is illustrated as follows:

100 shares at $40.................$4,000
100 shares at $30.................. 3,000
  Total investment $7,000

Average cost of 200 shares $35

The theory behind such thinking is that you are better off owning 200 shares at an average cost of $35 than 100 shares at a cost of $40. This makes sense only if the stock is going up in market value. If it is going down, it is—temporarily at least—a bad investment. Under these conditions you should sell the stock, not buy more.

14. Reinvest all dividends while you are still employed. Human frailty being what it is, most investors spend their dividends. Money received is easily dissipated, especially if it comes in small amounts at various times during the year, which is how stock dividends are paid.

There are two ways in which dividends can be saved automatically. One is to instruct the corporation to reinvest your dividends automatically in additional shares. In this case, the corporation will send you a notice of the number of additional shares you have purchased rather than a dividend check. Corporations are increasingly willing to do this. The other way is to hold your stock in a *street name* with your broker. This way the dividends will be mailed to the brokerage firm, not to you. You can then instruct your registered representative to hold the dividends in your account until you have decided where to invest them. In both of these ways, you do not receive the dividends directly, so you avoid the temptation to spend them.

15. Sell high and buy low. Selling high and buying low is what every investor in the stock market would like to do. Unfortunately, no one can sell at the *absolute high* of a bull market and buy in again at the *absolute low* of a subsequent bear market. The best you can hope to accomplish is to avoid doing the opposite.

Be satisfied and get out of the market and into cash after you make a good profit in a bull market. If the market goes higher after you have sold, you would have made more if you had waited; but be content with less.

At the same time, don't try to reinvest at the absolute low of a bear market. Wait until the market starts moving up, for there is still plenty of appreciation left. Many careful investors were caught napping in the bear market of 1980–1981. They thought the market had hit bottom when the DJIA declined to 875. It had not; it dropped below 750 in the summer of 1982. Those who went back in at 875 bought back too soon.

16. Sell your stock when it becomes fully valued. Too many investors become "married" to stocks that have done well for them. You must have an open mind toward your investments at all times. Admittedly, it is difficult to sell a stock that has justified your faith in it by going up handsomely. But remember, there comes a time when a stock becomes fully valued and that is when you should sell. It is not easy to determine when to sell, but if the stock you own starts falling in price—particularly if it is declining for no apparent reason and if it is acting against the general tone of the market—you had better dispose of it. You will have been wrong in selling if the stock later reverses itself. However, if this should happen, you can always buy the stock again.

17. Get rid of bad investments. Everyone makes a bad investment once in a while. To err is human, and this is never more true than in the marketplace. You will definitely make mistakes. You should reconcile yourself to this, and when you do make a mistake, you should sell that stock. Never for any reason ride a bad stock down. It will kill you. For example, if you buy 100 shares of stock at $150 and ride it down to $50, then sell, you will take a $10,000 loss. You should sell out long before this happens.

PREFERRED STOCK

As mentioned at the beginning of this chapter, the second way to invest in American industry is to buy preferred stock. **Preferred stock** represents only a limited ownership in a corporation. Preferred stockholders take less risk than common stockholders, and the return on their investments is generally limited to a stated amount of dividends.

Almost all preferred stocks are issued with a stated value printed on the face of the certificate, which is known as the par value. The par value is usually $100 a share. This par value has considerably more significance than the par value of a common stock. If a company issues a 6 percent preferred stock, the amount of that dividend will relate to its par value. If the par value is $100, then $6 per share will be paid. If the par value is $25, however, a 6 percent preferred stock will pay 6 percent of $25, or $1.50. If the preferred stock does not have a par value, the amount of the dividend will be expressed not in terms of a percentage but in terms of dollars, such as $5.

PREFERENCES ENJOYED BY PREFERRED STOCK

Most of the preemptive rights of common stockholders mentioned in Chapter 1 are not enjoyed by preferred stockholders. Nevertheless, they do enjoy certain advantages that common stockholders do not. These are the following:

1. *Priority as to dividends.* Without exception, preferred stockholders are entitled to receive a fixed amount of dividends before any dividends may be paid to common stockholders. If there are no profits, however, the board of directors will not declare dividends on the common stock and may also not declare dividends on the preferred stock. In other words, the preferred stock dividend must come from profits. The company is not obliged to pay dividends to stockholders in the same way it is required to pay interest on corporate bonds. If the company fails to pay the dividend, the preferred stockholder cannot force the corporation into bankruptcy. Preferred stockholders have none of the rights of creditors or bondholders.

2. *Prior claim on assets.* If the corporation is forced into bankruptcy, all of its valid bills must be paid first. Then the claims of the bondholders, if any, must be satisfied. Next in line are the preferred stockholders. If there are enough assets left, the preferred stockholders get paid in full; then the common stockholders divide what is left on a pro rata basis, depending on the number of common shares held. It should be noted that the preferred stockholder always has prior claim over the common stockholder in the event the company is dissolved.

FEATURES OF PREFERRED STOCK

Preferred stock may have a number of features, which are described in this section. Not all of these characteristics, however, apply to all preferred stock. Owners should refer to their stock certificates to determine which of these features apply to their shares.

Participating or Nonparticipating

Preferred stockholders are limited to an annual return by the amount stated on the stock certificate unless the stock is participating. After receiving their stated dividends, however, **participating preferred stockholders** are allowed to share profits with the common stockholders. Conditions under which preferred stockholders are allowed to participate in these profits vary. Usually the stated preferred dividend is paid first, then the common-stock dividend (in a predetermined amount) is paid, and then the common and preferred stockholders share equally in the remaining profits as declared by the board of directors.

Callable (Redeemable)

Preferred stocks do not have a maturity date as bonds do. Always remember that they are stocks and as such have no maturity. However, there are **callable preferred stocks**, which are redeemable at a certain price at the option of the issuing corporation. For example, a $100 par value preferred stock may be callable at $105. Corporations issue this type of preferred stock because they want the option of retiring this issue at some time in the future. The corporation's charter states the terms under which it may call its preferred stock and the earliest date at which it may exercise this option.

Convertible

Owners of **convertible preferred stocks** have the right to exchange their preferred stock for the common stock of the same company under certain conditions. The exercise of the option to convert is left up to the preferred stockholders. When a preferred stock is first offered to the public, it is sometimes necessary to confer on it some of the advantages of a common stock in order to make it more appealing.

For example, let us say you have purchased a convertible preferred stock at $105 with the right to convert it into five shares of common stock at $21. If the price of the common stock is quoted at $21, there is no reason for you to exercise the conversion privilege. If you did, after the conversion you would have five shares of common stock worth $105 instead of one share of preferred stock also worth $105, but you would have lost the fixed yield on your preferred stock. Therefore you should not exercise your conversion privilege so long as the stock is selling at $21 or below. However, if the common-stock price goes up to $30 per share, you could convert and buy five shares for $105, which would immediately be worth five times $30, or $150. You could then sell the common shares on the open market and make approximately 50 percent on your money.

Series Issues

A very large corporation, such as a big utility firm, might have several **series of preferred stock**. These are differentiated as *first preferred* and *second preferred, prior preferred,* or *preferred A* and *preferred B,* as each series is originally sold on different dates. They differ materially in their rate of return and in their prior claim on assets in the event that the corporation is dissolved.

REASONS FOR BUYING PREFERRED STOCK

Considering the various features of preferred stocks, it is obvious that under certain conditions they are a good buy. People buy preferred stocks for the following reasons:

1. *For the dividend income.* When the dividend is 1 percent above that of a good corporate bond, it might be advisable to buy preferred stock if income is your main objective. If a bond would yield the same amount, you should buy the bond instead because the interest on a bond is guaranteed. When you are a bondholder, you are also a creditor of the corporation, so it wouldn't make sense to buy the preferred stock for the same yield and get less protection.

2. *For cumulative dividends in arrears.* A great deal of money was made during the Great Depression when people bought preferred stocks of corporations that had not paid the dividend for a period of years. Great care has to be taken, however, when buying cumulative preferred stock for the dividends that are in arrears. One has to be convinced that the corporation is on the "comeback trail" and will start making good money again so that at some time in the future it can pay all the past arrears on the preferred stocks.

3. *For higher yield.* Although preferred stocks are usually issued at $100 per share, this price is affected by prevailing long-term interest rates, just as bond prices fluctuate according to the prevailing cost of borrowing money. The yield on the preferred stock must be higher than the stated dividend rate. For example, if the preferred stock is selling at $80 and calls for payment of a 5 percent dividend, the actual yield is 6¼ percent. The return is obtained by the simple arithmetic of dividing the $5 cash dividend by $80. At this point you must be careful

in your analysis. Is the preferred stock selling at $80 because the company is financially shaky and the 5 percent is liable not to be earned, or is it selling at $80 due to higher long-term interest rates? If the corporation is currently earning, after taxes, 20 to 30 times the amount owed the preferred stockholder, the dividend is well protected and the preferred stockholder is sure to receive the yield.

4. *For profit.* You may decide to buy preferred stock that is selling at a low price because you believe that in the near future long-term interest rates will be coming down. If long-term interest rates do go down, preferred-stock prices will go up, and you will be able to sell later at a profit.

As you will see in the next chapter, when interest rates go up, prices of preferred stocks and bonds go down. Conversely, when interest rates go down, bond and preferred-stock prices go up. The **prime rate**, which is the rate that commercial banks charge their best corporate customers and on which all other interest rates depend, is the interest charge to watch. Since the prime rate changes slowly and its movements are widely publicized, one has to keep track of it only a few times a year.

SUMMARY

Most people invest in American industry for growth, dividends, and protection over the long term from the inroads of inflation. Common stocks can provide all three. However, before investing, you should have a basic understanding of the difference between blue-chip stocks and growth stocks; the probable result of short-term trading compared with that of long-term trading; the bull and bear markets (to be aware that you should buy at the bottom of a bear market and sell near the top of a bull market); stock market averages and stock quotations; and yardsticks for evaluating common stock.

The stock market has its own peculiar terminology that you must learn in order to be on familiar ground when discussing investments with a stockbroker. You must understand how to calculate rates of return and how to follow the daily price fluctuations of your individual investments. And even then, you will have to follow time-tested rules if you are to have a chance for success.

Preferred stocks are an excellent investment too and should not be ignored. Most of the preemptive rights of common stockholders are not enjoyed by preferred stockholders. Nevertheless, preferred stockholders have a prior claim over common stockholders on dividends and assets. When income is the number one objective, you should consider preferred stocks.

ENDNOTES

1. Norman Dacey, *What's Wrong with Your Life Insurance* (New York: Crowell-Collier Press, 1963), 6.

2. *Ibid.*

3. This was the divisor in use on April 18, 1988.

2
REVIEW QUESTIONS
SHORT ESSAY

Name _____

Date _____ Points _____

Directions: Answer the following questions according to your instructor's directions.

1. Give the two basic reasons why investors buy common stock.

   a. _____

   b. _____

2. Name the four standards that must be met before a corporation's stock can be called "blue chip."

   a. _____

   _____

   b. _____

   _____

   c. _____

   _____

   d. _____

   _____

3. What is the chief characteristic of a growth stock?

   _____

   _____

4. What is the probable result of successful long-term investing over a period of ten years?

   _____

   _____

5. In your own words, describe a bull market.

   _____

   _____

   _____

6. In your own words, describe a bear market.

_____

_____

_____

7. When may it be reasonably decided that a bear market has come to an end?

_____

_____

8. How can you find out the price of a stock?

_____

_____

9. Name seven rules to follow after you invest in the stock market.

    a. _____

    b. _____

    c. _____

    d. _____

    e. _____

    f. _____

    g. _____

10. Why is a preferred stock referred to as a limited ownership of a corporation?

_____

_____

2

REVIEW QUESTIONS
MULTIPLE CHOICE

Name _____

Date _____ Points _____

Directions: For each of the following, select the best answer and place the letter that represents it in the Answers column.

ANSWERS

1. The following corporations make their shares available to the general public:
   a. close corporations.
   b. open corporations organized for profit.
   c. nonprofit corporations.
   d. all corporations.   _____
2. In terms of total value, the following percentage of all common stock is traded on the New York Stock Exchange:
   a. more than 10 percent.
   b. more than 25 percent.
   c. more than 40 percent.
   d. more than 80 percent.   _____
3. One way to offset the effect of inflation is to buy
   a. common stocks.
   b. preferred stocks.
   c. municipal bonds.
   d. corporate bonds.   _____
4. There are two basic kinds of stock. They are
   a. blue-chip stocks and growth stocks.
   b. blue-chip stocks and cyclical stocks.
   c. defensive stocks and cyclical stocks.
   d. growth stocks and special situation stocks.   _____
5. A growth stock should be compounding its earnings at an annual rate of
   a. 5 percent.
   b. 10 percent.
   c. 15 percent.
   d. 30 percent.   _____
6. The topping of a bull market is
   a. easy to determine if you are a professional.
   b. very difficult to determine even for a professional.
   c. impossible to determine.
   d. easy for an investor to determine.   _____
7. A preferred stock
   a. pays a dividend if earned.
   b. seldom pays a dividend.
   c. never pays a dividend.
   d. none of the above.   _____

8. If a stock is earning $8 per share and the price-earnings ratio is 16 to 1, what is the stock's current market price?
   a. $8.
   b. $16.
   c. $64.
   d. $128.

9. The price-earnings ratio of the average stock is considered to be low at
   a. 10 to 1.
   b. 15 to 1.
   c. 20 to 1.
   d. 50 to 1.

10. An investment of $10,000 in 1928 in any one of the top 13 stocks in the DJIA was worth, by the end of 1986, more than
    a. $10,000.
    b. $25,000.
    c. $200,000.
    d. $500,000.

11. Volume is considered to be low on the New York Stock Exchange any day that the number of shares traded is
    a. 125 million.
    b. 150 million.
    c. 200 million.
    d. 250 million.

12. A $1 par value common stock has a market value of $75. The earnings are $5 a share, and for the past year it has paid quarterly dividends as follows: 50 cents, 75 cents, 75 cents, and $1. Based on these four dividends, what is the current return?
    a. 4 percent.
    b. 5 percent.
    c. 5⅔ percent.
    d. 6⅔ percent.

13. An industrial concern announces a two-for-one stock split. The split doubles the
    a. number and value of shares.
    b. number of shares but does not affect their total value.
    c. value of shares but does not affect their number.
    d. number of stockholders.

14. The dividend on a 6 percent preferred stock with a par value of $100 would be
    a. $6.
    b. $60.
    c. $100.
    d. $600.

15. Preferred stockholders differ from common stockholders in that they
    a. take a greater risk and therefore receive greater returns.
    b. are lenders, not owners.
    c. are entitled to a fixed amount of dividends when dividends are declared.
    d. can force the corporation into receivership.

2

REVIEW QUESTIONS
TRUE-FALSE

Name _____

Date _____ Points _____

Directions: Circle T or F to indicate whether each statement is true or false.

ANSWERS

1. Equity is another word for ownership.   T F

2. "Blue chip" describes stocks of strong, well-established companies with long dividend-paying records.   T F

3. The ability to pay bills promptly is important to a young company.   T F

4. A bull market exists when the broad trend of the market is down.   T F

5. A daily stock quotation gives a stock's price-earnings ratio.   T F

6. There are a total of 20 stocks in the Dow Jones industrial average.   T F

7. Only government sources provide industry data.   T F

8. The volume of daily trading is not important when watching the stock market.   T F

9. Defensive stocks are issued by companies that have defense contracts with the Pentagon.   T F

10. "Special situation" is a term applied to a stock when something unusual occurs to enhance its value.   T F

11. Corporations split their stock to lower the stock's price.   T F

12. A stock warrant is an option granted to the holder to buy additional shares of common stock.   T F

13. One should never commit all of his or her excess funds in the market.   T F

14. Once in a while an individual investor can trust to luck and buy stocks on a hunch.   T F

15. When choosing a growth stock, one should not set her or his sights too high.   T F

16. Short-term trading is a must for individual investors.   T F

17. A stock should always be bought when its price is going down.   T F

18. The dollar cost averaging method should be used only when the price of one's stock is going up.   **T   F**

19. One should buy high and sell low in the stock market.   **T   F**

20. An individual investor should sell stocks that have turned out to be bad investments.   **T   F**

21. Most of the preemptive rights of common stockholders are shared by preferred stockholders.   **T   F**

22. If dividends are declared by the board of directors, preferred stockholders are paid before common stockholders.   **T   F**

23. Participating preferred stockholders are limited to an annual return of the amount stated on the stock certificate.   **T   F**

24. A corporation's charter states that a preferred stockholder may redeem callable stocks at the stockholder's option.   **T   F**

25. When interest rates go up, prices of preferred stocks go down.   **T   F**

2

PROJECT

Mary and Tom Baldwin have been successful in their dry cleaning business and now want to make their first small investment in the stock market. The following conditions exist:

1. The stock market is in the first stage of a bull market.
2. They are young, in their early thirties.
3. They don't need any more income than the profit from their dry cleaning business.
4. They now have two children instead of one.

Answer the following questions. In each instance, explain the reasoning behind your decision. (Use the space below and on the back of this page, if necessary.)

1. Should they invest now or wait for a more favorable market?
2. Should they buy a growth stock or a blue-chip stock?
3. A friend has told them that a certain stock is due for a stock split. Should this influence their decision?
4. A stockbroker suggests that they buy a defensive stock. Should they?
5. One stock they are considering does not pay a dividend. Should this be a factor in their decision?

CHAPTER 3
OUTLINE

I. **MAJOR CATEGORIES OF BONDS**
  A. Bonds Classified as to Issuer
      1. Corporate Bonds
      2. Municipal Bonds
      3. U.S. Government Bonds
  B. Bonds Classified as to Method of Making the Interest Payment
      1. Income Bonds
      2. Registered Bonds
      3. Coupon or Bearer Bonds
  C. Bonds Classified as to Method of Repaying the Principal
      1. Sinking Fund Bonds
      2. Serial Bonds
      3. Callable Bonds
      4. Convertible Bonds

II. **BOND QUOTATIONS AND PRICES**
  A. Market Price Quotations
      1. Fractional Price of Corporate Bonds
      2. Fractional Price of Government, Agency, and Miscellaneous Securities
  B. Quotations on an "And Interest" Basis
      1. Calculating Accrued Interest by Using a Formula
      2. Calculating Accrued Interest by Using Bond Interest Tables

III. **BOND YIELDS**
  A. Nominal Yield
  B. Current Yield
  C. Yield to Maturity

IV. **BOND RATINGS**
  A. Classifications by Investment Advisory Services
  B. Interpretation of Bond Ratings

3

FUNDAMENTALS OF BONDS

The two basic types of securities are stocks and bonds. Stocks, both common and preferred, were discussed in the previous chapter. This chapter will deal with bonds.

A **bond** is an interest-bearing certificate of indebtedness issued by a corporation or a government. It is almost always issued at a face value of $1,000. The following three facts should be remembered about bonds:

1. A bond is an evidence of a debt.
2. The corporation or government issuing a bond is a borrower.
3. The investor purchasing the bond is a creditor.

A bond states the issuer's promise to pay the lender a certain sum of money at a specified time known as the *maturity date*. It also promises to pay interest on the principal of the loan at a specified rate. Failure of the issuer to pay either the principal or the interest when due constitutes a *legal default*. Therefore, court proceedings may be instituted by the bondholder.

Bonds are known as *senior securities*, and stocks as *junior securities*. The term *senior* is used in connection with bonds because bondholders have a prior legal claim over the common and preferred stockholders on both the income and the assets of a corporation. The bondholders must be paid their interest in full before the stockholders are entitled to receive any dividends, if and when they are declared by the board of directors. In the event the firm is dissolved, the bondholders must be paid their principal before the stockholders are entitled to receive any of the assets of the corporation.

Sometimes bonds are better understood when stocks and bonds are compared to real estate. One could think of common stocks as property owned and bonds as a mortgage on the property. Dividends on the common stocks could be considered as the net rent, and interest on the bonds as interest on the mortgage.

MAJOR CATEGORIES OF BONDS

Bonds may be classified arbitrarily into several categories: (1) according to the type of issuer, (2) according to the method of making the interest payment, and (3) according to the method of repaying the principal. Each of these categories is described below.

BONDS CLASSIFIED AS TO ISSUER

Bonds classified according to the type of issuer include corporate bonds, municipal bonds, and U.S. government bonds.

Corporate Bonds

The issuers of **corporate bonds** are private enterprises. These enterprises may be utility, railroad, or industrial companies. There are different kinds of corporate bonds, depending upon the type of collateral offered as security or upon the addition of incentives to them. *Incentives* are sometimes added so that the bonds will sell better when they are first offered to the public, just as incentives are added to the initial offering of preferred stock. Some of the most common corporate bonds are discussed below.

Mortgage Bonds.   Bonds that are secured by a specific mortgage on some or all of the corporation's real property are called **mortgage bonds**. This real property consists of the land and buildings that the corporation owns. A **first-mortgage bond** is backed up by a mortgage on a specific property. A **general-mortgage bond** is backed up by a blanket mortgage on all of the corporation's fixed capital assets. Figure 3-1 shows a first-mortgage bond of the American Computer Corporation.

Debenture Bonds.   Not backed up by a mortgage or lien on any of the corporation's assets, **debenture bonds** are simply long-term notes that are only as good as the credit rating of the company that offers them. Therefore, debenture bonds should be purchased only from the best blue-chip companies. International Business Machines Corporation, for instance, can offer debentures to its stockholders, and they are immediately oversubscribed because of the financial soundness of the company.

Guaranteed Bonds.   Mergers of one company into another are frequent these days, and the bondholders might not agree to the merger if their position were jeopardized in any way. When a merger takes place, the dominant company usually guarantees the payment of either the interest or the principal of the bonds originally issued by the absorbed company. That is, the guarantee may extend only to the interest, or only to the principal, but not to both. Thus, **guaranteed bonds** are bonds guaranteed by a corporation other than the one that originally issued them. The value of guaranteed bonds rests with the earning power and the soundness of the guaranteeing company. For this reason, the word "guarantee" can be misleading to the investor.

Equipment Trust Certificates.   Quite often issued by airlines and railroads, **equipment trust certificates** come in serial form so that they mature at stated intervals. Jet aircraft cost millions of dollars each, and it is difficult for airline companies to finance them. When equipment trust certificates are issued, the airlines pledge title to the aircraft to a trustee. The bondholder's interest is protected by having the bonds mature long before the equipment is fully depreciated in value. Equipment trust certificates are not to be confused with voting trust certificates, which were discussed under common stocks in Chapter 2.

Municipal Bonds

Some people are confused about municipal bonds because of their name. A municipality is a small town; therefore, one could assume by the name that municipal bonds are issued only by small communities. This is not so. **Municipal bonds**, or **municipals** as they are more commonly called, is the term applied to the obligations of states, local governments, and authorities. Bonds issued by the state of California are municipal bonds, and so are bonds issued by the Pennsylvania Turnpike (an authority) or school bonds issued by Podunk, any small town in the United States.

Municipal bonds are bought because they have all of a bond's basic ingredients of safety as to principal and interest, plus one additional attraction: *the interest from these bonds is exempt from federal income taxes.* This feature is important to people who are in a very high income-tax bracket of 33 percent. A 33 percent tax bracket means that your *taxable* income, if filing a joint return, must be between $71,900 and $149,250. Or,

FIGURE 3-1 First-Mortgage Bond

if single, your taxable income must be between $43,150 and $89,560.

Obviously, very few taxpayers are in this high tax bracket. But if you are, and you own a *corporate* bond on which you receive an interest rate of 10 percent, you would have to pay 33 percent of the interest in income taxes—which leaves you with only 6.7 percent (10 percent less 3.3 percent equals 6.7 percent) in interest after paying the Internal Revenue Service. But if you own a tax-free *municipal* bond and receive 8 percent in interest, you don't pay any federal income taxes, so you retain the entire 8 percent for yourself. Thus, you are 1.3 percent (8 percent less 6.7 percent equals 1.3 percent) better off with a municipal bond. Municipal bonds are subject to state income taxes unless they are issued in the state where you live. Like corporate bonds, municipal bonds are fixed dollars, which don't offer any protection from inflation.

There are two principal kinds of municipal bonds: general obligation bonds and revenue bonds.

General Obligation Bonds.
States, cities, towns, and other political subdivisions issue **general obligation bonds** and back them up by their full credit and general taxing power. Counties, cities, and towns depend on real estate taxes for their principal source of revenue.

Revenue Bonds.
When issued, **revenue bonds** are backed up by a specific revenue, such as income from tunnels, turnpikes, and bridges that charge a toll for their use. The theory underlying the issuance of revenue bonds is that the cost of a particular construction project should be borne by those who are going to use it. A good example is the Golden Gate Bridge in San Francisco. When you buy revenue bonds, you incur more risk than when you buy general obligation bonds.

U.S. Government Bonds

As stated in Chapter 1, the debt of the federal government is divided into two classes: (1) nonmarketable debt and (2) marketable debt.

Nonmarketable Debt.
The nonmarketable debt of the federal government consists of U.S. savings bonds, which are sold to people who want to save money in safe, fixed dollars. As discussed in Chapter 1, savings bonds fall into two categories: (1) EE bonds, which compound the interest every six months from the date of purchase, and (2) HH bonds, which pay the interest to the investor every six months by Treasury checks from Washington, DC.

Marketable Debt.
The **marketable debt** of the federal government consists of U.S. Treasury bills, Treasury certificates, Treasury notes, and Treasury bonds. Treasury bills and Treasury certificates are *noninterest-bearing obligations* and therefore will not be described in this chapter.

Treasury notes are issued with maturities ranging from one to seven years. They are issued for their face amount and carry coupons for the interest payments. Treasury notes make excellent investments for commercial banks.

Treasury bonds are issued with maturity dates from five years up to 30 years. These bonds may be purchased in either coupon or registered form, and they are bought and sold through stockbrokers. If purchased through a bank, the bank in turn will have to place the order with a stockbrokerage firm. It should be noted here that of all the forms of marketable debt of the federal government, the average investor buys only Treasury bonds.

BONDS CLASSIFIED AS TO METHOD OF MAKING THE INTEREST PAYMENT

Bonds that are classified according to the method by which interest is paid to the bondholder fall into three types: income bonds, registered bonds, and coupon or bearer bonds.

Income Bonds

The term *income bonds* is a misnomer. One would think from their name that such bonds would be guaranteed as to their income, but they are not. **Income bonds** are guaranteed only as to payment of principal at maturity, and the interest on them is paid only when and if it is earned.

Registered Bonds

When a bond is sold, the buyer's name may or may not be registered on the books of the corporation as the owner. The choice, however, is not up to the buyer. The decision was made by the corporation when it first issued the bond. Most bonds are *not* registered. Investors prefer this type of ownership because bonds that are not registered can be bought and sold more easily.

Fully Registered Bonds.
The name and address of the owner of a **fully registered**

bond are recorded on the books of the issuing corporation. The owner's name also appears on the face of the bond. Interest, when due, is mailed to the bondholder. Furthermore, the bond may be cashed only when the bondholder endorses it and surrenders the endorsed bond to the issuing company.

Partly Registered Bonds. A partly registered bond has the owner's name listed on the books of the corporation. The owner's name also appears on the face of the bond. Unlike the fully registered bond, however, a **partly registered bond** is registered only as to principal, not as to interest. Coupons are attached to the bond for each interest payment. When the interest date is due, the coupons are detached from the bonds and presented to a bank teller for cashing. But when the bond is sold, it must be endorsed by the registered owner.

Coupon or Bearer Bonds

A coupon bond is not registered. That is, the owner's name is not recorded on the books of the issuing corporation. It is called a **coupon bond** because coupons with interest dates are attached to the bonds for each interest payment. Interest is obtained by clipping the coupons and presenting them to a bank, just as with the coupons attached to partly registered bonds.

A coupon bond is also known as a **bearer bond** because whoever is in possession of it (the bearer) may cash it. For this reason, great care has to be exercised when handling coupon bonds since ownership is transferred from one person to another by simple delivery of the certificates. No endorsement is required.

BONDS CLASSIFIED AS TO METHOD OF REPAYING THE PRINCIPAL

There are several methods by which the repayment of principal is made to certain bondholders. Depending on which method is used, these bonds are called sinking fund bonds, serial bonds, callable bonds, or convertible bonds.

Sinking Fund Bonds

When bonds have a *sinking fund* feature, the corporation issuing them is required to set aside, at regular intervals, a specific amount of money for the purpose of retiring all or part of the entire bond issue before or at maturity. **Sinking fund bonds** are originally issued to obtain the necessary money to buy excessively expensive machinery and equipment. In order to have enough cash to meet the maturity date and amount, the corporation has to accumulate the necessary sum on a regular basis over the course of many years.

Serial Bonds

Bonds that have a serial feature may be issued by a corporation or a government body. **Serial bonds** mature at different times and on successive dates as specified by the serial numbers on the bonds. Serial bonds with the shortest maturity date carry the lowest interest rates. Those with the longest maturity date carry the highest interest rates. As mentioned earlier, equipment trust certificates are serial issues.

Callable Bonds

When bonds may be redeemed at the option of the corporation, they are known as **callable bonds**. This is not a desirable feature as far as the investor is concerned because the company would call the issue only under conditions that would be advantageous to it. For example, when existing conditions of the money market allow the company to borrow money for less interest, then it would probably redeem the bonds. If the company calls the bonds, this is known as a **refunding operation**.

Convertible Bonds

When bonds have a *convertible* feature, they may be converted at the option of the holder during a specified period of time into another type of security—usually common stock. **Convertible bonds**, as such, have all the advantages of a bond and some of the speculative characteristics of common stock. This is an example of an incentive mentioned earlier in this chapter. You should also note that convertible bonds are usually debentures, although this is not necessarily so.

BOND QUOTATIONS AND PRICES

Remember that bonds are issued with a face value of $1,000 each. Also remember that at maturity they will be worth $1,000 each, but when you buy them in the open market, they are seldom worth exactly $1,000. Why? Because interest rates vary from time to time, depending on how much or how little money is made available by the Federal Reserve Board (FED). When business is good and danger of serious inflation is at hand, the FED tightens up the money supply, causing interest rates to rise and thereby making money less attractive to borrowers. Conversely, when the economy turns down, the FED increases the amount of money in circulation, thereby causing interest rates to go down.

Bond prices vary inversely with long-term interest rates. This means that when interest rates go up, bond prices go down; and when interest rates go down, bond prices go up. Let us say you own a $1,000 bond that pays 6 percent and long-term interest rates go up to 8 percent. Under these circumstances your 6 percent bond will no longer command a market price of $1,000. It will go down in value because no one will pay $1,000 for a 6 percent bond when 8 percent can be obtained elsewhere. Your bond will have to be sold at a *discount,* or for less than $1,000. On the other hand, if you own a bond that pays 8 percent and long-term interest rates go down to 6 percent, you will be able to sell your bond for more than $1,000, or at a *premium.*

MARKET PRICE QUOTATIONS

The market prices of corporate bonds and government bonds are quoted every day in *The Wall Street Journal.* Municipal bonds are not quoted in that publication. This is because there are so many thousands of municipal bonds that the best way for an investor to determine the price of a particular issue of municipals is to obtain it from a stockbrokerage firm or a bank.

The market price of corporate and government bonds is expressed in two parts: (1) in round figures as a percentage of face value and (2) as a fraction of $10. For example, a bond quoted at 92 is selling at $920—or 92 percent of its face value of $1,000. The reason for quoting this bond at 92 lies in simplicity, both in publishing its price and in quoting it over the telephone. Each point that a bond increases or decreases in value is a difference of $10. Thus, if the bond selling at 92 ($920) falls in price to 91 ($910), that bond has incurred a loss in value of $10.

The second part of the market price of a bond is expressed as a fraction of $10. This is determined differently for corporate bonds on the one hand and for government bonds on the other, as explained below.

Fractional Price of Corporate Bonds

The fraction that is used in the market price of a corporate bond is expressed in eighths of a point, or eighths of $10. An eighth of $10 is $10 ÷ 8 = $1.25.

To illustrate how the exact market price of a corporate bond is determined, take as an example the bonds of Georgia Power listed on the 20th line, middle column, of Figure 3-2. Disregarding commission and Securities and Exchange Commission registration fees, the closing price of these bonds is quoted as 95⅛. In computing the exact market price, bear in mind that a zero must be added to the whole number and that the fraction represents eighths of $10. The price is computed as follows:

```
Add a zero to 95, making
    it $950........................$950.00
Add ⅛ of $10, which is
    1 × $1.25 = $1.25..............   1.25
Exact market price..............$951.25
```

For another example, take the Holly Farms bonds on the last line of the middle column in Figure 3-2. Note that the closing price of these bonds is quoted as 73. Since there is no fraction quoted, simply add a zero to 73 to obtain the exact price of $730.

For a detailed explanation of how to read all the columns of a corporate bond quotation, see Figure 3-3 and the explanatory notes accompanying it.

Fractional Price of Government, Agency, and Miscellaneous Securities

Government, agency, and miscellaneous securities are also quoted in round

FIGURE 3-2 Quotations for New York Exchange Bonds

NEW YORK EXCHANGE BONDS

Wednesday, April 13, 1988

Total Volume $34,020,000

SALES SINCE JANUARY 1

1988	1987	1986
$2,235,288,000	$2,886,442,000	$3,476,179,000

	Domestic Wed.	Domestic Tue.	All Issues Wed.	All Issues Tue.
Issues traded	703	693	706	698
Advances	282	255	283	257
Declines	260	272	262	274
Unchanged	161	166	161	167
New highs	8	13	8	13
New lows	11	8	11	8

Dow Jones Bond Averages

–1986– High	–1986– Low	–1987– High	–1987– Low	–1988– High	–1988– Low		Wednesday –1988–		Wednesday –1987–		Wednesday –1986–	
93.65	83.73	95.51	81.26	91.25	86.92	20 Bonds	89.55	–0.15	90.59	–0.78	91.67	+0.12
95.79	81.85	98.23	79.51	91.88	86.65	10 Utilities	89.48	+0.18	91.23	–1.51	92.20	+0.22
91.64	84.82	93.10	83.00	90.64	86.96	10 Industrial	89.61	–0.49	89.94	–0.05	91.15	+0.03

Bonds	Cur Yld	Vol	Close	Net Chg.
Coastl 11¾06	11.6	7	101⅛	– ⅛
Coastl 8.48s91	8.9	31	95½	+ ⅞
Coleco 14⅜02f	...	63	31	– ⅛
Coleco 11s89f	cv	113	35	...
Coleco 11⅛01f	...	79	30¼	– ¾
ColuG 9s94	9.1	3	98⅜	– 1
ColuG 9⅛95	9.3	5	98⅝	– ⅜
ColuG 11¾99	11.4	2	103	...
ColuG 12¾00	12.0	10	106	– ¾
Cmdis 9.65s02	10.5	14	91½	+ ½
CmlCr 8¾91	8.8	10	100	...
CmwE 8¾05	10.0	5	87¾	– 1¼
CmwE 9⅜04	9.9	3	94⅜	– ⅜
CmwE 11⅛10	10.6	1	104⅝	+ ⅝
CmwE 17½88	16.7	14	104½	– ¾
CmwE 13⅜13	11.9	6	112¼	+ ⅜
CmwE 11¾15	10.9	3	107⅜	...
CmpAsc 5¾12	cv	5	131	+ 1½
ConEd 4⅜92v r	5.2	5	84⅛	...
ConEd 9⅜00	9.3	7	100½	+ ⅛
ConEd 7.9s01	9.0	25	88⅛	+ ⅜
ConEd 7¾03	9.0	2	86½	...
ConEd 9⅛04	9.5	10	96⅜	+ ¼
CnPw 4⅝89	4.9	1	95	...
CnPw 8⅝00	9.6	20	90	– 1½
CnPw 8⅛01	9.5	12	85⅞	– 1⅛
CnPw 7½2020	9.1	5	82	+ ⅜
CnPw 9¾06	10.2	22	95½	...
CnPw 8⅝07	9.9	1	87¼	+ ¼
CnPw 9s08	10.1	34	88¾	...
CtIllCp 6.85s89t	7.2	6	95¼	+ 3¾
Ct IC zr89	...	16	87	...
CtlDat 12¾91	11.9	10	106¾	– 1⅛
CtlDat 8½11	cv	35	116	...
CoopCo 8⅝05	cv	15	65	...
CntryCr 7s11	cv	100	83	– 1
Crane 7s94	8.2	11	85½	– ½
Crane 10½94	10.5	4	100⅛	+ ⅛
CrayRs 6⅛11	cv	10	109½	– ½
CritAc 12¼14	12.0	1	102¼	+ ⅛
CritAc 12.35s14	12.0	5	102½	...
Dana dc5⅞06	cv	1	91¼	– ¾

Bonds	Cur Yld	Vol	Close	Net Chg.
GMA 7¼90	7.4	155	98⅛	– ⅛
GMA 7⅞97	8.6	10	91½	+ ¼
GM 8⅝s05	9.3	4	92⅞	+ ¾
GM 8⅛91	8.1	10	100⅝	+ ¾
GTE 9⅜99	9.4	16	100	...
Gene 14¼94	14.1	10	101	+ 1
Genrad 7¼11	cv	35	82	– 1
GaPw 7⅜01	9.0	17	82¼	...
GaPw 8⅛01	9.5	1	85⅞	+ ⅞
GaPw 7½02J	9.1	35	82½	+ ½
GaPw 7½02D	9.1	15	82	– ½
GaPw 8⅝04	9.6	10	89¾	+ ¼
GaPw 11⅝00	11.3	31	102¾	– ½
GaPw 11¾05	11.3	4	104	– ⅜
GaPw 9¾08	10.1	5	96¼	+ ⅝
GaPw 10½09	10.4	5	101	– ⅜
GaPw 11s09	10.6	38	104	+ 1⅞
GaPw 13¼13	12.4	20	107¼	+ ⅛
GaPw 16s14	14.6	50	109¼	– ⅝
GaPw 10s16A	10.5	10	95⅛	– ¼
GaPw 10¾17	10.8	7	100	...
GibFn 9¼08	cv	12	75½	– 2
vjGloM dc16s01f	...	2	25	– ⅜
vjGloMr 16⅛02f	...	2	24¾	...
vjGloM dc13s03f	cv	136	23¾	+ 1¼
GldNug 8⅜92	9.3	13	89⅞	+ 3⅞
Grace 4¼90	cv	8	104	– 1¼
Grace 12¾90	12.4	40	103	– 1
GreyF zr94	...	32	51½	...
Grolr 13⅝03	13.3	200	102⅝	+ 1⅞
GrowGp 8½06	cv	1	93	+ 1
Grumn 9¼09	cv	6	101½	...
GlfWn 6s88	6.1	15	99	...
GlfWn 7s03B	9.0	25	78	– ¼
Harns dc12s04	12.0	10	100⅜	+ ¼
Hartfd 8½96	9.1	3	93¾	– ¼
Hawn 9s2000	9.2	10	97½	...
Hawn 7⅝02	9.0	10	85	+ 1
HltNJ 10⅝94	10.4	5	102	– 2
Holidy 10½94	10.6	271	98¾	+ ¼
Holidy 11s99	11.4	292	96⅝	+ ¼
HollyFar 6s17	cv	53	73	+ ¾

Bonds	Cur Yld	Vol	Close	Net Chg.
MerLy zr91	...	20	74¼	– ¼
MesaCap 12s96	12.0	35	99⅞	– ⅛
MichB 9.6s08	9.7	10	98¾	– ⅝
MichB 8⅛15	9.5	75	85¾	+ 1
MichB 9⅛18	9.6	8	94⅞	– ⅛
MPac 4¼90	4.5	7	95	+ ⅞
MPac 4¼05	7.7	5	55	...
MoAl 8.4505	9.2	2	91⅜	+ ⅛
Mobil 8½01	9.0	66	94½	– ⅜
Mobil 14.4s04	13.3	146	107⅞	+ ⅜
Mobil 8¾88	...	20	100 1/32	– 5/32
Mobil 7⅛92	7.4	25	96⅛	– ⅜
Mobil 8⅝94	8.6	33	99⅞	+ ⅛
Mobil 8.7s91	8.5	10	102	+ 1
Monon 6s07f	...	1	55⅛	– 4⅞
Mons 9⅛00	9.3	2	98⅛	– ⅞
MntWC 7⅜88	7.4	10	99 11/16	+ 3/16
MntWC 9s89	9.0	9	100¼	– ½
Moran 8¾08f	cv	4	58	– ½
MtSTl 7⅜11	9.2	17	80⅛	– ⅞
MtSTl 7¾13	9.4	14	82⅜	– ⅝
MtSTl 9¾12	9.8	24	100	– 1
MtSTl 9⅝15	9.8	25	97¾	– 1¼
MtSTl 7⅞16	9.5	10	83⅛	+ ⅛
MtSTl 8s17	9.5	10	84½	...
NBD 8¼10	cv	5	125	– 1
NBI 8¼07	cv	32	48½	+ ¼
Nabis 7¾s01	8.5	15	91	+ 2⅞
NCash 7.7s94	8.1	2	95⅝	– 2⅜
NConv 9s08	cv	68	79	– ½
NtEdu 6½11	cv	64	115¼	+ ¼
NtGyp zr04	...	187	63¼	+ ¼
NInd 10s99	11.0	10	90½	– ⅛
NMed 9s06	cv	14	105	– ½
NMed 8s08	cv	78	95¼	+ ¼
NMed 12¾99A	12.3	7	103½	– ¼
NMEd 12s00	12.0	93	100⅜	– 1⅝
NMed 12½00	12.0	4	104	+ 1
NMed zr04	...	38	29½	...
NRUt 9¼92	9.1	3	102.	...
Navstr 9s04	10.5	199	86	– ⅜
NavFin 8⅝91	8.8	6	98	+ 1¾

Source: Reprinted by permission of *The Wall Street Journal*, © Dow Jones & Company, Inc. (1988). All Rights Reserved.

FIGURE 3-3 How to Read Corporate Bond Quotations

1. The abbreviated name of the company issuing the bond is listed—in this case, Financial Corporation.
2. This column shows the rate of interest paid on each bond and its maturity date—for Fuqual 9⅞ percent per year, maturing in 1997.
3. Bonds having the letters "cv" are convertible bonds. That is, they may be converted to stocks at a predetermined ratio.
4. The Volume column shows the number of bonds traded for the day—for General Mills, 94 bonds were purchased.

Bonds	Cur Yld	Vol	Close	Net Chg.
Fldcst 6s12	cv	10	65¾	...
FinCpA 11⅞98	24.7	7	48⅛	− ⅜
FinCpA 6s10	15.6	23	38½	+ 3½
FinCp dc11½02	cv	39	36½	− ½
FtRepub 8¼99	cv	402	17½	− 2½
FtRep 9⅜01	24.0	71	39	+ 1
FtRep 8.6s04t	27.7	15	31	− 6
FishF 6½94	cv	1	57	...
FlowGn 14.30s04	14.3	5	100	...
FlyTigr 9s91	9.4	5	96	− ½
FrdC 7½91	7.7	5	97	...
FrdC 8.7s99	8.8	13	98½	+ 2
FrdC 7⅞89	7.8	10	100½	− ⅛
FrdC 8½02	9.1	25	93½	...
Fruf 13½96	17.3	464	78⅛	+ ¼
Fruf 13¾01	17.5	248	78⅜	+ ⅜
Fuqua 9⅞97	10.3	5	96	...
GAF 11⅜95	11.4	52	100	...
GATX 11½96	11.0	14	105	...
GnDev 12⅝05	13.5	39	93¼	− ¼
GnEl 7½96	8.0	10	93¼	+ ⅝
GElCr 8¼97	8.5	15	96⅝	...
GnInst 7¼12	cv	30	106	− ½
GMills 8⅞95	8.8	94	101	+ ½
GMA 6¼88	6.3	5	99 17/32	...
GMA 7⅛90	7.3	3	98	− ⅛
GMA 8s93M	8.3	242	96¾	− ¼
GMA 7¾94	8.3	100	93½	+ ½
GMA 7¼95	8.0	5	90¼	+ ⅛
GMA 7⅛92	7.6	20	93¾	− ¾
GMA 7.85s98	8.7	65	89¾	+ ½
GMA 8⅞99	9.2	178	96⅛	+ ⅛
GMA 8¾s01	9.4	10	93⅛	− 1⅜
GMA 8⅛96	8.7	43	93⅜	+ ⅛
GMA 8.65s08	9.7	10	89¼	− 1⅜
GMA 9¾03	9.8	74	99¾	...
GMA 9.4s04	9.7	19	97¼	− ⅛
GMA 12s05fb	11.2	23	107½	...
GMA dc6s11	9.1	10	66¼	− ¼
GMA zr12	...	29	100	...
GMA zr15	...	25	83	+ ¾
GMA 10¼90	10.2	5	100½	...
GMA 9¼93	9.1	80	101¼	− ¼
GMA 8⅞96	9.1	68	98	...
GMA 8s90	8.0	90	100	...
GMA 8⅛92	8.2	112	98¾	− ⅛
GMA 8s93J	8.3	95	96¾	...
GMA 8s93O	8.2	10	97	+ ¼

Bonds	Cur Yld	Vol	Close	Net Chg.
vjJonsLl 6¾94f	...	2	29	− ½
vjJoneL 9⅞95f	...	7	68¼	...
K mart 12⅛95	...	12	114	− ⅜
KerrGl 13s96	12.9	115	101	...
KogerP 9¼03	cv	21	94¾	+ ¼
vjLTV 5s88f	...	31	34	− ½
vjLTV 9¼97f	...	5	41	+ ⅛
vjLTV 11s07f	...	22	33⅜	+ ¾
vjLTV 13⅞02f	...	6	40	− 1
vjLTV 14s04f	...	160	42	− ½
vjLTV 11½97f	...	2	34⅞	+ ⅛
vjLTV 7⅞98f	...	4	29	− 1
vjLTV 8¾98f	...	10	29⅝	− ⅝
LaQuin 10s02	cv	32	97	+ 1
Litton 11½95	10.6	10	108	+ 1
LomN zr01	...	14	30	...
LomN 9s10	cv	34	97½	+ 1
LomN 7s11	cv	29	76	+ 1½
LglsLt 13½13	13.1	5	102⅞	+ ⅜
LglsLt 17½89	16.7	5	105	− 1
LglsLt 13¼95	12.9	85	102¾	+ ½
Loral 7¼10	cv	20	103¾	+ ¾
Lorilld 6⅞93	7.5	37	92¼	− ⅛
LouLE 8½00	cv	1	88⅝	+ ⅜
vjLykes 7½94f	...	32	29	...
MACOM 9¼06	cv	10	84	...
MCorp 9⅜01	15.4	50	61	...
MGMUA 12⅝93	12.4	7	101¾	...
MGMUA 13s96	13.1	85	99	− ½
MacMl 5½12	cv	11	104½	− ½
MeYk 8½02	9.3	10	91	+ ⅝
MfrH 8⅛04	9.9	3	82	+ 1¾
MfrH 8⅛07	10.1	1	80½	+ 1½
MarO 9½94	9.6	99	99⅜	+ ⅛
Masco 5¼12	6.0	30	87	+ ½
Mattel 11⅝03	13.5	5	86¼	+ ¼
MayDC 9s89	9.0	35	100¼	− ¼
McCro 7¾95	13.5	4	57½	− ½
McDlnv 8s11	cv	10	84	+ 1½
McDnl zr94	...	33	61¾	+ ¼
McKes 9¾06	cv	9	151	− 1¾
vjMcLn 12s03f	...	1	7¾	+ ¼
vjMcLn 14¼94f	...	4	8½	...
Mead 6s12	cv	22	101¼	+ 3¼
Melln 8.6s09	10.6	53	81	− 1⅝
Melln 7¼99	8.6	10	84	+ ½
MLCPS 15¾06	13.5	2	117	− 1
MerLy zr06	...	122	23⅞	− ⅛

EXPLANATORY NOTES
(For New York and American Bonds)
Yield is current yield.
cv-Convertible bond. cf-Certificates. dc-Deep discount. ec-European currency units. f-Dealt in flat. kd-Danish kroner. m-Matured bonds, negotiability impaired by maturity. na-No accrual. r-Registered. rp-Reduced principal. st-Stamped. t-Floating rate. wd-When distributed. ww-With warrants. x-Ex interest. xw-Without warrants. zr-Zero coupon.
vj-In bankruptcy or receivership or being reorganized under the Bankruptcy Act, or securities assumed by such companies.

figures and in fractions. But the fraction used is not the same as that used for corporate bonds. The fraction for government securities is expressed in thirty-seconds of \$10. One thirty-second of \$10 is $\$10 \div 32 =$ \$0.3125, or 31¼ cents.

To determine the exact market price of a government security, let us take as an example the Federal Home Loan Bank bonds listed in the second column, third from last line, in Figure 3-4.

Note that these bonds carry 10.75 percent interest, mature in May of 1993, and have an asked price of 109.17. In computing the exact market price, use the asked price but bear in mind that a zero must be added to the whole number and that the fraction represents 17/32 of \$10.

Add a zero to 109, making it \$1,090	\$1,090.00
Add 17/32 of \$10, which is 17 × \$0.3125	5.31
Exact market price	\$1,095.31

For another example, take the quotation for Federal Home Loan Bank bonds on the 11th line from the bottom of the second column in Figure 3-4. Note that these bonds bear 10.6 percent interest, mature in October of 1992, and have an asked price of

FIGURE 3-4 Quotations for Government, Agency, and Miscellaneous Securities

GOVERNMENT AGENCY ISSUES

Wednesday, April 13, 1988
Mid-afternoon Over-the-Counter quotations usually based on large transactions, sometimes $1 million or more. Decimals in bid-and-asked represent 32nds; 101.1 means 101 1/32. a-Plus 1/64. b-Yield to call date. d-Minus 1/64.
Source: Bloomberg Financial Markets

Fed. Home Loan Bank

Rate	Mat	Bid	Asked	Yld
10.15	4-88	100.1	100.4	5.78
10.38	4-88	100.1	100.5	5.01
7.38	5-88	100	100.3	6.36
10.15	5-88	100.9	100.13	6.31
7.25	6-88	100.1	100.4	6.49
8.80	6-88	100.11	100.14	6.45
10.80	6-88	100.24	100.27	6.38
9.15	7-88	100.18	100.22	6.52
6.90	7-88	99.31	100.2	6.57
6.35	8-88	99.26	99.30	6.47
7.15	8-88	100.1	100.5	6.55
11.63	8-88	101.21	101.25	6.51
9.45	8-88	100.28	101	6.55
8.00	9-88	100.15	100.19	6.61
6.35	10-88	99.18	99.24	6.83
8.90	10-88	100.28	101	6.94
11.40	10-88	102.6	102.10	6.88
9.55	10-88	101.8	101.12	6.86
8.90	11-88	101.1	101.4	6.97
14.20	11-88	104.5	104.9	6.92
7.50	11-88	100.7	100.10	6.95
10.70	12-88	102.11	102.15	7.01
7.80	12-88	100.12	100.16	7.03
7.40	1-89	100.3	100.7	7.09
11.38	1-89	103.1	103.5	7.11
6.50	2-89	99.11	99.15	7.13
6.95	2-89	99.21	99.25	7.20
8.30	2-89	100.26	100.30	7.15
10.80	2-89	102.28	103	7.16
15.10	2-89	106.2	106.19	7.11
6.90	3-89	99.19	99.23	7.20
7.45	3-89	100.2	100.7	7.20
6.90	4-89	99.13	99.23	7.18
7.38	4-89	99.31	100.5	7.21
14.25	4-89	106.20	106.30	7.14
7.40	5-89	99.30	100.4	7.27
10.20	5-89	102.28	103.2	7.27
7.70	6-89	100.9	100.13	7.33
7.00	7-89	99.11	99.21	7.27
14.13	7-89	107.31	108.5	7.31
6.75	9-89	99.5	99.15	7.14
12.50	9-89	106.21	106.31	7.33
14.55	9-89	109.9	109.19	7.43
9.35	10-89	102.12	102.16	7.59
6.60	11-89	98.21	98.27	7.36
11.55	11-89	105.17	105.27	7.63
8.13	11-89	100.21	100.27	7.55
6.55	12-89	98.21	98.27	7.28
8.25	12-89	100.29	101.1	7.58
11.20	1-90	105.23	105.29	7.58
6.55	1-90	98.7	98.13	7.51
6.70	3-90	98.13	98.19	7.49
7.30	3-90	99.15	99.19	7.52
11.90	3-90	107.11	107.21	7.60
7.05	4-90	98.25	98.31	7.61
8.25	5-90	101.3	101.9	7.58
7.75	6-90	99.23	100.1	7.73
9.50	6-90	103.11	103.21	7.65
9.75	7-90	103.27	104.5	7.72
7.80	7-90	99.29	100.3	7.75
8.10	8-90	100.17	100.23	7.76
8.88	9-90	102.7	102.13	7.77
12.50	9-90	109.31	110.9	7.80
10.30	9-90	105.7	105.17	7.77
7.05	10-90	98.7	98.13	7.75
8.40	11-90	101.3	101.9	7.84
13.70	11-90	113.5	113.15	7.89
10.90	12-90	106.25	107.3	7.92
8.70	12-90	101.27	102.5	7.79
8.30	1-91	100.25	100.31	7.90
9.10	1-91	102.25	103.3	7.83
7.10	2-91	97.27	98.1	7.88
7.65	2-91	99.7	99.11	7.90
11.88	2-91	109.19	109.29	7.93
7.75	3-91	99.1	99.11	7.90
7.35	4-91	98.3	98.13	7.95
7.88	5-91	99.9	99.19	8.02

FNMA Issues

Rate	Mat	Bid	Asked	Yld
10.50	5-88	100.7	100.10	5.89
10.50	6-88	100.16	100.20	6.22
9.40	8-88	100.24	100.28	6.52
16.38	8-88	102.27	103.2	6.48
8.55	9-88	100.17	100.23	6.70
13.20	9-88	102.13	102.17	6.79
9.50	10-88	101.5	101.8	6.85
12.75	10-88	102.19	102.25	6.86
8.95	11-88	101.1	101.5	6.84
11.00	11-88	102.5	102.8	6.90
11.70	11-88	102.17	102.21	6.86
11.25	12-88	102.19	102.23	6.94
11.75	12-88	102.30	103.2	6.90
11.10	1-89	102.24	102.28	7.01
11.60	2-89	103.13	103.17	7.07
12.10	3-89	104.3	104.11	7.05
7.55	4-89	100.7	100.13	7.12
9.30	6-89	102.3	102.9	7.20
9.50	6-89	102.9	102.15	7.23
8.00	7-89	100.19	100.29	7.21
10.05	8-89	103.2	103.12	7.31
13.13	8-89	106.28	107.2	7.40
12.10	10-89	106.9	106.15	7.43
12.75	10-89	107.5	107.11	7.45
9.85	11-89	103.9	103.15	7.46
11.80	11-89	106.1	106.7	7.52
11.30	12-89	105.13	105.23	7.55
6.50	12-89	98.13	98.19	7.41
11.45	1-90	106.1	106.11	7.48
11.05	2-90	105.23	106.1	7.45
8.65	3-90	101.29	102.3	7.45
7.35	4-90	99.9	99.19	7.57
10.30	5-90	105.1	105.7	7.53
11.15	5-90	106.19	106.25	7.55
9.85	7-90	104.5	104.15	7.63
10.00	9-90	104.21	104.31	7.69
10.15	10-90	104.29	105.3	7.86
7.00	11-90	98.3	98.9	7.74
10.90	11-90	106.23	107.1	7.83
8.40	12-90	101.5	101.9	7.85
11.80	12-90	108.27	109.5	7.90
8.75	1-91	101.25	102.3	7.88
8.38	1-91	101.7	101.11	7.81
6.90	2-91	97.15	97.25	7.78
7.65	2-91	99.15	99.21	7.78
12.00	3-91	110.3	110.13	7.92
12.50	3-91	111.11	111.21	7.94
7.20	4-91	98.1	98.7	7.88
8.00	4-91	100.7	100.11	7.87
7.45	5-91	98.15	98.21	7.95
8.55	6-91	101.9	101.19	7.96
7.65	7-91	98.27	99.5	7.94
8.70	8-91	101.31	102.5	7.94
8.40	8-91	101.3	101.9	7.95
7.00	9-91	96.17	96.27	8.07
7.80	10-91	99.11	99.21	7.91
7.38	10-91	97.19	97.29	8.08
9.55	11-91	104.5	104.11	8.12
11.75	12-91	110.23	111.1	8.19
8.50	1-92	100.29	101.1	8.17
7.00	3-92	96.1	96.11	8.11
12.00	4-92	112.21	112.27	8.16
8.45	5-92	100.19	100.25	8.22
7.05	6-92	95.27	96.5	8.15
10.13	6-92	106.19	106.25	8.16
8.45	7-92	100.17	100.27	8.20
10.60	10-92	108.7	108.17	8.29
9.88	12-92	105.9	105.19	8.39
10.90	1-93	109.7	109.17	8.41
7.95	2-93	98.17	98.21	8.29
7.90	3-93	98.5	98.15	8.28
10.95	3-93	109.23	110.1	8.41
7.55	4-93	96.16	96.22	8.37
10.88	4-93	109.24	109.30	8.40
10.75	5-93	109.11	109.17	8.40
7.75	11-93	96.25	96.31	8.44
7.38	12-93	95.3	95.9	8.44

108.17. The exact market price of these bonds is computed as follows:

Add a zero to 108, making it $1,080	$1,080.00
Add 17/32 of $10, which is 17 × $0.3125	5.31
Exact market price	$1,085.31

QUOTATIONS ON AN "AND INTEREST" BASIS

Bonds are quoted on an "and interest" basis because the buyer has to pay the seller not only the quoted price but also the interest that the bond has earned since the last interest payment date. This is done so that corporate bonds may be sold at any time without any loss of interest to the seller or, conversely, without any advantage to the buyer.

For example, a $1,000 government bond bearing 5 percent interest, with interest payment dates of January 1 and July 1, is sold on June 10 for delivery on June 13. In addition to the market price of the bond, the buyer would pay the seller the accrued interest from January 1 to June 12, the day before the date of delivery. The interest accrues up to, but not including, June 13. The total number of days of accrued interest would be 163, calculated as follows:

January	31
February (not leap year)	28
March	31
April	30
May	31
June	12
	163 days

It should be noted here that accrued interest for government bonds is computed for the *actual* number of days involved, as illustrated above. For corporate bonds, accrued interest is computed on the basis of a 30-day month and a 360-day year. If interest is not being paid on a bond, then it is in default and of course there will be no accrued interest. Such a bond is quoted as **trading flat**.

There are two ways of calculating the amount of accrued interest: (1) by the use of a formula and (2) by the use of a bond interest table.

Calculating Accrued Interest by Using a Formula

The formula for calculating simple interest is:

$$\text{Principal} \times \text{Rate} \times \text{Time} = \text{Interest}$$

If our previous example of a $1,000 bond at 5 percent were a corporate bond, the accrued interest would be for 162 days (30 × 5 + 12) and would be computed as follows:

$$\$1,000 \times \tfrac{5}{100} \times \tfrac{162}{360} = \$22.50 \text{ (accrued interest)}$$

Calculating Accrued Interest by Using Bond Interest Tables

Bond interest tables are widely used by stockbrokers as an easier way to determine the amount of interest that has accrued on a bond since the last interest payment date.

A bond interest table is illustrated in Table 3-1.

When using a bond interest table, the first items to check are the columnar headings for the time and the interest rate. If the time period is less than 30 days, the interest can be found for the exact days involved. If the time period is 30 days or more, the interest can be found by locating the months involved.

To illustrate, let us take the corporate bond in the previous example. The time for the number of days in June is 12, and five months have elapsed since the last payment date on January 1. By consulting Table 3-1, we find that:

The interest for 12 days at
  5 percent.....................$ 1.6667
The interest for 5 months at
  5 percent 20.8333
Total accrued interest $22.5000

This is the same amount of accrued interest that was obtained by using the formula P × R × T = I.

With either method of calculating accrued interest, a seller obtains all interest up to the date of delivery because this interest is added to the quoted price of the bond.

TABLE 3-1 Accrued Interest on $1,000 (360-Day basis)

Days	5%	6%	Days	5%	6%	Months	5%	6%
1	.1389	.1667	16	2.2222	2.6667	1	4.1667	5.0000
2	.2778	.3333	17	2.3611	2.8333	2	8.3333	10.0000
3	.4167	.5000	18	2.5000	3.0000	3	12.5000	15.0000
4	.5556	.6667	19	2.6389	3.1667	4	16.6667	20.0000
5	.6944	.8333	20	2.7778	3.3333	5	20.8333	25.0000
6	.8333	1.0000	21	2.9167	3.5000	6	25.0000	30.0000
7	.9722	1.1667	22	3.0556	3.6667	7	29.1667	35.0000
8	1.1111	1.3333	23	3.1944	3.8333	8	33.3333	40.0000
9	1.2500	1.5000	24	3.3333	4.0000	9	37.5000	45.0000
10	1.3889	1.6667	25	3.4722	4.1667	10	41.6667	50.0000
11	1.5278	1.8333	26	3.6111	4.3333	11	45.8333	55.0000
12	1.6667	2.0000	27	3.7500	4.5000	12	50.0000	60.0000
13	1.8056	2.1667	28	3.8889	4.6667			
14	1.9444	2.3333	29	4.0278	4.8333			
15	2.0833	2.5000	30	4.1667	5.0000			

The buyer does not lose anything because the $22.50 of accrued interest is recovered when $25 for the full six months is paid on the due date, July 1. The amount of $25 actually reimburses the accrued interest of $22.50 and gives $2.50 in interest for the 18 days (June 13, the date of delivery, to July 1, the interest due date), which is the length of time the buyer owned the bond.

BOND YIELDS

We have seen that the interest a bond earns is stated on the face of the bond certificate. If the bond is bought for its face value of $1,000, the buyer knows exactly what the interest will be. However, we have also seen that bonds fluctuate in value with changes in long-term interest rates. Because of these fluctuations, several different kinds of yields, or interest, may be obtained from bonds. These various interest rates are called nominal yield, current yield, and yield to maturity.

NOMINAL YIELD

The **nominal yield** is the interest that is paid per $1,000—or the interest stated on the face of the bond. It is important to remember that regardless of the price that is paid for a bond, it will pay the interest as stated. A $1,000 bond at 7 percent will pay $70 a year. It does not matter whether the market price is $960, $1,000, or $1,060; the bond will still pay its nominal yield.

CURRENT YIELD

The **current yield** is the interest that takes into consideration the current market price. If a $1,000 bond at 5 percent is bought at a discount, it will yield more than 5 percent. If the same bond is bought at a premium, it will yield less than 5 percent. Calculations of current yield are given below. Remember that the current yield equals the annual income divided by the investment.

Example: What is the current yield on a bond that is selling at 97 and carrying 5 percent interest?

97% of $1,000 = $970 market price
5% of $1,000   = $50 annual income
Current yield = $50 ÷ $970 = .0515
                 or 5.15%

Since the market price was less than $1,000, the bond was selling at a discount. In this case, the current yield is 5.15 percent, which is more than the 5 percent nominal yield.

If the bond is selling at 105, or at a premium, the calculations for its current yield are as follows:

105% of
$1,000   = $1,050 market price
5% of $1,000   = $50 annual income
Current yield = $50 ÷ $1,050 = .0476
                 or 4.76%

YIELD TO MATURITY

The **yield to maturity** considers the nominal yield, market price, and time period during which the bond is held. Remember that bonds have a maturity date. When a bond matures, it will be worth its face amount no matter how much it may have fluctuated in market price in the meantime. Like anything that is selling at a discount, if you buy it for less and later sell it for its full value, you obviously gain the difference. With a corporate bond, you know *when* you will gain the difference because you know its maturity date.

For example, if you purchase a 5 percent bond selling for $970 that will mature in three years, you know that you will gain $30 in three years. The amount of $30 represents the increase in the value of the bond bought at a discount, and this is called its **accumulation**. Now divide $30 by 3 years to obtain the annual accumulation of $10. The amount of $10 constitutes 1 percent of $1,000—the face value of the bond. This means that 1 percent will be added to the nominal 5 percent yield if you hold the bond to maturity. Therefore, you average 6 percent a year, not 5 percent. The adjusted annual income of the bond is $60, while its nominal income is $50. The calculations for this example are given below.

$1,000 face value
$\underline{- \quad 970}$ market price
$\overline{\$ \quad 30}$ profit in 3 years

$30 ÷ 3 $\quad$ = $10 a year
$10 ÷ $1,000 = .01, or 1% yield on the face amount of the bond

5% of $1,000 = $50 nominal income
$\underline{1\% \text{ of } \$1,000 = \$10}$ annual accumulation
6% of $1,000 = $60 adjusted annual income

The above example of obtaining the yield to maturity is only a rule-of-thumb method. It is not precise, for it does not take into consideration the average cost of holding the bond to maturity. To find the precise, or net, yield to maturity, there are published bond value tables that can be consulted. Lacking these tables, the following formula to approximate the net yield to maturity is given in three steps:

Step 1. Add the nominal interest income and the annual accumulation to obtain the adjusted annual income.

$$\$50 + \$10 = \$60$$

Step 2. Add the face value and the current market price, then divide by 2 to obtain the adjusted average cost.

$$(\$1,000 + \$970) ÷ 2 = \$985$$

Step 3. Divide the adjusted annual income by the adjusted average cost to obtain the net yield to maturity.

$$\$60 ÷ \$985 = .0609 \text{ or } 6.09\%$$

When a bond is bought at a premium, the decrease in the value of the bond is called its **amortization**. To find the net yield to maturity in this case, the same calculations are made except that in Step 1 the annual loss is subtracted from the nominal interest income to obtain the adjusted annual income.

Now you know why a bond is bought or quoted at a discount. The previous examples illustrate the importance of computing correctly the yield on a bond because the interest that you will receive is the main reason for purchasing it.

BOND RATINGS

Bond ratings help the investor decide on the quality of bonds. Safety and assurance that the income will be paid are paramount. Certainly no one wants to buy a bond that may default sometime in the future, either by not meeting the interest payment on time or by failing to pay the face amount upon maturity.

CLASSIFICATIONS BY INVESTMENT ADVISORY SERVICES

The two best-known advisory services that publish bond ratings are Moody's Investors Service and Standard & Poor's Corpora-

tion. These services rate bonds as a school paper is graded: A, B, C, and D. The rating A is the highest. Each grade, however, has three classifications, as illustrated in Table 3-2. Within each grade the triple letter has the highest rating and the single letter has the lowest rating.

INTERPRETATION OF BOND RATINGS

When rating bonds, the most important item being evaluated is the probable risk factor. That is, what are the chances of a possible loss? Experienced bond buyers will

TABLE 3-2 Comparative Ratings of Moody's and Standard & Poor's

Moody's	Standard & Poor's	Interpretation
Aaa	AAA	Highest grade
Aa	AA	High grade
A	A	Upper medium; medium grade; sound
Baa	BBB	Medium; good grade; some uncertainty
Ba	BB	Fair to good; lower medium; uncertainty
B	B	Fair; speculative features
Caa	CCC	Outright speculation; poor standing
Ca	CC	Outright speculation; marked weakness
C	C	Best defaulted issues; highly speculative
Daa	DDD	In default
Da	DD	Assets of little value
D	D	No apparent value

not normally buy bonds rated below the A classification.

As can be seen from the Interpretation column in Table 3-2, bonds rated triple B are considered to be only medium or good grade, with some uncertainty. Bonds rated C are considered to be speculative. Bonds rated triple D and lower are already in default. However, both Moody's and Standard & Poor's warn investors that their ratings are only a help in determining the right bonds to buy. These investment advisory services state that their ratings are subject to miscalculation and human error.

As when making any investment, bond buyers should obtain the facts themselves. They should be sure that the issuing corporation or the issuing government body is fiscally sound and that the source of revenue for payment of the bond interest is secure.

SUMMARY

There are several major categories of bonds. When classified as to issuer, the least safe to the safest are corporate bonds, municipal bonds, and government bonds. When classified as to method of making the interest payment, there are income bonds, registered bonds, and coupon or bearer bonds. Most bonds are bearer bonds. The person who is in actual possession of these bonds is the owner. As a consequence, great care should be exercised when handling coupon bonds. They should be kept in a safe place. When classified as to method of repaying the principal, there are sinking fund bonds, serial bonds, callable bonds, and convertible bonds.

It is important to remember that bond prices fluctuate; they vary inversely with long-term interest rates. When long-term interest rates go up, bond prices go down; and when long-term interest rates go down, bond prices go up.

Quotations for corporate and government bonds are found in *The Wall Street Journal*. To understand these quotations, an investor must realize that a zero should be added to the listed whole number to obtain the approximate price. The investor must also understand that the fractions are in terms of eighths of $10 for corporate bonds and thirty-seconds of $10 for government bonds. In addition, the bond buyer has to pay the seller the accrued interest on the bond from the last interest payment date. Bonds are traded "flat," or at no accrued interest, if they are in default.

Since bonds are purchased primarily for income, knowing their net yield to maturity is important. The income that a bond buyer will receive is related to the current market price and the maturity date of the bond. The bondholder will at all times be paid the amount of interest that the bond calls for on its face amount, but the true yield will not be that amount unless the bond is bought for $1,000.

Advisory services publish bond ratings as a guide to determine the right bonds to buy. The two best-known services are Moody's Investors Service and Standard & Poor's Corporation. They rate bonds in grades of A, B, C, and D, with three classifications within each grade.

3

REVIEW QUESTIONS
SHORT ESSAY

Name _____

Date _____ Points _____

Directions: Answer the following questions according to your instructor's directions.

1. Three basic facts concerning bonds should be considered before investing. What are they?

    a. _____

    b. _____

    c. _____

2. Why is a bond known as a senior security?

    _____

    _____

    _____

3. Name the three major categories of bonds according to the type of issuer.

    a. _____

    b. _____

    c. _____

4. In your own words, define a municipal bond.

    _____

    _____

5. Bond prices vary inversely with interest rates. Explain in your own words what this means.

    _____

    _____

6. The market price of a bond is quoted in *The Wall Street Journal* as 92. What are the two reasons for not quoting the actual selling price?

a. _____

b. _____

7. A bond is quoted at 95⅝. Calculate its market price.

8. Calculate how much you would have to pay for a U.S. Treasury bond that is quoted at 76.8.

9. Using Table 3-1 on page 67, what is the accrued interest due for 7 months and 24 days on a $1,000 bond paying 6 percent interest?

10. What is meant by nominal yield?

_____

_____

_____

_____

3

REVIEW QUESTIONS
MULTIPLE CHOICE

Name _____

Date _____ Points _____

Directions: For each of the following, select the best answer and place the letter that represents it in the Answers column.

ANSWERS

1. The security behind general obligation bonds is the
   a. general obligation of the voters.
   b. full taxing power of the political subdivision that issues them.
   c. general revenue from all toll bridges.
   d. general revenue from all property taxes.   _____

2. One of the following statements describes a principal difference between coupon bonds and registered bonds:
   a. coupon bonds are more easily bought and sold.
   b. the principal of coupon bonds is paid on the maturity date.
   c. the interest on registered bonds is payable only on demand.
   d. registered bonds are bought and sold at a discount.   _____

3. A partly registered bond is registered only
   a. as to the interest.
   b. as to the principal.
   c. at the option of the bondholder.
   d. in the name of the bondholder's bank.   _____

4. The market price of bonds is seldom quoted at $1,000 because
   a. few people want to pay that much for them.
   b. they are usually sold at a discount.
   c. they are usually sold at a premium.
   d. long-term interest rates fluctuate.   _____

5. The market price of corporate bonds is expressed as a
   a. whole number, plus eighths of $10.
   b. whole number, plus thirty-seconds of $10.
   c. whole number.
   d. fraction.   _____

6. "And interest," when applied to bonds, means that the
   a. buyer of these bonds will get extra cash.
   b. seller must pay the buyer the interest.
   c. accrued interest from the last payment date must be added to the price of the bond.
   d. interest payment is deferred until the bond matures.   _____

7. When computing market price, one way to determine the accrued interest on a bond is to
   a. multiply the interest rate by the bond's face value.
   b. divide the number of days and months involved by the bond's face value.
   c. use the formula $P \times R = I$.
   d. use a bond interest table.   _____

8. A $1,000 corporate bond is quoted at 97 "and interest." Interest at 6 percent is paid twice a year on January 1 and July 1. The bond is sold on May 15 for delivery on May 19. How much does the buyer have to pay for the bond?
    a. $970.00.
    b. $992.83.
    c. $993.00.
    d. $1,000.00.

9. The interest on a $1,000 corporate bond for 73 days at 5 percent is
    a. $8.3333.
    b. $9.1389.
    c. $10.0000.
    d. $10.1389.

10. Nominal yield signifies that a bond is paying
    a. what the company can nominally afford.
    b. its current yield.
    c. what the bond calls for on the face of its certificate.
    d. accrued interest.

11. To determine the current yield of a bond, you would need to know the
    a. market price and coupon rate.
    b. face value, coupon rate, and maturity date.
    c. market price and maturity date.
    d. coupon rate and maturity date.

12. A bond is quoted at 97 and carries a 5 percent coupon. Current yield is determined by
    a. dividing 97 by 5.
    b. dividing 5 by 97.
    c. multiplying 97 by 5 and dividing the result by 100.
    d. dividing 97 by 5 and multiplying the result by 100.

13. One of the following is the best bond rating:
    a. A.
    b. AAA.
    c. BBB.
    d. C.

14. Bond ratings by Moody's Investors Service and Standard & Poor's Corporation can be relied upon
    a. with 100 percent accuracy.
    b. more than corporate financial reports.
    c. to the extent that they are a help in buying bonds.
    d. when speculating.

15. One of the following bond ratings is considered to be speculative:
    a. AAA.
    b. BBB.
    c. CCC.
    d. DDD.

<table>
<tr><td>

3

REVIEW QUESTIONS
TRUE-FALSE

</td><td>

Name _____

Date _____ Points _____

</td></tr>
</table>

Directions: Circle T or F to indicate whether each statement is true or false.

ANSWERS

1. Bonds are known as senior securities because, for the most part, only older, well-established people can afford them.   T   F

2. A general mortgage bond is a blanket mortgage on all of a corporation's fixed assets.   T   F

3. A debenture is only as good as the credit rating of the corporation that issues it.   T   F

4. A guaranteed bond is the best bond that you could buy.   T   F

5. Equipment trust certificates are securities placed in a trust for the protection of the creditor.   T   F

6. Municipal bonds are attractive to investors in a high income tax bracket because these bonds are free from federal income tax.   T   F

7. Revenue bonds are guaranteed by the tax revenue of the state that issues them.   T   F

8. U.S. Treasury notes are issued with a 10-year maturity.   T   F

9. U.S. Treasury bonds are a part of the nonmarketable debt of the federal government.   T   F

10. Income bonds are guaranteed only as to payment of their principal at maturity.   T   F

11. Fully registered bonds are registered with the U.S. government.   T   F

12. Bearer bonds may be cashed by whoever has possession of them.   T   F

13. Sinking fund bonds are issued to purchase excessively expensive machinery and equipment.   T   F

14. A refunding operation takes place when a corporation repays accumulated interest on defaulted bonds.   T   F

15. The Federal Reserve Board controls credit by controlling the money supply.   T   F

16. The market price of bonds is quoted in two parts.   **T**   **F**

17. The buyer of a bond quoted on an "and interest" basis receives interest from the last interest payment date to the day before delivery. **T F**

18. The formula for calculating simple interest is $P \times I \times T = R$. **T F**

19. Yield to maturity must take into consideration the nominal yield, the market price, and the time period during which the bond is held. **T F**

20. Precise yield to maturity cannot be calculated without knowing the average cost of holding a bond to maturity. **T F**

21. When a bond is bought at a premium, the decrease in the value of the bond is called its amortization. **T F**

22. When bonds are being rated, the probable risk factor is the most important consideration. **T F**

23. The letters AA signify the highest bond rating by Standard & Poor's. **T F**

24. Bonds rated D should not be purchased, for they have no apparent value. **T F**

25. As with any investment, bond buyers themselves should obtain the facts about the issuing corporation or the issuing government. **T F**

3

PROJECT

Mary and Tom Baldwin are continuing to prosper in their dry cleaning business. They have always been conservative, so they feel they should balance their common-stock portfolio by buying some bonds. They are considering investing $5,000 in a certain issue. The bond is quoted at 85, carries a 9 percent coupon, and will mature in six years.

Many bond buyers are content to use the rule-of-thumb method, which is a quick way of determining approximate bond yield to maturity. Mary and Tom are not satisfied with this method.

In this project you are to determine for them the precise yield to maturity for the bond they are considering. You are also to show all of the arithmetic that you used to arrive at your answer.

CHAPTER 4
OUTLINE

I. **MAJOR CATEGORIES OF MUTUAL FUNDS**

   A. Funds Classified According to How They Sell Shares

   B. Funds Classified as to How They Invest

II. **OPERATION AND ADVANTAGES OF MUTUAL FUNDS**

   A. The Pool Diagram

   B. Advantages of Mutual Funds

III. **MUTUAL FUND CHARGES**

   A. Sales Charge

   B. Quantity Discount Sales Charge

   C. Management Fee

IV. **INVESTING IN MUTUAL FUNDS**

   A. Quotation of Mutual Fund Prices

   B. Opening a Mutual Fund Account

   C. How Funds Pay Out Dividends and Capital Gains Distributions

IV. **PERFORMANCE OF MUTUAL FUNDS**

   A. Ten-Year Record of a Lump-Sum Investment

   B. Twenty-Year Record of a Lump-Sum Investment

V. **NINE GUIDELINES FOR INVESTORS IN MUTUAL FUNDS**

   A. Before You Invest

   B. After You Invest

VI. **MAJOR CATEGORIES OF MONEY-MARKET FUNDS**

   A. Money-Market Funds Classified According to How They Sell Shares

   B. Money-Market Funds Classified as to How They Invest

VII. **INVESTING IN MONEY-MARKET FUNDS**

   A. Quotations of Money-Market Funds

   B. How Money-Market Funds Pay Out Dividends

4

MUTUAL FUNDS

What is a mutual fund? A **mutual fund** is essentially a pool of money contributed by many people and invested for them by specialists in a cross section of American industry. The Investment Company Institute, the trade organization of the investment company industry, defines a mutual fund as follows:

> . . . a company that makes investments on behalf of individuals and institutions with similar financial goals. Pooling is the key to mutual fund investing. By pooling the financial resources of thousands of shareholders—each with a different amount to invest—investors gain access to the expertise of the country's top money managers and wide diversification of ownership in the securities markets.[1]

Arthur Wiesenberger and Company, a recognized authority in the field, defines a mutual fund as follows:

> It is a corporation or trust whose only business is the proper investment of its shareholders' money, generally in common stock or a combination of stock and bonds, in the hope of achieving a specific investment goal. And it undertakes to do a better job of investing those funds and managing the investments than the people, individually, could do for themselves.[2]

So, if you do not have the time to watch the securities markets, you can buy mutual fund shares. Over 54 million individual investors have invested approximately $769 billion in over 2,300 mutual funds. As a result, mutual funds have become the nation's fourth largest type of financial institution. Only commercial banks, savings and loan institutions, and life insurance companies are larger in terms of assets.

Because of the large number of mutual funds, it has become almost as difficult for an investor to select the right mutual fund company as it is for that individual to choose personally the correct stocks and bonds to buy. To help you make a decision, we will discuss the different kinds of mutual funds in this chapter, their advantages and disadvantages, their past performance, and nine basic guidelines to follow—both before and after you have made your decision.

MAJOR CATEGORIES OF MUTUAL FUNDS

Mutual funds may be classified in two ways: (1) according to how they sell shares and (2) according to the nature of their investment portfolios (or how the funds invest).

FUNDS CLASSIFIED ACCORDING TO HOW THEY SELL SHARES

When funds are classified according to how they sell shares, there are two types: (1) open-end funds and (2) closed-end funds.

Open-End Funds

An **open-end fund** continuously and aggressively offers new shares to the investing public and stands ready to redeem those shares at their true or asset value at any time. Open-end funds offer their shares to the public in three different ways, as described below.

1. Most open-end funds sell shares through stockbrokerage commission houses (whose major business is selling individual stocks and bonds) and through broker/dealers who specialize in selling mutual fund shares. An open-end fund using this method enters into sales agreements with these firms and grants them dealers' terms. Such terms vary from one fund to another. From these terms, the commission houses and the broker/dealers derive their profit and pay their representatives a commission.

2. A small number of open-end funds sell their shares through their own sales force. An open-end fund using this method hires its own representatives who exclusively sell its particular group of funds. Insurance companies are the principal users of this method of distribution.

3. Many open-end funds employ no sales force at all. That is, they neither have a sales force of their own nor utilize the sales forces of commission houses and broker/dealers. Such funds sell what are known as **no-load funds**, the term *no load* meaning "no sales commission."

Closed-End Funds

A **closed-end fund** does not sell its own shares, nor does it stand ready to redeem them. A prospective buyer of closed-end shares must buy them from someone who already owns them. In this respect, closed-end shares are similar to individual stocks. A seller of closed-end shares must sell them to whomever wants to buy them, quite often at a discount. Because of their relatively small impact—and because the general public is interested mainly in buying open-end shares—closed-end funds will not be further discussed in this chapter.

FUNDS CLASSIFIED AS TO HOW THEY INVEST

All mutual funds state their investment objectives in the first few pages of their official prospectus. The individual investor should choose a fund whose stated objectives most nearly coincide with her or his own.

There are seven major groups of mutual funds: (1) aggressive growth funds, (2) growth funds, (3) growth and income funds, (4) balance funds, (5) income funds, (6) municipal bond funds, and (7) money market funds. In addition, there are many specialty funds, such as gold funds, international funds, U.S. government income funds, U.S. government agency mortgage funds, and some even more fragmented types of mutual funds. It has been said that with this proliferation investors can find a mutual fund for most any investment objective.

Aggressive Growth Funds

The investment objective of **aggressive growth funds** is to seek maximum capital gains. Income is not a factor, as this type of mutual fund is mainly confined to younger growth companies that do not pay a dividend. The risks should be obvious to the investor, but so should the possibility of greater reward.

Growth Funds

A **growth fund** invests in the common stocks of the more established companies. However, increase in the value of the investment is still its primary objective.

Growth and Income Funds

A **growth and income fund** invests mainly in the blue-chip companies, which have an established niche in a solid industry and have a record of consistent dividends. The name of this type of mutual fund indicates its objectives.

Balanced Funds

A **balanced fund** invests in common stocks, preferred stocks, and bonds of established companies. Balanced funds have three objectives: (1) safety of principal, (2) modest income, and (3) an increase in the value of the shares, consistent with the first two concerns.

Income Funds

An **income fund** seeks a high current income primarily through a portfolio of fixed-income securities, although some high-dividend-paying common stocks could

be included. Income funds invest mostly in corporate bonds. Some of them may invest in U.S. government bonds as well. Those income funds that are called *high yield* or *high income* will invest in bonds rated BBB or lower by Standard & Poor's Corporation or Baa or lower by Moody's Investors Service; therefore, their risk is higher.

Municipal Bond Funds

A **municipal bond fund** invests in municipal bonds, which are free from federal income tax. If this fund is domiciled where the investor lives, as stated earlier in this text, the municipal bond is free from state income tax as well. Because of their tax-free feature, income from these funds is usually lower than that derived from income funds.

Money-Market Funds

A money-market fund invests for the short term. Money-market funds will be discussed in more detail later in this chapter because of the amount of money invested in them—$228 billion—which is almost one-third of the amount invested in all other types of mutual funds.

OPERATION AND ADVANTAGES OF MUTUAL FUNDS

A good way to understand how a mutual fund operates is illustrated in Figure 4-1. It shows a pool diagram and also lists the nine advantages offered by mutual funds.

THE POOL DIAGRAM

The person in the upper right-hand corner of the pool diagram represents an individual investor. Any sum of money may be invested (initially or later) along the line where $10,000 is depicted as a typical beginning amount. Bear in mind that some funds require only $100 to open an account. Once the account has been established, these funds allow as little as $10 to be invested at any time thereafter.

The grid on the upper left of the pool diagram represents the investments comprising the portfolio of a mutual fund. The two X's in the lower left portion of the grid indicate how a fund manager might remove an investment from the portfolio and add another one to take its place. At this point it must be emphasized that the individual investor's money does not go into any one security. Furthermore, after an initial investment the shareholder immediately starts to participate in the overall performance of the fund. This means that the shareholder receives dividends and realizes gains when they are declared. And the investor's shares increase or decrease in value with the changing fortunes of the investments in the fund's

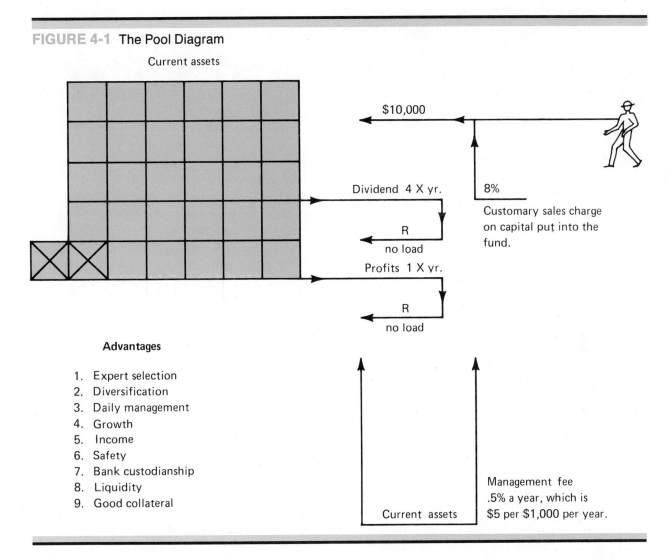

FIGURE 4-1 The Pool Diagram

ADVANTAGES OF MUTUAL FUNDS

Mutual funds offer advantages that formerly were available only to the millionaire.

portfolio and with the overall rise or fall of the stock market as a whole.

The two arrows extending out from the grid on the right demonstrate that most balanced funds and growth-income funds pay a dividend four times a year and a year-end capital gains distribution once a year. These distributions may be received in cash or, as the pool diagram shows, reinvested in additional shares of the fund, in most cases without paying a sales load.

The sales charge on investments and the management fee of .5 percent a year are explained in detail on pages 86 and 92–94.

The nine advantages listed in Figure 4-1 are made possible because of the pooling arrangement, whereby the funds of thousands of investors are managed as one complete whole. These advantages evoke sound principles of investing that have stood the test of time. Five of these advantages are briefly discussed below.

Expert Selection

As mentioned earlier, it is difficult for the average investor to choose a stock that will meet his or her investment goals. Investing in mutual funds relieves the average investor from this difficult task because mutual funds employ expert investment analysts and portfolio managers. These experts work full time to choose investments that will meet the fund's stated investment objectives. Most of the larger mutual funds have dozens of specialists, many of whom have advanced college degrees. The funds maintain up-to-date libraries and chart the day-by-day performance of hundreds of stocks and bonds by using the most modern computers. Of course, no one person or group of persons is infallible. Mutual fund managers do make mistakes in selection, but for the most part their mistakes are minor.

Diversification

Mutual funds provide average investors with greater diversification of investments than they could possibly obtain by themselves. The diversification provided by mutual funds is demonstrated in Figure 4-2, which shows the portfolio of Pioneer Fund, Inc., a large growth and income fund.

Bank Custodianship

The assets of all mutual funds must have bank custodianship. This is a part of their safety feature and is required by the federal Investment Company Act of 1940. However, bank custody of all securities and cash of a mutual fund merely provides safekeeping. Bank custodianship of the assets of a mutual fund should not be regarded in the same light as insurance that is provided by the Federal Deposit Insurance Corporation on bank deposits. Mutual fund shares are *not* insured by any agency of the federal government. But bank custodianship of mutual fund shares does and should give a feeling of security to a mutual fund shareholder by ensuring that the fund management cannot abscond with any of the fund's assets.

Liquidity

A mutual fund is liquid; that is, a fund shareholder may redeem her or his shares at any time at their net asset value. The shareholder redeems an account by mailing a request for redemption of the shares to the fund's custodian bank. The shareholder must also enclose any stock certificate that has been issued, including a signed stock power of attorney. To be acceptable, the shareholder's signature on the stock power of attorney must be guaranteed by a commercial bank or by a stockbrokerage firm.

Good Collateral

Mutual fund shares are considered to be excellent collateral as security for a loan. This is because bankers know that the investments in the fund's portfolio are widely diversified and are chosen by proven professionals. Mutual fund shares as collateral, therefore, are much better than individual stocks, no matter how blue chip the latter may be.

MUTUAL FUND CHARGES

All mutual funds charge fees in spite of the fact that mutual funds are classified as either *load* or *no-load funds*. A **load** refers to a front-end sales charge. No-load funds do not have this type of fee.

SALES CHARGE

In the past, other charges have been scattered throughout the prospectuses of mutual funds that have made it difficult for an investor to determine how much it actually costs to buy a particular mutual fund. One of these charges, usually deducted by no-load funds, is the right to deduct distribution costs from the net assets of the fund on an annual basis. The funds that imposed this charge were called *12b-1 funds*; 12b-1 was the regulation of the SEC that permitted this practice. To end this confusion, as of May 1, 1988, the SEC required all mutual funds to report their charges under two categories: transaction expenses and operating expenses.

Transaction expenses are primarily the usual sales charge (typically 8 percent on the first $10,000). These expenses include sales charges for the reinvestment of dividends, any deferred sales load, redemption fees, and exchange fees (charges for transferring shares to another fund offered by the

FIGURE 4-2 (page 1) Portfolio of Pioneer Fund, Inc., as of December 31, 1987

PIONEER FUND CONSOLIDATED
SCHEDULE OF INVESTMENTS
DECEMBER 31, 1987

Principal Amount		PIONEER FUND (Excluding Scout) Cost (Notes 1 and 2)	Market Value*	PIONEER SCOUT Market Value*	CONSOLIDATED Market Value*
	CONVERTIBLE DEBENTURES—1.7%				
$3,000,000	Deere & Co., Sub. Conv. Deb., 9%, 2008	$ 3,010,000	$ 3,273,750		$ 3,273,750
800,000	Independence Bancorp, Sub. Conv. Deb., 7%, 2011	792,500	730,000		730,000
9,500,000	International Business Machines Corp., Conv. Deb., 7.875%, 2004	10,631,760	9,713,750		9,713,750
5,000,000	Tenax Co., Sub. Conv. Deb., 8.375%, 2010	4,700,000	5,675,000		5,675,000
2,000,000	Air Wisconsin Service, Inc., Conv. Sub. Deb., 7³/₄%, 2010			$ 1,250,000	1,250,000
700,000	Hudson Foods, Inc., Conv. Deb., 8%, 2006			367,500	367,500
		$ 19,134,260	$ 19,392,500	$ 1,617,500	$ 21,010,000

Shares

	PREFERRED STOCKS—2.6%				
48,000	Cameron Iron Works, Inc., $3.50, Conv.	$ 2,728,360	$ 1,848,000		$ 1,848,000
600,000	Greif Bros. Corp. (Class A)	521,282	19,200,000		19,200,000
90,000	National Semiconductor Corp., $4.00, Conv.	4,515,050	4,545,000		4,545,000
58,630	Union Pacific Corp., $7.25, Conv.	1,479,369	6,376,013		6,376,013
65,000	Presidio Oil Co., 9.5%, Cum. Conv.			$ 390,000	390,000
		$ 9,244,061	$ 31,969,013	$ 390,000	$ 32,359,013

	COMMON STOCKS—94.6% **Chemicals and Drugs—6.2%**				
159,400	Air Products and Chemicals, Inc.	$ 1,834,855	$ 6,495,550		$ 6,495,550
281,500	Cabot Corp.	824,508	9,183,938		9,183,938
240,400	Engelhard Corp.	6,046,005	4,777,950		4,777,950
240,800	Hercules, Inc.	4,494,511	11,317,600		11,317,600
123,500	Monsanto Co.	5,229,531	10,250,500		10,250,500
157,200	Olin Corp.	2,529,625	6,602,400		6,602,400
54,000	PPG Industries, Inc.	2,396,155	1,788,750		1,788,750
238,260	A. Schulman, Inc.			$ 8,756,055	8,756,055
136,702	Block Drug Company, Inc. (Class A)			3,622,603	3,622,603
147,400	Crompton & Knowles Corp.			2,984,850	2,984,850
106,000	Essex Chemical Corp.			1,841,750	1,841,750
62,000	Fuller Company (H.B.)			2,247,500	2,247,500
56,250	Guardsman Products, Inc.			646,875	646,875
61,083	Lilly Industrial Coatings, Inc. (Class A)			839,891	839,891
126,300	Pratt & Lambert, Inc.			2,068,163	2,068,163
63,000	Quaker Chemical Corp.			1,323,000	1,323,000
281,900	The West Co., Inc.			4,721,825	4,721,825
		$ 23,355,190	$ 50,416,688	$ 29,052,512	$ 79,469,200

	Consumer Goods and Services—9.5%				
354,800	Armstrong World Industries, Inc.	$ 2,643,989	$ 11,442,300		$ 11,442,300
151,600	R. R. Donnelley & Sons Co.	4,595,381	4,945,950		4,945,950
381,150	Eastman Kodak Co.	12,348,081	18,676,350		18,676,350
65,000	General Motors Corp.	4,293,920	3,989,375		3,989,375
189,800	Johnson & Johnson	7,515,686	14,258,725		14,258,725

FIGURE 4-2 (page 2)

PIONEER FUND CONSOLIDATED
SCHEDULE OF INVESTMENTS
(CONTINUED)

Shares		PIONEER FUND (Excluding Scout)		PIONEER SCOUT	CONSOLIDATED
		Cost (Notes 1 and 2)	Market Value*	Market Value*	Market Value*
	Consumer Goods and Services — (Continued)				
109,500	Maclean Hunter Ltd. (Class X)	$ 1,788,198	$ 1,656,188		$ 1,656,188
284,600	MCA Inc.	11,420,593	9,818,700		9,818,700
137,000	McGraw-Hill, Inc.	8,205,100	6,610,250		6,610,250
50,000	New York Times Co. (Class A)	1,286,150	1,550,000		1,550,000
501,900	Standex International Corp.	1,804,134	7,089,338		7,089,338
311,250	The Stanley Works	2,967,079	8,053,594		8,053,594
320,000	Thames Television PLC (ORD)	1,961,819	2,140,000		2,140,000
94,000	West Point-Pepperell, Inc.	2,568,690	2,455,750		2,455,750
180,000	Anglia Television Group p.l.c. (ORD)**			$ 1,181,250	1,181,250
900,200	Baton Broadcasting, Inc.			8,551,900	8,551,900
39,800	Camco Inc.			228,850	228,850
72,000	Chubu Nippon Broadcasting Corp.**			607,500	607,500
16,500	Helene Curtis Industries, Inc.			420,750	420,750
28,000	Huffy Corp.			518,000	518,000
148,900	John Wiley & Sons, Inc. (Class A)			3,573,600	3,573,600
141,625	Lancaster Colony Corp.			2,478,438	2,478,438
1,100	McGraw Hill Ryerson Ltd.			22,000	22,000
269,200	Oxford Industries, Inc.			2,961,200	2,961,200
20,980	Redken Laboratories, Inc.			451,070	451,070
7,838	Rosenthal A.G. (ORD)**			848,464	848,464
28,930	William H. Sadlier, Inc.			151,883	151,883
165,000	Scottish Television p.l.c.**			1,103,438	1,103,438
6,321	Stauffer Communications, Inc.			821,730	821,730
189,800	Tele-Metropole, Inc. (Class B)			3,511,300	3,511,300
74,800	Wynn's International, Inc.			1,309,000	1,309,000
		$ 63,398,820	$ 92,686,520	$ 28,740,373	$121,426,893
	Electrical, Electronics, Instruments—7.5%				
344,800	General Electric Co.	$ 3,524,683	$ 15,257,400		$ 15,257,400
159,300	General Signal Corp.	6,079,494	7,487,100		7,487,100
90,700	International Business Machines Corp.	3,928,210	10,487,188		10,487,188
263,300	Motorola, Inc.	4,628,045	13,099,175		13,099,175
153,200	Philips Incandescent Lamp Works Holding Co. NV	3,926,585	2,221,400		2,221,400
331,200	Raytheon Corp.	20,587,948	22,066,200		22,066,200
576,300	Unisys Corp.	6,931,740	19,378,088		19,378,088
100,000	Anaren Microwave, Inc.**			$ 575,000	575,000
21,000	Astro-Med, Inc.			217,875	217,875
33,400	DICKEY-john Corp.			651,300	651,300
166,500	Dranetz Technologies, Inc.			1,540,125	1,540,125
38,900	High Voltage Engineering Corp.			525,150	525,150
19,000	Moore Products Co.			541,500	541,500
63,500	Radiation Systems, Inc.			531,813	531,813
24,885	RAI Research Corp.			161,753	161,753
83,000	WEIGH-TRONIX, Inc.			1,162,000	1,162,000
		$ 49,606,705	$ 89,996,551	$ 5,906,516	$ 95,903,067
	Engineering and Construction—4.6%				
287,800	Dover Corp.	$ 8,107,084	$ 18,023,475		$ 18,023,475
601,400	Foster Wheeler Corp.	4,727,815	8,269,250		8,269,250
79,930	Imo Delaval Inc.	638,891	2,407,891		2,407,891
257,200	Stone & Webster, Inc.	7,145,032	17,361,000		17,361,000

FIGURE 4-2 (page 3)

PIONEER FUND CONSOLIDATED
SCHEDULE OF INVESTMENTS
(CONTINUED)

Shares		PIONEER FUND (Excluding Scout) Cost (Notes 1 and 2)	Market Value*	PIONEER SCOUT Market Value*	CONSOLIDATED Market Value*
	Engineering and Construction — (Continued)				
221,700	Ameron, Inc.			$ 7,094,400	$ 7,094,400
140,000	Gilbert Associates, Inc. (Class A)			2,450,000	2,450,000
75,600	Kewaunee Scientific Corp.			595,350	595,350
101,250	Noland Co.			1,721,250	1,721,250
7,500	Palmer G. Lewis Co., Inc.			48,750	48,750
		$ 20,618,822	$ 46,061,616	$ 11,909,750	$ 57,971,366
	Financial and Insurance—9.4%				
502,100	Bank of New York Co., Inc.	$ 11,071,722	$ 12,929,075		$ 12,929,075
272,400	CIGNA Corp.	9,532,857	11,951,550		11,951,550
55,000	CoreStates Financial Corp.	2,149,375	1,849,375		1,849,375
173,500	Indiana National Corp.	6,700,375	5,465,250		5,465,250
192,500	Midlantic Corp.	8,994,620	6,424,688		6,424,688
712,762	National City Corp.	11,687,802	20,759,193		20,759,193
39,000	Ohio Casualty Corp.	1,576,500	1,413,750		1,413,750
132,700	PNC Financial Corp.	6,243,120	4,943,075		4,943,075
489,600	SAFECO Corp.	4,153,225	13,586,400		13,586,400
130,600	Signet Banking Corp.	4,718,424	3,101,750		3,101,750
95,000	Sovran Financial Corp.	3,463,750	3,206,250		3,206,250
739,300	Transamerica Corp.	13,601,392	21,994,175		21,994,175
62,000	Bank of Delaware Corp.			$ 1,395,000	1,395,000
136,200	Employers Casualty Co.			4,528,650	4,528,650
16,500	First Ohio Bancshares, Inc.			396,000	396,000
15,000	Framingham Savings Bank			155,625	155,625
36,600	Indiana Federal Savings & Loan Association			375,150	375,150
15,000	Milwaukee Insurance Group, Inc.**			146,250	146,250
273,333	SouthTrust Corp.			4,988,327	4,988,327
25,000	West Newton Savings Bank**			225,000	225,000
		$ 83,893,162	$107,624,531	$ 12,210,002	$119,834,533
	Food Products—6.3%				
786,482	Archer Daniels Midland Co.	$ 5,575,549	$ 16,712,743		$ 16,712,743
282,400	Campbell Soup Company	9,693,501	7,871,900		7,871,900
100,000	Dean Foods Co.	2,498,707	2,462,500		2,462,500
171,800	Fleming Cos., Inc.	6,717,950	4,681,550		4,681,550
720,950	International Multifoods Corp.	20,446,969	19,285,413		19,285,413
145,000	Kraft, Inc.	8,485,975	6,869,375		6,869,375
15,000	Sara Lee Corp.	501,050	532,500		532,500
404,300	Staley Continental, Inc.	7,940,064	8,591,375		8,591,375
20,000	Sysco Corp.	520,765	542,500		542,500
20,600	Campbell Soup Company Ltd.			$ 278,100	278,100
53,500	Dinner Bell Foods, Inc.†			1,257,250	1,257,250
80,000	Hudson Foods, Inc.			470,000	470,000
205,000	Nash Finch Co.			3,792,500	3,792,500
83,400	Pueblo International, Inc.††			1,928,625	1,928,625
233,400	Super Food Services, Inc.			5,163,975	5,163,975
		$ 62,380,530	$ 67,549,856	$ 12,890,450	$ 80,440,306

FIGURE 4-2 (page 4)

PIONEER FUND CONSOLIDATED
SCHEDULE OF INVESTMENTS
(CONTINUED)

Shares		PIONEER FUND (Excluding Scout) Cost (Notes 1 and 2)	PIONEER FUND (Excluding Scout) Market Value*	PIONEER SCOUT Market Value*	CONSOLIDATED Market Value*
	Forest Products—2.3%				
21,000	Consolidated Papers, Inc.	$ 1,048,750	$ 1,181,250		$ 1,181,250
285,600	Union Camp Corp.	4,153,489	10,353,000		10,353,000
420,400	Weyerhaeuser Co.	11,172,682	16,395,600		16,395,600
39,511	Badger Paper Mills, Inc.			$ 622,298	622,298
32,500	Mosinee Paper Corp.			341,250	341,250
29,500	Perkins Papers, Ltd.			136,438	136,438
10,000	Sealright Co., Inc.			200,000	200,000
		$ 16,374,921	$ 27,929,850	$ 1,299,986	$ 29,229,836
	Industrial Equipment—12.1%				
535,400	Alco Standard Corp.	$ 11,971,139	$ 10,908,775		$ 10,908,775
433,700	Caterpiller, Inc.	19,130,247	26,889,400		26,889,400
383,600	Deere & Co.	8,948,849	13,473,950		13,473,950
306,500	Echlin Inc.	5,215,227	4,291,000		4,291,000
349,600	Johnson Controls, Inc.	10,205,369	8,958,500		8,958,500
242,600	McDonnell Douglas Corp.	20,122,535	14,434,700		14,434,700
390,700	Norton Co.	10,257,635	18,069,875		18,069,875
533,350	Parker Hannifin Corp.	13,905,359	19,400,606		19,400,606
28,300	Tecumseh Products Co.	1,525,050	3,650,700		3,650,700
303,500	The Timken Co.	12,993,652	18,285,875		18,285,875
23,000	Arrow Automotive Industries, Inc.			$ 126,500	126,500
4,400	Athey Products Corp.			59,400	59,400
35,200	Cimco			378,400	378,400
23,300	Hako Minuteman, Inc.			186,400	186,400
22,400	McGill Manufacturing Co., Inc.			593,600	593,600
66,000	Milton Roy Co.			643,500	643,500
127,800	Mine Safety Appliances Co.			3,418,650	3,418,650
8,500	Monarch Machine Tool Co.			144,500	144,500
1,000	O'Sullivan Corp.			17,375	17,375
281,050	Raymond Corp.			3,864,438	3,864,438
32,000	Rexworks, Inc.			152,000	152,000
40,000	Robbins & Meyers, Inc.**			300,000	300,000
104,400	Superior Surgical Mfg. Co., Inc.			2,009,700	2,009,700
101,500	Tennant Co.			2,385,250	2,385,250
65,000	Walbro Corp.			1,470,625	1,470,625
		$114,275,062	$138,363,381	$ 15,750,338	$154,113,719
	Mining and Metals—5.6%				
316,350	Alcan Aluminum Ltd.	$ 2,907,695	$ 8,501,906		$ 8,501,906
341,600	Handy & Harman	999,942	5,380,200		5,380,200
260,000	INCO Ltd.	2,923,772	5,720,000		5,720,000
211,200	Inland Steel Industries, Inc.**	5,011,050	6,415,200		6,415,200
458,500	Magma Copper Co. (Class B)	2,089,981	3,209,500		3,209,500
191,250	Newmont Mining Corp.	0	6,741,563		6,741,563
461,250	Nucor Corp.	6,934,168	18,277,031		18,277,031
100,000	Placer Dome, Inc.	1,516,500	1,525,000		1,525,000
1,828,125	Western Mining Corp. Holdings Ltd. (A.D.R.)	1,069,453	8,226,563		8,226,563
1,719,500	Ashton Mining Ltd. (A.D.R.)			$ 1,857,060	1,857,060
41,726	Baukol-Noonan, Inc.			584,164	584,164
304,078	Lac Minerals Ltd.			3,078,790	3,078,790
20,000	Mascot Gold Mines Ltd.			203,750	203,750
121,750	Roanoke Electric Steel Corp.			2,008,875	2,008,875
		$ 23,452,561	$ 63,996,963	$ 7,732,639	$ 71,729,602

FIGURE 4-2 (page 5)

PIONEER FUND CONSOLIDATED
SCHEDULE OF INVESTMENTS
(CONTINUED)

Shares		PIONEER FUND (Excluding Scout) Cost (Notes 1 and 2)	Market Value*	PIONEER SCOUT Market Value*	CONSOLIDATED Market Value*
	Office Products—0.8%				
250,000	The Standard Register Co.	$ 4,093,125	$ 5,000,000		$ 5,000,000
42,400	American Building Maintenance Industries, Inc.			$ 826,800	826,800
189,100	Barry Wright Corp.			1,914,638	1,914,638
35,000	Bowne & Co., Inc.			371,875	371,875
77,100	Ennis Business Forms, Inc.			1,946,775	1,946,775
30,000	Mars Graphic Services, Inc.			86,250	86,250
		$ 4,093,125	$ 5,000,000	$ 5,146,338	$ 10,146,338
	Oil/Gas and Related Services—10.4%				
272,440	Atlantic Richfield Co.	$ 6,512,481	$ 18,866,470		$ 18,866,470
35,000	Chevron Corp.	1,315,575	1,386,875		1,386,875
520,200	Kerr-McGee Corp.	15,197,684	18,857,250		18,857,250
641,700	Mobil Corp.	20,232,811	25,106,513		25,106,513
346,900	Permian Basin Royalty Trust	2,454,737	2,081,400		2,081,400
553,900	Sabine Corp.	9,839,026	7,269,938		7,269,938
85,200	Sabine Royalty Trust	1,036,666	979,800		979,800
1,606,300	San Juan Basin Royalty Trust	8,983,405	12,850,400		12,850,400
313,700	Schlumberger Ltd.	13,160,134	9,058,088		9,058,088
591,600	Sonat, Inc.	17,196,409	13,532,850		13,532,850
367,526	Unocal Corp.	9,985,336	10,382,610		10,382,610
238,900	Conwest Exploration Co., Ltd. (Class B)			$ 1,926,131	1,926,131
96,600	Howell Corp.			809,025	809,025
124,600	McFarland Energy, Inc.**			965,650	965,650
54,300	North European Oil Royalty Trust			889,163	889,163
113,820	Plains Petroleum Co.			2,447,130	2,447,130
45,500	Texas Pacific Land Trust			1,126,125	1,126,125
242,100	The Wiser Oil Co.			3,389,400	3,389,400
		$105,914,264	$120,372,194	$ 11,552,624	$131,924,818
	Public Utilities—11.5%				
346,300	Allegheny Power System, Inc.	$ 15,923,617	$ 12,856,388		$ 12,856,388
1,026,000	American Telephone & Telegraph Co.	17,096,459	27,830,250		27,830,250
260,000	Bell Atlantic Corp.	18,319,455	16,900,000		16,900,000
65,000	BellSouth Corp.	2,494,675	2,364,375		2,364,375
236,200	Eastern Gas & Fuel Associates	3,973,878	5,373,550		5,373,550
697,050	GTE Corp.	13,037,520	24,745,275		24,745,275
278,000	Oklahoma Gas & Electric Co.	9,338,172	8,131,500		8,131,500
585,300	Public Service Co. of New Mexico	19,906,463	10,974,375		10,974,375
530,000	United Telecommunications, Inc.	15,472,050	13,051,250		13,051,250
7,000	Connecticut Energy Corp.			$ 143,500	143,500
30,000	E'Town Corp.			1,170,000	1,170,000
220,000	Iowa Southern Utilities Co.			5,940,000	5,940,000
188,000	Lincoln Telecommunications Co.			4,982,000	4,982,000
72,600	Northwest Natural Gas Co.			1,397,550	1,397,550
119,750	NUI Corp.			2,395,000	2,395,000
122,000	Public Service of North Carolina, Inc.			1,570,750	1,570,750
132,700	The Hydraulic Co.			3,433,613	3,433,613
65,600	TNP Enterprises, Inc.			1,213,600	1,213,600
50,000	Upper Peninsula Power Co.			1,325,000	1,325,000
		$115,562,289	$122,226,963	$ 23,571,013	$145,797,976

FIGURE 4-2 (page 6)

PIONEER FUND CONSOLIDATED
SCHEDULE OF INVESTMENTS
(CONTINUED)

Shares		PIONEER FUND (Excluding Scout) Cost (Notes 1 and 2)	PIONEER FUND (Excluding Scout) Market Value*	PIONEER SCOUT Market Value*	CONSOLIDATED Market Value*
	Retail—5.6%				
315,200	Dayton Hudson Corp.	$ 14,166,964	$ 8,825,600		$ 8,825,600
867,500	Payless Cashways, Inc.	20,117,784	9,867,813		9,867,813
307,400	J.C. Penney Company, Inc.	7,445,284	13,371,900		13,371,900
287,200	Rite Aid Corp.	8,666,251	10,339,200		10,339,200
690,500	Stop & Shop Companies, Inc.	13,854,317	14,673,125		14,673,125
177,200	Walgreen Co.	5,469,004	5,448,900		5,448,900
147,000	Delchamps, Inc.			$ 2,940,000	2,940,000
45,000	Paul Harris Stores, Inc.**			236,250	236,250
22,500	Paul Harris Stores, Inc. (Class B)**			118,125	118,125
561,000	Rose's Stores, Inc. (Class B)			5,329,500	5,329,500
		$ 69,719,604	$ 62,526,538	$ 8,623,875	$ 71,150,413
	Transportation—2.7%				
155,000	CSX Corp.	$ 1,252,666	$ 4,514,375		$ 4,514,375
208,300	Delta Air Lines, Inc.	8,656,656	7,733,138		7,733,138
100,000	Roadway Services, Inc.	3,675,000	3,200,000		3,200,000
139,820	Union Pacific Corp.	945,817	7,550,280		7,550,280
217,900	USAir Group, Inc.	6,137,289	7,354,125		7,354,125
156,600	Arkansas Best Corp.			$ 1,683,450	1,683,450
73,200	Carolina Freight Corp.			1,518,900	1,518,900
29,000	Midway Airlines, Inc.**			319,000	319,000
		$ 20,667,428	$ 30,351,918	$ 3,521,350	$ 33,873,268
	Miscellaneous—0.1%				
22,500	Arthur D. Little, Inc.			$ 765,000	$ 765,000
	TOTAL COMMON STOCKS	$773,312,483	$1,025,103,569	$178,672,766	$1,203,776,335
	TOTAL INVESTMENT IN SECURITIES	$801,690,804	$1,076,465,082	$180,680,266	$1,257,145,348

** Represents non-income producing securities.
 † Investment held by the Fund representing 5% or more of the outstanding voting stock of such company.
†† 49,900 shares of Pueblo International, Inc. on loan to broker at December 31, 1987 (See Note 7).

same management group). **Operating expenses** include management fees (typically ½ of 1 percent of the total assets of the fund), 12b-1 fees, and other expenses.

To facilitate comparison of mutual fund charges, the SEC requires an example of the costs based on an investment of $1,000 over one-year, five-year, and ten-year periods, assuming a 5 percent annual return and redemption at the end of each period. Obviously, by this comparison method, charges will vary from fund to fund. (*A word of cau-*

tion: An investor should not choose a fund solely because of a comparatively low fee. The reasons for a choice should rank as follows: first, because the fund meets the investor's objectives; second, because of the fund's past performance; and finally, because of the fee.)

As stated earlier, the maximum sales load is normally 8 percent, and by law it cannot be more than 9 percent. However, there are several ways to reduce the amount of this charge, as discussed below.

QUANTITY DISCOUNT SALES CHARGE

Under any one of several conditions, a **quantity discount sales charge** allows a person to invest a larger sum of money at less than the customary sales charge. These conditions are (1) reaching the required breakpoint, (2) qualifying for a combination privilege, (3) qualifying for an accumulation privilege, (4) qualifying for a family privilege, and (5) signing a statement of intention. Each of these conditions is explained below.

Reaching the Required Breakpoint

A **breakpoint** is the point at which an investor is granted a quantity discount sales charge because of the amount of money invested. The sum at which the breakpoint occurs varies from fund to fund. It is granted most frequently at the $10,000 level. Successive breakpoints in the sales charge are also granted as more and more money is invested. Table 4-1 demonstrates how Pioneer Fund, Inc.'s sales charges are reduced at different breakpoints.

Qualifying for a Combination Privilege

When one and the same company manages more than one fund, frequently it grants a **combination privilege**. This privilege allows a shareholder to combine investments in all of the funds managed by that company to determine whether she or he qualifies for a quantity discount sales charge.

For example, assume that Company X manages both Fund A and Fund B shares and offers reduced sales charges as given in Table 4-1. If an investor buys $5,000 of Fund A shares and $5,000 of Fund B shares, he or she would be granted a quantity discount sales charge at the $10,000 level of 7.75 percent on the total investment.

Qualifying for an Accumulation Privilege

A mutual fund grants an **accumulation privilege** when it allows the graduated sales charges to apply not only to the initial purchase in the amount stated, but also to any subsequent purchase by the same shareholder where the aggregate investment becomes large enough to qualify for the quantity discount sales charge.

For example, assume that a mutual fund offers the graduated sales charges listed in Table 4-1. If an investor makes an initial investment of $5,000, the sales charge on this amount would be 8.50 percent. If the same investor makes a subsequent investment of $6,000, where an accumulation privilege is granted, the sales charge on the $6,000 investment would be

---

TABLE 4-1 Pioneer Fund's Sales Charges

Amount of Purchase	Sales Charge as % of	
	Offering Price	Amount Invested
Less than $10,000	8.50	9.29
$10,000 but less than $25,000	7.75	8.40
$25,000 but less than $50,000	6.00	6.38
$50,000 but less than $100,000	4.50	4.71
$100,000 but less than $250,000	3.50	3.63
$250,000 but less than $400,000	2.50	2.56
$400,000 but less than $600,000	2.00	2.04
$600,000 or more	1.00	1.01

Source: Pioneer Fund, Inc., 60 State Street, Boston, MA 02109.

7.75 percent since the investor's aggregate investment is now more than $10,000. The accumulation privilege, however, is granted by only a few of the existing mutual funds.

Qualifying for the Family Privilege

When the **family privilege** is granted, it applies to the investor, the investor's spouse, and any child who is under 21 years of age. If the combined investments of all these members of the family are of a sufficient amount to qualify, a quantity discount sales charge will be granted.

Signing a Statement of Intention

A **statement of intention** is a form letter provided by the fund's underwriter stating that the shareholder intends to invest a sufficient sum over a 13-month period to qualify for the quantity discount sales charge. If the shareholder does not invest a sufficient sum within the stated period to qualify for the quantity discount, no penalty will be assessed. The statement of intention is not a binding obligation upon the investor to purchase, nor on the fund to sell, the full amount indicated therein. Nevertheless, the investor should read carefully the provisions of the statement of intention before signing it.

The necessary amount to be invested over the ensuing 13-month period indicated in a statement of intention varies from fund to fund. Some funds require only $10,000; others require $25,000 or $50,000.

For example, assume that a person makes an initial investment of $5,000 in a mutual fund and submits a signed statement of intention indicating that he or she intends to invest a total of $50,000 during the next 13 months. (The statement of intention may be submitted any time within 90 days of the date of the initial investment.) Also assume that the mutual fund offers the same graduated sales charges listed in Table 4-1. During the ensuing 13-month period, the shareholder invests $5,000, $20,000, and $25,000 at different dates to fulfill the total amount of $50,000 specified in the statement of intention. A 4.5 percent sales charge will be applied to all of the investments just as though a single application for a $50,000 investment had been signed. In other words, the adjusted sales charge on the investor's total investment of $50,000 will amount to only $2,250 (or $50,000 × .045). Should the amount actually purchased during the 13-month period be *more* or *less* than that indicated in the letter, an adjustment in the sales charge would be made.

MANAGEMENT FEE

All funds charge a management fee of approximately .5 percent a year of the fund's average daily net assets. The fee is reduced slightly when the fund's assets reach a certain level, usually at $250 million, with the exact amount varying from fund to fund.

INVESTING IN MUTUAL FUNDS

As stated earlier, a mutual fund is a corporation. Like the stock prices of other corporations, mutual fund prices are quoted in daily papers and *The Wall Street Journal*. When you invest in a mutual fund, you buy shares of that fund. And if the fund is successful, it pays dividends and a capital gains distribution.

QUOTATION OF MUTUAL FUND PRICES

The price per share of a mutual fund is computed every day. It is calculated by adding up the value of all the investments, including any accumulated dividends, and dividing this sum by the number of outstanding shares. The result is the net asset value (NAV) of a share that day. Figure 4-3 illustrates a quotation of mutual funds.

As you will note from Figure 4-3, there are two prices quoted on mutual funds: (1) the selling price and (2) the buying price. If only the selling price is shown in the daily quotation and the letters "NL" appear in the Buy column, this means that the fund is a no-load fund.

Selling Price

The selling price of a mutual fund share is the net asset value (NAV) of a share of the fund and is the lower of the two prices that are quoted every day. It is the price at which a shareholder would redeem her or his shares upon sending a written request to the custodian bank of the fund.

Buying Price

The buying price of a mutual fund share, also called the offering price, is the higher of the two prices quoted. It is the price at which an investor would buy the shares that day.

For example, take Putnam High Yield Fund in Figure 4-3. The selling price is

---

FIGURE 4-3 Mutual Funds Quotation

	Sell	Buy	Chg
AssetA	9.56	10.04	−.05
BlueC	12.65	13.28	−.09
Direct	19.23	21.02	−.20
Eqinc	8.25	9.02	−.04
GNMA	13.57	14.25	+.02
Global	23.01	25.15	+.13
Gold	13.91	13.02	−.19
Hi Yld	15.77	16.91	−.18
NY Tax	11.79	12.38	−.01
90-10	15.17	16.44	+.05
OTC Fd	16.50	17.32	−.10
Oppen	7.99	8.73	−.05
Prem	21.88	23.91	−.09
Rgcy	12.01	13.13	−.08
Specl	15.94	17.42	−.10
Target	14.97	15.72	−.08
Tx Fre	9.15	9.61	−.01
Time	14.60	15.96	−.10
TotR	6.28	6.59	−.04
USGvt	9.61	10.31	−.01
OTC Sec	15.75	16.40	−.05
Pacific Horizon:			
Agrsv	13.17	13.79	−.10
Calif	13.33	13.96	−.03
Hi Yld	14.89	15.59	
PIMIT LD	9.96	NL	−.01
PIMIT Tr	9.94	NL	−.01
Paine Webber:			
AstAll r	9.76	NL	−.02
Atlas	14.05	15.36	+.03
Amer	12.85	14.04	−.04
CalTx	10.66	11.13	−.01
GNMA	9.34	9.75	−.01
HiYld	8.99	9.39	+.01
HYMu	9.52	9.94	−.02
InvGd	9.62	10.05	−.01
MstEU	10.27	NL	−.10
MstGi r	11.15	NL	+.02
MstGt r	10.06	NL	−.09
Mstln r	9.00	NL	
Olymp	10.61	11.60	−.02
TaxEx	10.87	11.35	−.01
ParkAv	18.34	NL	−.03
Parnasus	20.30	21.04	−.09
PasadG	14.59	NL	−.06
PatrlCC	48.51	49.00	
PaxWld	12.14	NL	−.03
Penn Sq	8.72	NL	−.03
Penn Mu	6.31	NL	−.01
PermPrt	15.02	NL	−.04
Phila	5.33	5.83	−.04
Phoenix Series:			
Balan	12.03	13.15	−.05
CvFd	15.53	16.97	−.12
Grwth	15.18	16.59	−.12
HiQual	9.03	9.48	−.03
HiYld	8.89	9.33	
Stock	11.19	12.23	−.07
TotRet	12.58	13.21	−.06
Pilgrim Grp:			
CpCsh	10.00	NL	
FGvSc	9.37	9.66	
FHiln	8.71	8.98	
GNMA	14.20	14.91	+.01
HiYld	7.30	7.66	
Mag	8.66	9.09	−.06
PAR	19.14	19.43	−.06
Prefd	20.68	20.99	−.16
RisPrf	8.21	8.62	−.08

	Sell	Buy	Chg
Eqinc r	8.86	NL	−.06
FIAg r	9.34	NL	−.04
FICn r	9.34	NL	−.03
GNMA r	14.82	NL	−.02
Globl r	9.94	NL	−.02
GlbGn r	10.78	NL	−.02
GlbR r	9.10	NL	−.09
GvPl r	9.51	NL	−.01
GvPll r	8.97	NL	−.02
GvtSc	10.17	NL	−.02
GtOp r	10.73	NL	−.06
HiYld r	9.98	NL	−.01
InVer r	10.12	NL	−.07
MuAz r	10.68	NL	−.02
MuGa r	10.93	NL	−.01
MunHi r	10.06	NL	−.01
Muln r	10.13	NL	−.02
MuMd r	10.19	NL	−.01
MuMa r	10.50	NL	−.02
MuMn r	10.77	NL	
MuMi r	10.47	NL	−.01
MNC r	10.29	NL	−.01
MuNY r	10.54	NL	−.01
MuOr r	10.69	NL	
MuOh r	10.45	NL	−.02
MuPa r	9.39	NL	−.01
NtMu r	14.71	NL	−.02
OptG r	7.82	NL	−.05
Rsch r	12.33	NL	−.09
Util r	12.99	NL	−.10
Putnam Funds:			
CCArp	41.60	42.67	+.01
CCDsp	41.40	42.46	−.05
CalTx	14.90	15.64	−.05
Capit	5.45	NL	−.04
CaPrs	11.81	12.40	
Conv	14.37	15.70	−.04
EngRs	13.61	14.87	−.11
GNMA	9.98	10.48	−.01
Georg	12.18	13.31	−.07
Globl	16.19	17.00	+.03
GroInc	10.57	11.55	−.05
Health	18.04	19.72	−.18
Hilnco	10.54	11.30	−.01
Hi Yld	14.59	15.65	−.01
HiYdll	11.20	12.01	
Incom	6.78	7.27	−.01
InfoSc	15.53	16.97	−.13
Int Eq	25.51	27.88	−.06
Invest	6.71	7.33	−.05
MaTx r	11.69	NL	−.03
MiTx r	11.68	NL	−.02
MnTx r	11.54	NL	−.02
OhTx r	11.60	NL	−.04
NYTx	16.19	17.00	−.04
OTC E	25.45	27.29	−.21
Optn	8.50	9.29	−.06
Optnll	9.21	10.07	−.06
Tax Ex	24.23	25.44	−.09
TFHY r	13.53	NL	−.02
TFIns r	13.68	NL	−.05
USGtd	13.93	14.62	−.01
Vovag	19.30	21.09	−.17
QuestF	25.05	NL	−.08
RNC Group:			
CvSec	9.13	9.59	−.04
Regcv	11.69	12.27	−.05
Wstwnd	9.25	9.71	+.03

	Sell	Buy	Chg
Devel	20.88	NL	−.17
Eqtvln	10.54	NL	−.06
Gen90	10.32	NL	−.01
Globl	14.05	NL	−.04
GNMA	14.46	NL	−.02
Grwln	12.75	NL	−.08
Incom	12.48	NL	−.02
Intl Fd	34.20	NL	−.01
MMB	8.31	NL	−.01
NYTax	10.38	NL	−.01
TxFHi	10.60	NL	−.02
TxFr90	10.16	NL	
TxFr93	10.63	NL	−.01
TxFr96	10.74	NL	−.02
Seagint	10.12	NL	−.01
Security Funds:			
Action	8.45		−.05
Bond	7.64	8.02	−.02
Equity	4.36	4.77	−.03
Invest	8.36	9.14	−.01
OmniFd	2.38	2.60	−.04
Ultra	6.02	6.58	−.06
Selected Funds:			
Am Shs	12.14	NL	−.09
Spl Shs	18.33	NL	−.17
Seligman Group:			
CapFd	10.97	11.52	−.08
ColoTx	6.70	7.03	−.01
CmStk	11.38	11.95	−.09
Comun	10.36	10.88	−.09
FLTax	6.47	6.79	−.01
Growth	4.26	4.47	−.03
Inco	12.18	12.79	−.04
LaTx	7.61	7.99	−.02
MassTx	7.51	7.88	−.01
MdTx	7.23	7.59	
MichTx	7.74	8.13	
MinnTx	7.34	7.71	−.01
MO Tx	6.96	7.31	
NatlTx	7.33	7.70	−.01
NJ TE	6.77	7.11	−.02
NY Tax	7.40	7.77	−.01
OhioTx	7.55	7.93	−.01
OrTE	6.64	6.97	−.01
PaTxQ	7.14	7.50	−.01
CaTax	6.13	6.42	−.02
CaTxQ	6.20	6.49	−.01
GovGtd	7.22	7.58	−.01
HYdBd	7.24	7.60	
MtgSec	6.81	7.15	
Sentinel Group:			
Balan	11.83	12.93	−.05
Bond	9.42	10.30	
Com S	21.73	23.75	−.19
GvSecs	9.42	10.30	−.02
Grwth	11.31	12.36	−.10
Sequoia	37.72	NL	−.18
Sentry	10.94	11.89	−.07
Shearson Funds:			
ATIG r	46.12	NL	−.29
ATIln r	91.73	NL	−.55
AgrGr	13.91	14.64	−.14
Appre	26.88	28.29	−.18
CaiMu	14.97	15.76	−.03
FdVal	5.61	5.91	−.02
Global	24.02	25.28	−.03
HiYld	18.00	18.95	−.01
LehCa	17.19	18.09	−.17
Lehln	15.21	16.01	−.09

	Sell	Buy	Chg
TaxEx	9.95	10.42	−.03
US Gov	4.77	5.02	−.06
St FarmFds:			
Balan	18.37	NL	−.04
Gwth	12.87	NL	−.13
Muni	7.70	NL	−.01
StStreet Resh:			
Exch	124.70	NL	−1.15
Grwth r	73.22	NL	−.58
Inv	73.96	74.33	−.48
Steadman Funds:			
Am Ind	2.15	NL	−.01
Assoc	.61	NL	−.01
Invest	1.33	NL	−.01
Ocean	3.62	NL	−.03
Stein Roe Fds:			
Cap Op	22.97	NL	+.81
Discv	9.09	NL	−.08
GvtPlu	9.58	NL	−.02
HYMu	11.22	NL	−.01
HYBds	9.51	NL	−.02
IntMu	10.43	NL	−.01
MgdBd	8.49	NL	−.02
MgdM	8.54	NL	−.02
PrimE	8.40	NL	−.03
Specl	14.12	NL	−.12
Stock	14.61	NL	−.08
TotRet	22.48	NL	−.12
Univ	13.24	NL	−.12
StkMkt	17.84	18.68	−.12
Strategic Funds:			
Capit	5.78	6.32	−.03
Invst	3.95	4.32	−.06
Silvr	4.26	4.77	−.03
StratmDv	24.76	NL	−.11
Strat Gth	19.43	NL	−.19
Strong Funds:			
GovSc	10.01	NL	
Inco	11.95	NL	−.01
Invst	17.86	18.04	−.01
Oppty	17.11	17.46	−.01
ST Bd	10.19	NL	−.03
TFInc	9.22	NL	−.01
Total	19.27	19.46	−.04
Templeton Group:			
Frgn	19.04	20.81	−.11
Glob I	38.95		−.25
Glob II	12.05	13.17	−.03
Grwth	12.81	14.00	−.09
Inco	10.31	11.27	−.01
World	13.76	15.04	−.09
Thomson McKinn:			
Global r	10.14	NL	−.03
Gwth r	13.20	NL	−.11
Inco r	9.72	NL	
Opor r	11.56	NL	−.07
TaxEx r	10.59	NL	−.02
USGv r	9.49	NL	−.01
Trnsatln	11.73	NL	−.01
TrnstGr	14.16	NL	
TreasFt	9.88	NL	
TrustFunds:			
Bdldx	9.49	NL	−.01
ShtGov	9.73	NL	−.01
IntGvt	9.59	NL	−.01
Eqldx	9.49	NL	−.07
Value	8.90	NL	−.07
20th Century:			
Gift r	7.08	7.11	−.06

	Sell	Buy	Chg
Prspc r	.71	NL	
RIEst	8.98	NL	−.03
US TF	10.64	NL	−.03
UST Int	8.67	NL	
ValFrg r	9.94	NL	
Value Line Fd:			
Aggrln	8.19	NL	+.01
Conv	10.20	NL	+.01
Fund	13.03	NL	+.12
Incom	5.70	NL	+.01
Lev Gt	18.67	NL	−.11
MunBd	10.11	NL	
Spl Sit	12.02	NL	−.09
US Gvt	11.86	NL	−.01
Van Eck:			
GoldR	5.19	5.51	−.04
Intlnv	13.47	14.72	+.18
WdInc	10.04	10.85	+.02
WldTr	13.78	14.90	+.02
VanKampen Mer:			
CalTF	14.89	15.66	+.07
Gwth	14.56	15.31	+.09
HiYls	13.62	14.32	+.07
InTxF	16.89	17.76	
TxFrH	16.05	16.88	
US Gvt	15.03	15.60	+.01
Vance Exchange:			
CapE	95.58	NL	+.58
DBst	54.11	NL	+.37
Diver	101.91	NL	+.73
ExFd	142.63	NL	+.58
ExBo	127.72	NL	+.65
FidEst	80.16	NL	+.66
SeFid	79.55	NL	+.47
Vanguard Group:			
BdMkt	9.21	NL	−.02
Convrt	8.74	NL	−.02
Explr	28.28	NL	−.02
Explll	19.42	NL	−.02
Morg	10.57	NL	+.06
NaesT	34.94	NL	+.15
Prmcp	44.94	NL	+.17
VHYS	12.94	NL	−.05
V Pref	7.91	NL	−.03
V ARP	20.88	NL	
Quant	10.27	NL	−.07
STAR	10.46	NL	−.04
TC Int	30.86	NL	−.02
TCUsa	25.59	NL	−.01
GNMA	9.44	NL	
HiYbd	8.54	NL	
IGBnd	7.85	NL	−.03
ShrtTr	10.37	NL	
STGovt	9.98	NL	
US Tr	9.10	NL	−.02
IdxExt	11.28	NL	−.08
Indx 500	25.41	NL	−.17
MuHY	9.56	NL	−.02
Muint	11.67	NL	−.04
MunLd	10.17	NL	−.01
MuLg	9.94	NL	−.02
MInLg	11.04	NL	−.02
MuSht	15.30	NL	
Cal Ins	9.48	NL	−.01
NYIns	9.02	NL	−.02
Pennln	9.51	NL	−.03
VSPE r	11.50	NL	−.07
VSPG r	10.10	NL	−.01
VSPH r	17.27	NL	−.12

$14.59 and the buying price is $15.65. At these prices a buyer would pay $1,565 for 100 shares (or 100 × $15.65). If six months later the two prices had not changed and the buyer decided to sell the 100 shares, that person would receive $1,459 (or $14.59 × 100). The difference of $1.06 per share is the sales charge, which is approximately 7¾ percent.[3]

OPENING A MUTUAL FUND ACCOUNT

There are several ways to establish a mutual fund account: (1) by a lump-sum account, (2) by an accumulation account, and (3) by dollar cost averaging.

Lump-Sum Account

A **lump-sum account** is a single investment. Although any lump sum may be utilized, the account will hardly be worthwhile unless at least several hundred dollars are invested. That is, the single investment must be a sufficient sum of money so that the expected dividends and capital gains distribution would be sufficient to warrant opening the account in the first place.

If a large sum of money is contemplated, such as $20,000, $30,000, or more, the investor should *not* invest near the top of a bull market. If the investor does, he or she may have to wait many years before the value of the investment is recovered. In the meantime, in the subsequent bear market, the shareholder can become considerably upset about losses in the value of the investment. Although these losses will be only paper losses if the shareholder doesn't sell the shares, such a situation can be annoying, to say the least. Therefore, the lump-sum mutual fund buyer should, like the individual stock buyer, try to buy at low prices.

Accumulation Account

An **accumulation account** is a small account initially, with the investor having every intention of adding to it at later dates. One who opens an accumulation account is most likely gainfully employed and is trying to build an account for future delivery. Since the initial amount is small, it makes no difference whether the account is opened at a high or low point of the stock market.

An accumulation account takes two forms: (1) the voluntary plan and (2) the contractual plan.

Voluntary Plan. Also called a **level charge account** or an **open account**, the **voluntary plan** allows an investor to make subsequent purchases whenever she or he desires to do so. This type of account is simplicity itself. The investor decides how much money to invest initially and then pays the appropriate sales charge. Thereafter, the shareholder adds to the account on a voluntary basis and, of course, pays the sales charge appropriate to each additional investment.

Many funds accept subsequent additions to the account as low as $10, while others require a minimum of $25. Under the voluntary plan, the shareholder agrees to add regularly to the account but signs no contract to do so.

Contractual Plan. The **contractual plan** is also called the **penalty**, **front-end load**, or **prepaid charge method** of acquiring mutual fund shares. This plan requires the investor to sign a contract to invest a fixed number of dollars each month for a stated number of years and charges a front-end load. The duration of the contract is usually ten or 15 years, and the front-end load is generally a 50 percent charge. A 50 percent front-end load means that the shareholder agrees that 50 percent of the first-year payments may be deducted and applied against the cost of completing the entire contract.

For example, if the contract calls for investing $100 per month, which is $1,200 per year, 50 percent of $1,200—or $600—will be deducted for the sales charge that year. Assuming that the price per share is the same at the end of the year as it was at the beginning of the year, the shareholder will have a value of just $600. If the account is then cashed out, the shareholder will have lost half of the $1,200 that was invested.

Considerable controversy has taken place in recent years about the advisability of using the contractual plan for investing in mutual fund shares. Those who argue against this plan maintain that too high a percentage of contractual plan holders cancel their plans at a loss, or continue only until they reach the break-even point. On the other hand, those who favor contractual plans maintain that most people need a contract with a penalty for early withdrawal attached to it because otherwise they would not save money at all. They contend that this has been proven to be true of all forms of cash value life insurance policies and face-amount certificate companies.

In favor of the contractual plan, too, is the undisputed fact that if the shareholder completes the contract, the shareholder pays the identical sales charge on the entire amount of money invested that he or she would in a voluntary plan.

For example, a contractual plan that calls for the eventual investment of $15,000 over the entire period of the contract requires no more of a sales charge than if the $15,000 were invested on a voluntary basis. Also, many mutual fund companies suggest that the investor take out a reducing term insurance policy that guarantees completion of the contract. This way, if the investor should die before completing the contract, the insurance company will make good on the remaining unpaid payments or will pay the commuted value of the policy to the beneficiary.

Because of this controversy, the Investment Company Act of 1940 was amended in 1970 with respect to contractual plans. Two amendments were made, which are explained below.

Under the first amendment, a contractual plan may be set up charging the 50 percent front-end load during the first year, provided that the investor is permitted to cancel the plan within 18 months and demand a partial refund. The shareholder who cancels would be paid the value of the account plus that part of the sales load that exceeds 15 percent of the total investment paid.

Under this amendment, a shareholder is given the right to cancel the contract within the first 45 days and pay no sales charge at all. Of course, the shareholder would get back only the current value of the redeemed account, and this could be *more* or *less* than the amount that was invested.

Under the second amendment, a contractual plan may be set up without allowing the 18-month partial refund, provided that the fund charges no more than 20 percent the first year and no more than a total of 64 percent over the first four years. In this case, the shareholder will *not* receive a refund of any sales charge because of an early redemption. The shareholder will simply receive the value of the account. As with the 50 percent front-end load amendment, the shareholder of the 20 percent front-end load plan may cancel within the first 45 days and not pay any sales charge.

Dollar Cost Averaging

Every investor, whether buying shares of mutual funds or common stock, would like to buy fewer shares when the price is high and more shares when the price is low. A way to do this is to use **dollar cost averaging**. By this method, a person invests the same number of dollars every month or every quarter and continues to invest regularly regardless of fluctuations in price.

Dollar cost averaging is utilized by shareholders who invest regularly in either voluntary or contractual plans of mutual funds and by investors who buy individual securities. To see how dollar cost averaging works, take the example of an investor who is investing $100 a month in mutual fund shares. For the sake of simplicity, only two $100 investments are illustrated below, deliberately using a price fluctuation that is greater than normal in order to better demonstrate a point.

Dollar Amount of Investment	Price per Share	Number of Shares
$100	$20	5
100	10	10
$200		15

This investor purchased five shares when the price was high and ten shares when the price was low. To find the average cost of all the 15 shares purchased, divide the total investment of $200 by 15 and obtain an answer of $13.33.

Note from the above example that dollar cost averaging means regularly investing the *same number of dollars,* not buying the same number of shares. The law requires that this method of investing be called just that—dollar cost averaging. It should never be called by such terms as "dollar averaging" or "averaging the dollar."

Figure 4-4 will give you an idea of the excellent summary results that can be obtained from an investment plan that employs the principle of dollar cost averaging. It shows performance figures of an investment program involving $100 a month, with income dividends and capital gains distributions accepted in additional shares, in Pioneer Fund, Inc., a growth and income fund. These performance figures presuppose two conditions:

1. That the shareholder was financially able to invest a set number of dollars regularly over a long period of time.
2. That the investor had the intestinal fortitude to continue to invest regularly during bear markets—a difficult thing to do even for the optimistic.

According to Figure 4-4, a total investment of $24,000 made in monthly installments was worth $91,239 at the end of 20 years. At the end of 30 years, a total investment of $36,000 was worth $287,731. These performance figures should be sufficiently impressive to satisfy the most skeptical investor as to the effectiveness of a long-term investment program in a mutual fund by employing the dollar cost averaging method.

HOW FUNDS PAY OUT DIVIDENDS AND CAPITAL GAINS DISTRIBUTIONS

Many mutual funds pay a dividend four times a year, and at the end of their fiscal year they also pay a capital gains distribution. The gain realized by the fund is derived from buying and selling the securities in its portfolio at a net profit during the course of the year. Note that the realized gain is normally a net profit. A **net profit** occurs when the profits at the end of the fund's fiscal year exceed the losses from security transactions.

Mutual Fund Application

On a **mutual fund application**, provided by all funds, the shareholder indicates how she or he elects to receive the income dividends and/or capital gains distributions that may be paid by the fund. Figure 4-5 shows a typical mutual fund application form. (A contractual plan, however, requires a different application form.) The application form sets forth the four methods by which a shareholder may choose to treat income dividends and capital gains distributions. These are:

1. By reinvestment of dividends and capital gains distributions in additional shares of the fund.
2. By payment of dividends in cash and reinvestment of capital gains distributions in additional shares of the fund.
3. By payment of dividends and capital gains distributions in cash.
4. By the use of a systematic withdrawal plan.

The first three methods listed above are self-explanatory. The fourth method—the systematic withdrawal plan—is discussed in more detail below.

Systematic Withdrawal Plan

Under the **systematic withdrawal plan**—also known as the **systematic payout plan**—a shareholder deliberately spends a part of his or her capital in a mutual fund account by redeeming some shares every year. The usual amount paid by the fund is 6 percent of the total money invested by the shareholder. Sometimes an 8 percent or a 10 percent systematic payout plan is used.

FIGURE 4-4 When Accumulating Dollars . . . Years Make a Difference

Summary Results of assumed investment programs
of $100 per month with income dividends and capital
gain distributions accepted in additional shares.

No. of Years	Period	Total Amount Invested	Income Dividends Reinvested	Total Cost	Value of Shares Acquired				
					Through Investments	Capital Gain	Subtotal	Through Dividends	Total
60	1928-87*	$71,800	$6,044,412	$6,116,212	$575,976	$12,380,321	$12,956,297	$7,696,306	**$20,652,603**
59	1929-87	70,800	5,673,953	5,744,753	556,011	11,622,679	12,178,690	7,212,251	**19,390,941**
58	1930-87	69,600	5,310,247	5,379,847	535,935	10,878,782	11,414,717	6,737,456	**18,152,173**
57	1931-87	68,400	4,937,275	5,005,675	514,344	10,115,830	10,630,174	6,251,498	**16,881,672**
56	1932-87	67,200	4,366,533	4,433,733	478,855	8,948,154	9,427,009	5,510,199	**14,937,208**
55	1933-87	66,000	3,631,351	3,697,351	428,639	7,443,838	7,872,477	4,559,666	**12,432,143**
54	1934-87	64,800	3,087,480	3,152,280	388,419	6,330,812	6,719,231	3,859,442	**10,578,672**
53	1935-87	63,600	2,639,015	2,702,615	352,810	5,412,878	5,765,688	3,284,374	**9,050,063**
52	1936-87	62,400	2,285,141	2,347,541	322,768	4,688,410	5,011,178	2,832,448	**7,843,626**
51	1937-87	61,200	2,030,906	2,092,106	299,922	4,167,800	4,467,723	2,508,933	**6,976,655**
50	1938-87	60,000	1,844,913	1,904,913	282,520	3,786,847	4,069,368	2,272,878	**6,342,246**
49	1939-87	58,800	1,518,940	1,577,740	250,012	3,119,046	3,369,058	1,861,096	**5,230,154**
48	1940-87	57,600	1,254,396	1,311,996	221,889	2,576,957	2,798,846	1,528,531	**4,327,377**
47	1941-87	56,400	1,027,505	1,083,905	196,189	2,111,883	2,308,072	1,244,732	**3,552,803**
46	1942-87	55,200	805,237	860,437	169,665	1,656,173	1,825,838	968,011	**2,793,849**
45	1943-87	54,000	623,594	677,594	146,038	1,283,569	1,429,607	743,649	**2,173,256**
44	1944-87	52,800	509,830	562,630	130,799	1,050,152	1,180,951	603,496	**1,784,447**
43	1945-87	51,600	429,353	480,953	119,444	884,944	1,004,388	504,853	**1,509,240**
42	1946-87	50,400	372,026	422,426	110,862	767,147	878,009	434,997	**1,313,006**
41	1947-87	49,200	331,302	380,502	104,460	683,418	787,878	385,589	**1,173,467**
40	1948-87	48,000	292,494	340,494	98,042	603,535	701,578	338,726	**1,040,304**
39	1949-87	46,800	255,710	302,510	91,562	527,828	619,390	294,524	**913,914**
38	1950-87	45,600	218,977	264,577	84,619	452,204	536,823	250,661	**787,484**
37	1951-87	44,400	188,705	233,105	78,512	389,852	468,364	214,751	**683,114**
36	1952-87	43,200	164,870	208,070	73,391	340,739	414,131	186,631	**600,762**
35	1953-87	42,000	143,555	185,555	68,582	296,808	365,390	161,608	**526,998**
34	1954-87	40,800	124,229	165,029	63,958	256,944	320,901	139,055	**459,956**
33	1955-87	39,600	107,843	147,443	59,768	223,110	282,878	120,054	**402,932**
32	1956-87	38,400	95,538	133,938	56,464	197,670	254,134	105,855	**359,989**
31	1957-87	37,200	84,834	122,034	53,430	175,548	228,978	93,552	**322,530**
30	1958-87	36,000	74,896	110,896	50,460	154,986	205,446	82,185	**287,631**
29	1959-87	34,800	65,378	100,178	47,427	135,290	182,718	71,355	**254,072**
28	1960-87	33,600	58,203	91,803	44,995	120,432	165,427	63,230	**228,657**
27	1961-87	32,400	51,244	83,644	42,476	106,005	148,482	55,383	**203,865**
26	1962-87	31,200	45,536	76,736	40,315	94,169	134,484	48,970	**183,455**
25	1963-87	30,000	39,870	69,870	38,013	82,454	120,467	42,629	**163,096**
24	1964-87	28,800	34,817	63,617	35,781	72,030	107,811	37,002	**144,813**
23	1965-87	27,600	30,329	57,929	33,650	62,777	96,427	32,032	**128,458**
22	1966-87	26,400	26,502	52,902	31,669	54,903	86,572	27,816	**114,387**
21	1967-87	25,200	23,109	48,309	29,770	47,944	77,713	24,092	**101,805**
20	1968-87	24,000	20,279	44,279	28,055	42,183	70,238	21,001	**91,239**
19	1969-87	22,800	18,055	40,855	26,592	37,666	64,258	18,580	**82,838**
18	1970-87	21,600	16,017	37,617	25,102	33,553	58,655	16,365	**75,021**
17	1971-87	20,400	13,644	34,044	23,136	28,851	51,987	13,805	**65,792**
16	1972-87	19,200	11,660	30,860	21,352	24,900	46,252	11,685	**57,936**
15	1973-87	18,000	9,952	27,952	19,687	21,501	41,188	9,875	**51,063**
14	1974-87	16,800	8,327	25,127	17,940	18,282	36,222	8,167	**44,389**
13	1975-87	15,600	6,603	22,203	15,842	14,881	30,723	6,386	**37,109**
12	1976-87	14,400	5,122	19,522	13,894	11,919	25,812	4,889	**30,701**
11	1977-87	13,200	4,034	17,234	12,327	9,697	22,024	3,808	**25,832**
10	1978-87	12,000	3,106	15,106	10,849	7,772	18,621	2,899	**21,520**
9	1979-87	10,800	2,302	13,102	9,402	6,072	15,474	2,126	**17,600**
8	1980-87	9,600	1,666	11,266	8,112	4,690	12,803	1,527	**14,330**
7	1981-87	8,400	1,194	9,594	7,004	3,620	10,624	1,086	**11,710**
6	1982-87	7,200	833	8,033	5,983	2,737	8,719	750	**9,470**
5	1983-87	6,000	497	6,497	4,749	1,859	6,609	444	**7,052**
4	1984-87	4,800	298	5,098	3,785	1,280	5,065	266	**5,331**
3	1985-87	3,600	147	3,747	2,754	758	3,511	131	**3,642**
2	1986-87	2,400	56	2,456	1,775	352	2,127	51	**2,178**
1	1987-87	1,200	14	1,214	900	80	980	14	**994**

*Beginning March 1, 1928.

Summary results should be reviewed in conjunction with the table on page 24

The total cost figures represent the cumulative total of monthly investment of $100 per month plus the cumulative amount of income dividends reinvested and capital gain distributions accepted in additional shares. A sales commission as described in the prospectus was included in the price of shares purchased through investment. Income dividends were invested at the net asset value.

No adjustment has been made for any income taxes payable by shareholders on capital gain distributions and dividends reinvested in shares

Source: Pioneer Fund, Inc., 60 State Street, Boston, MA 02109.

FIGURE 4-5 (page 1) Mutual Fund Application Form

THE PIONEER GROUP OF FUNDS

In accordance with the Account Provisions set forth on the reverse side of this application and the terms of the current Prospectus which I acknowledge receiving, Pioneering Services Corporation is authorized to act as my Agent for the investment dealer named below in the purchase of shares to establish an account in accordance with the instructions on this application. APPLICATIONS WHICH ARE NOT COMPLETED MAY BE REJECTED.

PSC USE ONLY

1 Choice of Funds

- ☐ Pioneer Fund
- ☐ Pioneer Three
- ☐ Pioneer II
- ☐ Pioneer Bond Fund
- ☐ Pioneer Municipal Bond Fund

2 Initial Investment

- ☐ Initial investment of $ _____ enclosed on _____ date
- ☐ Initial investment of $ _____ ordered by dealer on _____ date

A $1,000 initial investment is required for PIONEER THREE, PIONEER BOND FUND, and PIONEER MUNICIPAL BOND FUND. Shareholders may NOT purchase shares of PIONEER THREE if thereafter they would own shares with a net asset value in excess of $100,000. A $50 initial investment is required for PIONEER FUND and PIONEER II.

3 Distribution Option

Dividends and Capital Gain Distributions will be reinvested in shares unless an option is checked below.
- ☐ Reinvest my Dividends and Capital Gain Distributions in shares
- ☐ Pay my Dividends in cash and reinvest my Capital Gain Distributions in shares.
- ☐ Pay my Dividends and Capital Gain Distributions in cash

4 Account Registration

NAME(S) SHOULD APPEAR EXACTLY AS THE ACCOUNT IS TO BE REGISTERED.
The account of two or more co-owners will be registered as "joint tenants with right of survivorship" unless another form of ownership is specfied. If Trust, provide Trustee and Date of Trust.

- ☐ Individual
- ☐ Joint Tenant
- ☐ Custodian
- ☐ Other

5 Account Mailing Address

Street

City   State   Zip

6 Taxpayer Identification

My social security or taxpayer identification number is └─┴─┴─┴─┴─┴─┴─┴─┘ (If no number, write "Applied for" on this line _____)
I understand that if I do not provide a taxpayer identification number within 60 days, the Funds are required to withhold 20% of all reportable payments until I provide a number. For custodial accounts under the Uniform Gift to Minors Act, please give the minor's account number.

Check one:
- ☐ I am a citizen of the U.S. **OR** ☐ I am a citizen of the following country _____

If you are exempt from backup withholding on interest and dividend payments because you are an entity described in paragraph 9 of the Account Provisions. enter "exempt" in the following space _____ and cross out item (2) of the following certification.
CERTIFICATION — Under penalties of perjury, I (we) certify that the information provided in this section is true, correct, and complete and that
(1) The number shown on this form is my correct Social Security or Taxpayer Identification Number (or I am waiting for a number to be issued to me), and
(2) I am not subject to backup withholding either because I have not been notified by the Internal Revenue Service ("IRS") that I am subject to backup withholding as a result of a failure to report all interest or dividends, or the IRS has notified me that I am no longer subject to backup withholding.
Certification Instructions — You must cross out item (2) above if you have been notified by the IRS that you are subject to backup withholding because of underreporting interest or dividends on your tax return. However, if after being notified by the IRS that you were subject to backup withholding, you received another notification from the IRS that you are not longer subject to backup withholding, do not cross out item (2).

X

Account Signature(s) ▶ **X**

Signature of Shareholder   Date

Signature of Co-Owner. if any   Date

7 Reduced Sales Charge

For Right of Accumulation and/or Letter of Intention purposes. my account being established qualifies for a reduced sales charge. If claiming the reduced sales charge (See "Sales Charge" Section in the Prospectus) I have listed my accounts in the Pioneer Group of Funds below:
- ☐ My account qualifies for a reduced sales charge under Right of Accumulation.
- ☐ My account qualifies for a reduced sales charge under $ _____ Letter of Intention.

Account Name

Account Number

Account Name

Account Number

Account Name

Account Number   If additional space is needed. attach schedule showing Account Name(s) and Number(s)

COMPLETE *ONLY* FOR SYSTEMATIC WITHDRAWAL PLAN

8 Systematic Withdrawal Plan

Minimum Account Value: $5,000 in shares at the current public offering price
You are authorized to redeem in accordance with the terms of the Prospectus, sufficient shares to realize the amount indicated below at the net asset value in effect on the date of redemption.
You are directed to make Systematic Withdrawal Payments in the amount of $ _____
Monthly Commencing _____ Month   Quarterly Commencing _____ Month
NOTE — PROVIDE THE FOLLOWING INFORMATION ONLY IF NAME OF PAYEE IS DIFFERENT FROM ACCOUNT REGISTRATION.

Payable to

Payee's Name or Bank

Bank Account Number

Street

City   State   Zip

FOR COMPLETION BY YOUR INVESTMENT DEALER

9 Investment Dealer

I hereby authorize and direct you to act as my Agent in connection with transactions under the Account of the above Purchaser in accordance with the Dealer Agreement on the reverse side of this Application.

Authorized Signature ▶ **X**

Firm Name   Address

Authorized Signature of Dealer   City   State   Zip

PSC USE ONLY

Representative Number   Representative Last Name   First Name   Middle Initial

Mail Completed Application to: Pioneering Services Corporation, P.O. Box 9014, Boston, MA 02205-9014

FIGURE 4-5 (page 2)

PIONEER FUND
PIONEER SCOUT
60 State Street
Boston, Massachusetts 02109

TABLE OF CONTENTS

INVESTING ACCOUNT APPLICATION

ACCOUNT PROVISIONS

1. A PIONEER INVESTING ACCOUNT MAY BE OPENED by completing this application and forwarding it through an authorized investment dealer to Pioneering Services Corporation, referred to below as the Transfer Agent. The Application becomes effective only upon its acceptance by the Transfer Agent in Massachusetts and is to be construed under the laws of Massachusetts. Acceptance of this Application by the Transfer Agent does not create an option, warrant or right to purchase shares of the Fund and no penalty is incurred by any party if the intention declared is not fulfilled.

2. PURCHASE OF SHARES will be made by the Transfer Agent at the closing public offering price on the day an investment is received, or, if the New York Stock Exchange is closed on that day, on the next day on which said Exchange is open. Fractional shares carried to the third decimal will be utilized for this purpose.

3. CERTIFICATES will not be issued unless requested, but shares included under these Accounts will be placed to the credit of the Investor on the stock record books of the Fund and shall entitle him to full shareholder rights. At written request of the Investor, certificates will be issued for all or part of the full shares owned without in any way affecting the continued operation of the Investor's Pioneer Investing Account except that no certificate will be issued to a shareholder of Pioneer Fund or Pioneer II whose account has a net asset value of less than $500.

4. SYSTEMATIC WITHDRAWAL PLAN PAYMENTS shall be made from the proceeds of redeemed shares of the Fund. The Transfer Agent, as Agent for the Investor, will redeem as many shares as shall be necessary to obtain the funds needed for the scheduled payment. Such redemption of shares shall be made at the net asset value in effect at the close of business on the 19th day (or, if that day is not a business day, then the preceding business day) of each month.

Periodic checks of $25 or more will be sent to the Investor or any person designated by the Investor in the application either monthly or quarterly on or before the fifth business day following such redemption.

Investors should be cautioned that purchases of shares of the Fund at a time when the Investor has a Systematic Withdrawal Plan in effect would result in the payment of unnecessary commissions by the Investor and would appear to be disadvantageous to him.

5. SHARES MAY BE REDEEMED at any time upon written request of the Investor OR (except for Pioneer Bond Fund, Pioneer Three, and Pioneer Municipal Bond Fund) upon six months' notice to a shareholder whose account has a net asset value of less than $500 (or such lesser amount as the Board of Trustees of the Fund may determine) and whose account reflects, at the time of such notice, no purchases of shares of the Fund, other than reinvestments of dividends and capital gains during the previous six months, provided such shareholder does not increase his record ownership to the minimum level within six months after the notice is mailed. Shares in an account with an aggregate net asset value of less than $1,000, in the case of Pioneer Bond Fund and Pioneer Municipal Bond Fund, and $500, in the case of Pioneer Three (or such lesser amounts as the Board of Trustees of such Funds may determine), may be redeemed by such Funds if a shareholder does not increase the net asset value of such shares in the account to at least $1,000 (in the case of Pioneer Bond Fund and Pioneer Municipal Bond Fund) or $500 (in the case of Pioneer Three) within six months notice by Pioneer Bond Fund or Pioneer Municipal Bond Fund or two months notice by Pioneer Three to such shareholder of such Fund's intention to redeem such shareholder's shares.

6. A DISTRIBUTION OPTION MAY BE CHANGED at any time with written notice from an investor to the Transfer Agent. Upon receipt by the Transfer Agent of appropriate evidence of the investor(s) death(s), the Distribution Option will automatically be changed so that dividends are paid in cash and capital gain distributions are reinvested in additional shares of the Fund.

7. A PIONEER INVESTING ACCOUNT WILL BE CLOSED when all shares in the Account are redeemed or transferred. A Systematic Withdrawal Plan may

be terminated under the terms as described in the Prospectus. Upon closing of a Pioneer Investing Account or termination of a Withdrawal Plan, unless otherwise requested, fractional shares will automatically be redeemed at the net asset value effective at the time of such closing or termination, and certificates representing full shares will be delivered to the Investor or his duly appointed legal representative, together with any cash balance then held.

8. The Transfer Agent will act as Agent for the Dealer in purchasing shares from the Principal Underwriter, as Agent for the Principal Underwriter in purchasing shares from the Fund and as Agent for the Fund or PGI in repurchasing shares in certain accounts. In acting as Agent for the Dealer, the Transfer Agent shall incur no liability for any action taken or omitted in good faith and with due care.

The Fund bears the cost of the services which the Transfer Agent renders to the Investor and the cost of services which the Transfer Agent renders to the Dealer is borne by the Principal Underwriter. The Transfer Agent may charge the Investor for extra services performed at his request.

9. PAYEES EXEMPT FROM BACKUP WITHHOLDING. Payees specifically exempted from backup withholding on interest and dividend payments include the following:

- A corporation
- A financial institution
- An organization exempt from tax under Section 501(a), or an individual retirement plan
- The United States or any agency or instrumentality thereof
- A State, the District of Columbia, a possession of the United States, or any subdivision or instrumentality thereof
- A foreign government, a political subdivision of a foreign government, or any agency or instrumentality thereof
- An international organization of any agency or instrumentality thereof
- A registered dealer in securities or commodities in the U.S. or a possession of the U.S.
- A real estate investment trust
- A common trust fund operated by a bank under section 584(a)
- An exempt charitable remainder trust, or a non-exempt trust described in section 4947(a)(1)
- An entity registered at all times under the Investment Company Act of 1940
- A foreign central bank of issue
- A middleman known in the investment community as a nominee or listed in the most recent publication of the American Society of Corporate Secretaries, Inc., Nominee List.

DEALER AGREEMENT

The Dealer guarantees the signature(s) of the applicant(s); that to the best of the Dealer's knowledge and belief the Investor is of full age and is legally competent; that the Dealer may lawfully sell securities in the state which the Investor has designated in such Application as his mailing address; and that in the case of a Systematic Withdrawal Plan that he has reviewed with the applicant(s) the provisions of this Systematic Withdrawal Plan and the rate of withdrawal, and believes that the withdrawals requested are reasonable in light of the Investor's circumstances. The Dealer represents that he has entered into a Dealer Sales Agreement with The Pioneer Group, Inc., the Principal Underwriter, and in signing this Application appoints Pioneering Services Corporation as his Agent to execute the purchase transactions in accordance with the terms and the Pioneer Investing Account Application executed by the Investor or the Investor's Withdrawal Plan and to confirm each purchase to the Investor and Dealer. With respect to each purchase, Pioneering Services Corporation will remit semimonthly to the Dealer the amount of his concession.

Source: Pioneer Fund, Inc., 60 State Street, Boston, MA 02109.

The systematic payout plan is widely used by elderly widows, widowers, and retired people in order to receive a check every month that is more than what they normally would receive from quarterly dividends and a year-end capital gains distribution alone. This plan has evolved from the economic facts of life for these people. Today, because of inflation and high taxes, it is becoming increasingly difficult to build an estate of sufficient size to retire respectably. Any type of savings or investment account of $100,000 that pays an average of 5 percent—or $5,000 a year—does not provide adequate income for them. They do not want to get along on approximately $400 per month when they have already accumulated $100,000. They have had to discard the concept on which many of them were raised and on which they thought they would eventually retire—which was to keep their capital intact and spend only the income from it.

A Caution on Using the Systematic Withdrawal Plan. In a mutual fund systematic payout plan, the shareholder must carefully monitor her or his account in order to liquidate no more than the number of shares that was originally contemplated when the plan was established. In some years, because of a down market, the shareholder will redeem more shares than in other years to receive the same number of dollars per month. But as long as the average number of shares redeemed is not too great, the shareholder normally stays with the original monthly withdrawal.

It must be pointed out here that the main concern of the typical retired person is not to go broke before he or she dies. If this person spends some of the mutual fund shares during retirement, thereby leaving fewer shares to heirs, she or he doesn't care. This person's objective is to live better on the amount of money that can be withdrawn regularly.

The mutual fund shareholder on a systematic payout plan should be warned that if the withdrawal plan is kept up long enough, it is possible to use up all of the shares in the account. This can take place particularly if the shareholder had placed a large sum in mutual funds at the top of a bull market and then takes as high as a 10 percent payout.

It should also be understood that the withdrawal plan is *not* an annuity. In an *annuity contract,* the annuitant agrees that both the capital and the interest shall be paid back and exhausted. Most of the payment from an annuity is the return of the annuitant's own capital, and only a small portion of the payment is interest. The annuitant has one advantage: payment is guaranteed for life. In a systematic payout from a mutual fund account, the payments are not guaranteed to last a lifetime.

Advantage of the Systematic Withdrawal Plan. One great advantage of the systematic withdrawal plan is that it permits a change of payout at any time. If the shares are being used up too fast, the shareholder can reduce the payout. If the shares are not being used up fast enough to suit the shareholder's needs, the payout may be increased. Furthermore, like any mutual fund account, the shares in a systematic withdrawal account are liquid and the account may be closed out at any time.

PERFORMANCE OF MUTUAL FUNDS

Mutual funds are purchased because they undertake to do a better job of investing in the stock market than an individual can accomplish alone. Basically, an investment is not a good one if it cannot produce better results than fixed dollars that are kept in a bank deposit or a savings and loan account. In an effort to measure the performance of mutual funds, two periods of time are shown: (1) a ten-year period and (2) a 20-year period. The ten-year record will show that this is too short a period to show a consistently good performance from a lump-sum investment, especially if the market should experience two sharp downturns in that time frame. Any performance over a 20-year period could be viewed as likely to occur again.

TEN-YEAR RECORD OF A LUMP-SUM INVESTMENT

Over a ten-year period, a lump-sum investment in mutual funds can be disappointing. Certainly the ten-year record from 1966 to 1975 supports this contention. This ten-year period was a poor one for the stock market and therefore was just as bad for mutual funds. On February 9, 1966, the Dow Jones industrial average reached an intraday high of slightly over 1,000. But there were two severe bear markets during this period, one in 1970 and another in 1974. In October and again in December of 1974, the DJIA fell below 600. As a consequence, only two of the top five mutual funds during that ten-year period did better than a $10,000 account compounded annually at 8 percent. The figure for a savings account of $10,000 compounded annually at 8 percent for ten years was $21,590. The figures for the top five mutual funds with all earnings automatically reinvested were as follows:

Mathers	$23,264
Istel	$21,669
Financial Industrial Income	$21,389
Roe Price New Horizons Fund	$20,841
Pioneer Fund, Inc.	$18,241

Obviously, during the ten-year period from 1966 to 1975, those millions of shareholders who owned other mutual funds that did not do as well as the top five funds were even more disappointed.

However, the ten-year performance record from 1975 to 1984 for the top mutual funds was far better. Pioneer Fund's ten-year performance, for example, was $46,491 for the period ending December 31, 1984. But it should be noted that two of these years, 1983 and 1984, were excellent years for the stock market.

TWENTY-YEAR RECORD OF A LUMP-SUM INVESTMENT

Over any 20-year period a lump-sum investment in mutual funds should do very well. This is a long enough period of time for the investor to experience at least the average results from the built-in, long-term growth of the economy.

Figure 4-6 shows the 20-year periods of Pioneer Fund, Inc., from 1928 to 1987. This

FIGURE 4-6 Growth of Pioneer Funds During 20-Year Periods

20 Year Periods	Jan. 1-Dec. 31	Income Dividends Reinvested	Total Investment Cost	Capital Gain Distributions Taken in Shares†	Ending Value of Shares
...here's what	1928-47 *	$ 29,951	$ 39,951	$ 2,501	$ 111,001
your investment	1929-48	29,008	39,008	3,423	91,886
would have	1930-49	32,670	42,670	4,609	104,610
been worth had	1931-50	56,761	66,761	9,121	197,663
you invested	1932-51	85,250	95,250	16,806	306,098
$10,000 in any	1933-52	71,403	81,403	16,212	251,626
20 year period	1934-53	66,113	76,113	15,774	215,535
in the Fund's	1935-54	59,138	69,138	14,947	235,452
history	1936-55	47,760	57,760	14,674	200,709
	1937-56	40,012	50,012	14,347	165,515
	1938-57	79,915	89,915	32,136	266,817
	1939-58	72,772	82,772	32,025	306,041
	1940-59	69,023	79,023	33,049	296,667
	1941-60	75,193	85,193	38,966	295,697
	1942-61	68,266	78,266	45,673	303,504
	1943-62	63,493	73,493	47,705	233,412
	1944-63	45,800	55,800	36,833	173,469
	1945-64	35,062	45,062	31,082	137,940
	1946-65	25,502	35,502	25,128	113,650
	1947-66	24,875	34,875	27,614	96,054
	1948-67	26,691	36,691	31,898	128,890
	1949-68	29,458	39,458	39,542	165,083
	1950-69	28,603	38,603	40,162	121,016
	1951-70	25,399	35,399	38,023	97,078
	1952-71	24,036	34,036	34,185	93,590
	1953-72	23,962	33,962	34,247	96,921
	1954-73	25,199	35,199	36,692	88,982
	1955-74	20,221	30,221	29,592	52,130
	1956-75	19,007	29,007	25,561	61,035
	1957-76	19,056	29,056	23,782	74,829
	1958-77	23,533	33,533	28,366	84,997
	1959-78	18,739	28,739	21,848	67,334
	1960-79	18,688	28,688	20,891	75,437
	1961-80	21,210	31,210	22,890	96,712
	1962-81	20,001	30,001	20,185	75,039
	1963-82	25,085	35,085	26,240	91,426
	1964-83	25,110	35,110	26,600	99,674
	1965-84	24,939	34,939	26,727	86,131
	1966-85	22,601	32,601	24,579	86,872
	1967-86	26,251	36,251	47,447	101,573
	1968-87	21,164	31,164	41,762	77,755

Source: Pioneer Fund, Inc., 60 State Street, Boston, MA 02109.

investment company has been in existence since 1928 and has over $1 billion in net assets. The figure depicts what happened to a $10,000 lump-sum investment for every 20-year period since 1928 if income dividends and capital gains distributions were reinvested in additional shares.

According to Figure 4-6, the worst 20-year performance of Pioneer Fund, Inc., was during 1955–1974, when an investment of $10,000 was worth $52,130 at the end of 20 years. The best 20-year performance of Pioneer Fund, Inc., was during 1932–1951, when an investment of $10,000 was worth $306,098 at the end of 20 years. This out-

standing performance was partially the result of the low prices of stocks caused by the recession in 1932, followed by the stock market rise after World War II.

By comparison, the figure for a savings account of $10,000 compounded annually at 8 percent for 20 years was $46,661.

The results of many mutual funds compare favorably with the 20-year results shown in Figure 4-6. In any 20-year period, therefore, it would appear that a saver would be better off investing in mutual funds than having his or her money in savings accounts that earn 8 percent.

NINE GUIDELINES FOR INVESTORS IN MUTUAL FUNDS

Just as there are guidelines to follow when purchasing common stocks, there are guidelines that should give an investor a better-than-average chance for success when buying shares in mutual funds. Some of these guidelines may not be applicable to you at your age today, but they might be at some future date.

BEFORE YOU INVEST

1. Choose a mutual fund as carefully as you would an individual security. Past performance is important, and so are the investment objectives stated in a fund's official prospectus. But remember that past performance shows only how well the fund has done—it is not a guarantee of how well it will perform in the future.

2. When making a single lump-sum investment, timing is of the utmost importance. If at all possible, avoid making a large lump-sum investment at the crest of a long bull market. It's better to wait in a cash position, even for a fairly long period of time if necessary, in order to avoid making a serious mistake. An investor might never recover from a single large mutual fund commitment made at too high a price.

3. If you are young and have only a small amount to invest initially, and you plan on saving regularly every month, there is no better medium than a long-term, dollar cost averaging program in a growth and income or maximum capital appreciation fund. If you are serious about saving regularly over a long period of time in order to achieve better-than-average financial independence, you need only review Figure 4-7, which shows the results of an account that started with $500 and thereafter invested $100 per month for a period of 40 years. The result after 40 years was an account worth all the way from a minimum of $1,070,694 to $3,019,913. If this plan was started at age 25 and religiously adhered to until age 65, the results should be good enough to satisfy even the most sophisticated investor.

4. If your heirs are inexperienced or too young, invest in mutual funds so that they can inherit professional management and diversification, which they might badly need. Don't leave too much cash behind you. Cash is too easily spent by heirs, but often they will leave a sound investment alone.

5. If you have enough money, diversify your investment management and buy shares from several different funds. Note that this guideline applies only to the wealthy.

FIGURE 4-7 Pioneer Fund's Growth in 40-Year Periods

	Jan. 1 Dec. 31	Income Dividends Reinvested	Total Investment Cost	Capital Gain Distributions Taken in Shares†	Ending Value of Shares
40 YEAR	1928-67*	$ 552,412	$ 600,612	$ 620,335	**$2,501,039**
PERIODS	1929-68	578,792	627,192	726,716	**3,019,913**
	1930-69	607,250	655,650	795,011	**2,381,202**
Total Investments	1931-70	643,590	691,990	894,838	**2,268,831**
$48,400	1932-71	647,057	695,457	854,765	**2,317,355**
	1933-72	595,193	643,593	790,529	**2,212,041**
Results shown for	1934-73	561,120	609,520	757,933	**1,817,088**
every 40 year period	1935-74	533,104	581,504	722,955	**1,258,758**
in the Fund's history	1936-75	512,119	560,519	640,998	**1,505,813**
	1937-76	507,334	555,734	591,703	**1,821,589**
	1938-77	535,099	583,499	604,792	**1,764,479**
	1939-78	496,832	545,232	545,666	**1,632,794**
	1940-79	467,388	515,788	495,107	**1,731,267**
	1941-80	447,612	496,012	460,792	**1,881,780**
	1942-81	412,272	460,672	404,681	**1,437,336**
	1943-82	374,792	423,192	384,220	**1,278,138**
	1944-83	345,833	394,233	360,626	**1,291,070**
	1945-84	328,268	376,668	348,418	**1,070,694**
	1946-85	319,128	367,528	346,082	**1,162,102**
	1947-86	315,808	364,208	560,919	**1,158,306**
	1948-87	312,701	361,101	587,604	**1,039,661**
60 YEAR PERIOD	1928-87*	$6,346,563	$6,418,763	$11,685,239	**$21,294,165**
Total Investments $72,200					

Results shown on the life of the Fund, a 60 year period.
*Beginning March 1, 1928.

These summaries afford a representative picture of performance during a variety of stock market conditions. Considering these varied conditions all the results are productive and rewarding. The illustrations above are with income dividends and capital gains taken in shares.

Source: Pioneer Fund, Inc., 60 State Street, Boston, MA 02109.

AFTER YOU INVEST

6. Monitor your fund's performance as far as your individual account is concerned in relation to the record of other funds in the same category. In order to monitor your fund's performance, invest a few dollars each year in Wiesenberger Services' *Investment Companies.* This publication contains a wealth of information about mutual funds in general and the funds' individual performance in particular.

7. View your account as a liquid investment. You can't trade mutual funds as you do stocks, particularly if you have a small account subject to the maximum sales charge. But you shouldn't stay with a badly performing mutual fund for years just because you again have to pay a sales charge when you can buy another mutual fund that could do better for you.

8. If you need part of your capital in a down market, don't liquidate your shares at a loss. When this situation occurs, you should borrow against your stock certificates at your bank and then pay off the loan when your shares go up in value.

9. If you are retired or elderly and single, take as much as 8 percent using a systematic withdrawal plan. You need maximum cash flow to live better if you are retired or widowed. Take as much as 8 percent from your mutual fund. However, be sure to monitor your account so that you are not redeeming too many shares. Remember that if it should become necessary to tighten your belt temporarily, as during a bear market, you can take less money per month by redeeming fewer shares. You can then return to an 8 percent payout when economic conditions improve. Most of the time, however, don't try to get along on a payout of less than 8 percent in these days of inflation and high taxes merely because you want to leave your estate intact for your heirs.

MAJOR CATEGORIES OF MONEY-MARKET FUNDS

Since they came into being in 1974, money-market funds have demonstrated a continuous growth that is unprecedented in the mutual fund industry. In the short span of eight years, the assets of money-market funds grew from $1.7 billion to over $200 billion in 1982. On December 31, 1987, shareholder accounts in these funds numbered 15.6 million, which was nearly 90 times their number in 1976.

A **money-market fund** invests in short-term credit obligations (three months to one year) that yield high interest and provide relative safety. In many of these funds, a small investor can open an account for as little as $1,000 and thereafter add to the account in increments of $100. Thus, the small investor is able to obtain the high yields that before were available only to the affluent.

Each share in a money-market fund is issued at $1 and is redeemed at $1. Therefore, there is no change in the asset value of the shares. No commission is charged for the purchase or redemption of shares, and the shareholder may cash all or part of the account at any time without paying a penalty. In addition, the shareholder is granted a free check-writing privilege in the amount of $500 or more per check. Money-market funds, however, are not government insured.[4]

Money-market funds, like ordinary mutual funds, may be classified in two ways: (1) according to how they sell shares and (2) according to the nature of their investment portfolios.

MONEY-MARKET FUNDS CLASSIFIED ACCORDING TO HOW THEY SELL SHARES

When money-market funds are classified as to how they sell shares, there are three types: (1) general purpose funds, (2) broker/dealer funds, and (3) institutional funds.

General Purpose Money-Market Funds

Mutual fund organizations that cater to the small investor offer *general purpose money-market funds*. Over one-half of these individual shareholders view their accounts as part of their long-term savings program. This is evidenced by the small number of checks they write. Other objectives for in-

vesting in general purpose funds are to obtain higher income than can be obtained elsewhere while still retaining liquidity and to earn income for short periods when a temporary supply of cash is available.

Mutual fund organizations have a history of offering a wide variety of services to their shareholders, and general purpose money-market funds are no exception. They offer a transfer privilege to the other mutual funds that are in the same "family" of funds offered by their parent company, either free or for a small administrative fee—usually $5. The funds mail a statement to the investor any time there is an addition to or a withdrawal from the account.

Broker/Dealer Money-Market Funds

Stockbrokerage firms offer *broker/dealer money-market funds*. At first, general purpose money-market fund held 80 percent of all money-market fund assets. By 1986, however, over 69 percent of all money-market fund assets were in broker/dealer funds, and only 31 percent were in general purpose funds.

The larger accounts have always gravitated toward broker/dealer firms that deal primarily in stocks and bonds. Normally the larger investor already has a securities account with a broker/dealer. This investor is simply "parking" cash in the money-market fund to obtain a high rate of return and liquidity while awaiting a favorable time to invest in the stock market. Service on the money-market fund accounts is not an objective of the fund, nor is long-term savings an objective of the shareholder.

Institutional Money-Market Funds

Broker/dealers also offer *institutional money-market funds,* but only through their institutional departments. These funds are invested in by banks, big business corporations, pension funds, etc., who want a high yield on a short-term basis.

MONEY-MARKET FUNDS CLASSIFIED AS TO HOW THEY INVEST

When money-market funds are classified as to how they invest, there are three types: (1) diversified funds, (2) single purpose funds, and (3) tax-exempt funds.

Diversified Money-Market Funds

Diversified money-market funds invest in all types of short-term debt obligations, including U.S. Treasury obligations. Table 4-2 lists the various kinds of debt obligations in which these funds invest.

Single Purpose Money-Market Funds

Single purpose money-market funds invest only in U.S. Treasury obligations. The objective of investors in this case is high yield and liquidity with ultimate

security, which is obtained by investing solely in the obligations of the U.S. Treasury. In exchange for greater security, these investors sacrifice 1 or 2 percentage points in yield.

Since none of the money-market funds is government insured, safety lies in the quality of a money-market fund's portfolio. Obviously, the quality of the single purpose funds that invest only in obligations of the U. S. Treasury is greater than the quality of the portfolios of the diversified funds. Under conditions of economic uncertainty and volatility in the credit markets, more shareholders turn to single purpose funds for the ultimate in security that these funds provide.

Tax-Free Money-Market Funds

As the name implies, *tax-free money-market funds* invest exclusively in tax-exempt securities.

TABLE 4-2 Money-Market Funds, Assets Composition, Year-End 1981 (Billions of Dollars)

	1986
U.S. Treasury bills	$20,428.6
Other Treasury securities	7,602.9
Other U.S. securities	15,120.3
Repurchase agreements	32,160.2
Commercial bank CDs[a]	13,427.2
Other domestic CDs[b]	5,684.3
Eurodollar CDs[c]	22,168.4
Commercial paper	94,882.0
Bankers' acceptances	10,405.7
Cash reserves	(24.8)
Other	6,491.2
Total net assets	$228,345.8
Average maturity[d]	40
Number of funds	360

[a] Commercial banks are primarily business banks.
[b] Other domestic banks are savings banks and savings and loan associations.
[c] Eurodollar CDs are those issued by European banks.
[d] Average maturity is number of days.
Source: 1987 *Mutual Fund Fact Book,* Investment Company Institute, 1775 K Street, N.W., Washington, DC.

INVESTING IN MONEY-MARKET FUNDS

Of prime importance to the shareholder of a money-market fund are three factors: the fund's total assets, the share's average number of days to maturity, and the fund's yield. Of these three factors, the yield of a money-market fund is the most important.

QUOTATIONS OF MONEY-MARKET FUNDS

In any published quotation for a money-market fund, the price per share is not important because you buy at $1 per share and sell at $1 per share. Quotations for money-market funds can be found in two places: (1) *The Wall Street Journal* and (2) the big metropolitan daily newspapers.

The quotation of money-market funds in *The Wall Street Journal,* published every business day, shows a list of the money-market funds, their average maturity in days, their seven-day yield, their effective seven-day yield, and their assets. Figure 4-8 shows such a quotation.

HOW MONEY-MARKET FUNDS PAY OUT DIVIDENDS

The dividends earned by a money-market fund are credited to the shareholder's account daily in the form of additional shares. On request, the shares credited to the account during the month may be redeemed and the proceeds paid by check to the shareholder or to anyone this person designates. If the shareholder does not want to receive the dividends, they will be reinvested. The shareholder will then receive a monthly statement instead.

FIGURE 4-8 List of Money-Market Funds in *The Wall Street Journal*

Fund	Avg. Mat.	7Day Yld.	e7Day Yld.	Assets
PW RMA TaxF	20	3.89	3.97	1038.4
PW RMA USGv	63	5.95	6.13	300.5
RNC LiquidAsst	46	5.99	6.17	117.1
RodneySq MMP	28	6.34	6.54	374.6
RodneySq TE	23	4.06	4.14	465.9
RodneySq USG	26	6.06	6.24	292.8
TRowePPrm	45	6.09	6.27	3509.0
TRowePTxEx	47	4.14	4.23	1283.0
TRowePUST	48	5.70	5.86	260.0
Safeco MnyMk f	27	6.11	6.28	115.7
Safeco TF MM	33	3.89	3.95	36.2
StClair Prime	27	6.15	6.34	77.7
StClair TxFr	19	4.13	4.21	64.3
ScuddCashInv f	45	6.19	6.14	1408.7
ScuddCaTFM	21	3.77	3.84	51.8
ScuddNYTFM	50	3.73	3.80	29.1
ScuddrGvt Mny	50	5.54	5.69	157.1
ScuddrTaxFr cf	49	3.94	4.02	415.0
Seagt TEx	32	3.94	4.02	70.9
Seagt Trs	74	6.21	6.40	175.9
Secur Cash Fd	17	5.76	5.93	44.2
Select Mny Mkt	35	5.46		
Selig CalTE	5	3.07	3.12	16.0
SelgmnCM Prm	31	5.73	5.70	346.6
SeligmnGov Prt	5	5.57	5.53	33.9
Sentinel Cash	39	6.04	6.22	66.9
Shrsn Cal Dly	31	4.13	4.21	190.1
ShrsnDailyDiv f	57	6.20	6.39	4172.1
ShrsnDaily TxF	36	4.24	4.33	747.7
ShrsnFMA Cash	58	6.30	6.50	1674.5
ShrsnFMA Govt	61	6.34	6.54	666.1
ShrsnFMA Mun	34	4.20	4.29	1150.1
ShrsnGovt Agen	73	6.34	6.54	2027.1
Shrsn NY Dly	47	3.84	3.91	221.4
ShortTerm Govt	80	5.74	5.91	266.9
ShortTm Asset	21	6.30	6.50	163.1
ShortTerm MM	45	6.01	6.19	790.8
ShortTermYld a	(z)	(z)		
Sigma Moneyfd	12	5.88	6.06	33.5
SthFrmBur Csh	(z)	(z)		
Standby Reserv	32	6.13	6.32	370.7
StandbyTE Res	55	4.17	4.26	68.3
SteinRoeCsh Rs	44	6.09	6.28	951.7
SteinRoe Govt	38	5.95	6.13	46.1
SteinRoe Tax	24	3.98	4.07	295.1
StrongMM Fnd	110	6.56	6.78	235.4
Strong TF MM	87	4.51	4.61	74.7
Summit Cash	50	5.86	6.03	741.5
TaxExmpMM c	15	4.13	4.21	1850.9
TF CshRsv Gen	32	4.00	4.08	257.2
Tx Ex CA MM	12	3.69	3.76	102.5
TaxFrInst Tr	34	4.06	4.14	1612.0
TaxFree Mny c	36	3.99	4.05	1147.5
TempInvest Fd	58	6.63	6.85	6169.7

SUMMARY

Mutual funds are another widely used method of investing in the stock market. By pooling their money with thousands of other investors, shareholders of mutual fund companies can obtain advantages that were formerly reserved for millionaires.

There are two major categories of mutual funds. The first category classifies investment companies by how they sell shares. The second category classifies investment companies by how they invest.

Because mutual fund managers operate in a goldfish bowl, so to speak, their investment objectives and past performance can be more easily evaluated than the results obtained by other money managers. Some advantages of mutual funds over individual investments include professional selection, greater diversification, and daily professional management.

The sales charge for mutual funds must be understood. When compared with the commission charged for investing in individual securities, the sales charge for mutual funds is high. For this reason, mutual funds must be viewed as long-term investments.

As with stocks and bonds, mutual fund prices are quoted daily in publications like *The Wall Street Journal*. An investor can purchase mutual fund shares by investing in a lump-sum account or in an accumulation account. An accumulation account may be a voluntary plan or a contractual plan.

Unfortunately, many ten-year performances of a lump-sum investment in mutual funds have been unfavorable in the past due to the short period of time involved. However, if the prospective investor in mutual funds has time on her or his side, with 20 working years ahead before retirement, it would be difficult to find a better vehicle for investment, particularly if the principle of dollar cost averaging is used.

There are nine guidelines that make for successful investing in mutual funds. The guidelines should be studied carefully and, if adhered to, should give the mutual fund investor satisfaction from having made a wise decision.

Money-market funds should not be ignored by either the small or the large investor. During periods of high yield on short-term interest obligations (30 to 90 days), money-market funds can pay high interest, provide liquidity, and offer relative safety. If ultimate security is desired, the single purpose money-market funds should be considered, for they invest solely in obligations of the U.S. Treasury.

ENDNOTES

1. Trade publication—Investment Company Institute, New York, NY.

2. *Investment Companies* (New York: Arthur Wiesenberger Services, 1987), 3.

3. A sales charge can be computed in either of two ways: (1) as a percentage of the buying price or (2) as a percentage of the selling price.

4. Money-market deposit accounts are insured by an agency of the federal government. These are not to be confused with money-market funds.

<table>
<tr><td rowspan="2">

4

</td></tr>
</table>

<table>
<tr>
<td>

4

REVIEW QUESTIONS
SHORT ESSAY

</td>
<td>

Name _____

Date _____ Points _____

</td>
</tr>
</table>

Directions: Answer the following questions according to your instructor's directions.

1.   List the three ways by which open-end mutual funds offer shares to the public.

     a.   _____

     b.   _____

     c.   _____

2.   Name four broad categories of funds when classified as to how they invest.

     a.   _____

     b.   _____

     c.   _____

     d.   _____

3.   List four advantages provided by mutual funds.

     a.   _____

     b.   _____

     c   _____

     d.   _____

4.   Explain how a statement of intention provides a quantity discount sales charge.

     _____

     _____

     _____

5.   Explain the difference between a selling price and a buying price for mutual funds.

     _____

     _____

     _____

6. Explain the difference between a voluntary plan and a contractual plan for buying mutual fund shares.

   _____

   _____

   _____

7. Define the term "dollar cost averaging."

   _____

   _____

   _____

8. Name five guidelines for investors in mutual funds.

   a. _____

   b. _____

   c. _____

   d. _____

   e. _____

9. Name two objectives for investing in a general purpose money-market fund.

   a. _____

   b. _____

10. Name the three types of money-market funds classified as to how they invest.

   a. _____

   b. _____

   c. _____

4

REVIEW QUESTIONS
MULTIPLE CHOICE

Name _____

Date _____ Points _____

Directions: For each of the following, select the best answer and place the letter that represents it in the Answers column.

ANSWERS

1. An open-end fund is one that will
   a. leave its investments open.
   b. sell its shares only through its own captive sales force.
   c. stand ready to redeem its shares at any time.
   d. not sell its shares to the public. _____
2. A balanced fund invests in
   a. common stocks only.
   b. bonds only.
   c. preferred stocks and bonds.
   d. common stocks, preferred stocks, and bonds. _____
3. A growth and income fund invests its money in companies that
   a. are established and conservative.
   b. are new and currently popular.
   c. have a potential for maximum growth.
   d. provide little or no dividend. _____
4. Aggressive growth funds invest for
   a. assured growth.
   b. explosive growth.
   c. reasonable growth.
   d. long-term growth. _____
5. Through expert selection, mutual fund portfolio managers are able to
   a. change the fund's investment objectives.
   b. eliminate mistakes.
   c. make investments that meet the fund's long-term objectives.
   d. alter trends in the stock market. _____
6. The cash and securities of an open-end mutual fund are held by the
   a. bonded treasurer.
   b. underwriter of the fund.
   c. custodian bank of the fund.
   d. broker/dealer. _____
7. Mutual funds are
   a. poor collateral for a loan.
   b. good collateral for a loan.
   c. unacceptable as collateral for a loan.
   d. not as good collateral as a blue-chip stock. _____
8. Breakpoint refers to the amount of money invested in a mutual fund to qualify for a
   a. reduced sales charge.
   b. reduced management fee.
   c. purchase of a large block of stock at a discount.
   d. low interest rate on a loan for which mutual fund shares are collateral. _____

9. A combination privilege qualifies shareholders for
   a. a quantity discount charge when investments in different
      funds are managed by one company.
   b. determining in which combination of stocks their money will be
      invested.
   c. combining their investments with family members for a
      reduced sales charge.
   d. combining previous investments for a reduced sales charge.   _____

10. A mutual fund has a maximum sales charge of 8½ percent, which
    drops to 4½ percent at $50,000. An investor signs a statement of
    intention to invest $50,000 within the next 13 months. The fund
    holder invests $20,000 initially, $20,000 three months later, and
    $10,000 six months later. The adjusted sales charge is
    a. $2,250.
    b. $2,350.
    c. $3,150.
    d. $3,850.   _____

11. An investor who buys shares in a mutual fund and then redeems
    them in 60 days would probably lose the least money in one of the
    following plans:
    a. front-end load fund.
    b. prepaid charge plan.
    c. penalty plan.
    d. level charge plan.   _____

12. When dollar cost averaging, the investor
    a. buys the same number of shares regularly.
    b. invests the same number of dollars regularly.
    c. buys shares only when the price is low.
    d. invests nothing when the price is high.   _____

13. When a mutual fund shareholder is using a systematic payout plan,
    the most important thing to watch is the
    a. fluctuations in the stock market.
    b. number of shares left in the account.
    c. value of the shares owned.
    d. number of shares set aside for his or her heirs.   _____

14. An investment in a money-market fund should be made when
    interest rates are
    a. low.
    b. high.
    c. declining.
    d. forecast to drop lower.   _____

15. In reference to all money-market fund assets, the general purpose
    money-market funds in 1986 had the following percentage:
    a. 31 percent.
    b. 50 percent.
    c. 70 percent.
    d. 80 percent.   _____

4

REVIEW QUESTIONS
TRUE-FALSE

Name _____

Date _____ Points _____

Directions: Circle T or F to indicate whether each statement is true or false.

ANSWERS

1. It is almost as difficult for an investor to choose the right mutual fund as it is to choose individually the right stocks and bonds.   T F

2. About 46 million people have invested in mutual funds.   T F

3. Some mutual fund companies sell their shares through their own sales force.   T F

4. Closed-end funds will not redeem shares.   T F

5. A growth and income fund is a balanced fund.   T F

6. A pool diagram helps an investor understand how mutual funds manage their current assets.   T F

7. Mutual funds rarely change the stocks in their portfolios.   T F

8. A mutual fund does not guarantee the return of the investors' money.   T F

9. All mutual funds provide significant tax advantages.   T F

10. The maximum sales charge allowed by law is 8½ percent.   T F

11. A sales charge is paid when a fund account is opened but not when capital is subsequently added.   T F

12. A breakpoint is the point at which the shareholder is entitled to a reduced sales charge.   T F

13. An accumulation privilege allows a shareholder to accumulate accounts in several mutual funds.   T F

14. A statement of intention indicates that a mutual fund investor intends to open a lump-sum account.   T F

15. An investor buys shares when investing in a mutual fund.   T F

16. The letters "NL" in a mutual fund quotation mean "no load."   T F

17. The difference between the selling price and the buying price of a mutual fund is the charge for the customary sales load.   T F

18. Any contractual plan customer can redeem the account within 18 months without paying a sales charge.   T   F

19. When dollar cost averaging, the shareholder buys the same number of shares each month.   T   F

20. In a systematic payout plan the investor should realize that she or he is probably spending part of the capital that was invested.   T   F

21. An investor can expect a good performance from mutual funds over any ten-year period.   T   F

22. The poorest way for a young person to invest is to save regularly over a long period of time in a mutual fund.   T   F

23. If an investor needs part of his or her capital during a down market, shares in a mutual fund should not be liquidated at a loss.   T   F

24. A single purpose money-market fund invests solely in U.S. Treasury obligations.   T   F

25. The relative safety of a money-market fund depends upon the quality of its portfolio.   T   F

4
PROJECT

Mary and Tom Baldwin have not done well in their choice of two growth stocks, despite a rising stock market. Their stockbroker suggests that they consider mutual funds instead. They agree, so the stockbroker makes the following suggestions:

1. To narrow down their selection of which mutual fund to buy, the Baldwins should consider only growth funds or aggressive growth funds.
2. They should invest all of their cash reserves because, even if they should need some of the money later, they could borrow it at the bank using their mutual fund shares as collateral.
3. Even though the sales charge in buying mutual funds has been explained to them, they should ignore the higher cost of buying mutual fund shares.
4. Dollar cost averaging is fine for some people, but it isn't for the Baldwins. This method is too slow in producing results.

State whether each of the suggestions made by the stockbroker is a good or a poor one, and give your reasons why.

CHAPTER 5
OUTLINE

I. **HOME OWNERSHIP**
   A. Basics About Buying a Detached Individual Home
   B. Methods of Paying for a Home
   C. Transfer of Title
   D. Tax Advantages in Buying a Home
   E. Basics About Buying a Condominium

II. **RESIDENTIAL INCOME-PRODUCING PROPERTY**
   A. Buying a House for Profit
   B. Sources of Mortgage Funds
   C. Landlord-Tenant Relationships

III. **COMMERCIAL INCOME-PRODUCING PROPERTY**
   A. Real Estate Limited Partnerships
   B. Real Estate Investment Trusts (REITs)

5

FUNDAMENTALS OF INVESTING IN REAL ESTATE

The term **real estate** basically refers to land, but it also includes whatever is made a part of the land by nature or human beings, such as trees by nature or buildings by people. In our great industrial cities, skyscrapers dominate the landscape, so it is natural for city dwellers to think of real estate as buildings and its income as the rental these buildings produce. In the Midwest—the breadbasket of America—agriculture is dominant. Therefore, farmers view real estate as the land, and its income as the crops that can be grown upon it. Home owners everywhere think of real estate as their homes, which provide them with comfortable places in which to live.

Despite these varying images, real estate is, first of all, land. This fact is recognized by law, for the title to any parcel of real estate always identifies the land, never the buildings or the trees that may be on it.

For many people a home is the only real estate they will ever own. It is for this reason that the first part of this chapter gives some rules to follow when considering home ownership. But real estate is bought for income and profit, too, just as stocks and bonds are. Thus, the balance of this chapter discusses some fundamentals about investing in residential and commercial income-producing property.

HOME OWNERSHIP

Millions of Americans own their homes. Every year approximately one million Americans buy a home for the first time. A home is an important and sizable investment. For many, it is the largest single investment they will make in their lifetimes. This being the case, people should know a few rules about the different ways to buy a home and how to pay for it. They should also know what must be done to transfer the title to real estate property and what tax advantages there are in buying a home.

Buying a condominium is another way to own your own home. Because of high costs, many potential buyers of detached individual homes are turning to condominiums as the solution to their housing problem.

Therefore, people also need to know the rules for buying a condominium.

BASICS ABOUT BUYING A DETACHED INDIVIDUAL HOME

The purchase of a home should never be undertaken lightly, for two reasons. First, there is too much money involved. The nationwide median price of a home in the United States today is over $80,000. It is more than twice that amount in high-priced areas such as San Francisco and Boston. These costs are beyond the reach of millions. As a result, many prospective home buyers find that they cannot afford to buy a house at all because it has become too expensive.

Second, it might kill your incentive for any further investment in real estate if your initial venture in this field should prove to be a tragic mistake.

The first decision to make when considering home ownership is whether to buy an existing older home or a brand new one from a builder or a real estate developer.

Buying an Existing Older Home

The big demand for homes is in the resale of houses that have been purchased, occupied, and owned by someone else. When buying an existing home, the basic rules given below should be followed:

1. *Choose the neighborhood carefully.* You should look for neatness, sound construction, carefully maintained lawns, and houses that are at least comparable in price to others in the neighborhood. If you have a growing family, the proximity of good schools, shopping centers, and churches is important.
2. *Find out what future projects, if any, may affect the property you plan to buy.* For example, check with the local city or town hall to be sure that zoning prohibits the construction of multi-family or high-rise apartment buildings in the area. Or call the state highway planning department to inquire about any projected freeway adjacent to the home you plan to buy. Even though actual construction may be years away, the freeway will eventually detract from your enjoyment of the property and will depreciate its value.
3. *Don't pay more than you can afford.* If the total monthly costs for the mortgage payment, property taxes, insurance, and utilities are too much for you, consider buying a less expensive home or waiting until you have enough money to make a larger down payment. The maximum monthly payment should be no more than one-third of your income.
4. *Don't take the real estate agent's word for the age of the house; also inspect the property yourself.* A simple, little-known method can tell you approximately when the house was built. Lift up the porcelain top of the toilet tank in the bathroom. The tank's date of manufacture is always imprinted on the underside, and this will give you the approximate date the house was completed.

Watch out for wood rot, inadequate or no insulation, a faulty water heater, a wet basement, and the need of paint inside or out. To check water pressure, turn on the water all over the property and then flush one of the toilets to see if the pressure remains the same. Remember that there is no perfect house. Just be sure you know in advance the shortcomings of the home you plan to buy. Don't wait until after you move in to be shocked.

If after careful inspection you still have doubts, pay a small fee for a professional to check out the plumbing, the wiring, the basic construction, or the roof if any of these should concern you.

Buying a New Home

Many people like to own a home that has never been occupied by someone else. Furthermore, a new home is likely to provide the latest in conveniences. The first three rules for buying an existing older home also apply to buying a new home. In addition, follow the rules given below:

1. *Don't be overwhelmed by the appearance of a glittering model home.* Determine exactly what features will be in the house that you are considering and which are the "extras" displayed in the model.

2. *Check the lot size in advance.* Is it the size and setting you want for your home? After the bulldozer has arrived, it may be too late.

3. *Check other incidental costs.* If the new community is to have new street paving, sewer lines, and sidewalks, determine whether you or the builder will assume the costs. Find out also about charges for water and trash collection.

4. *Be sure the builder's contract is complete.* Obtain agreement on all the details of the transaction. Don't assume that an item is included, such as a dishwasher, only to discover later that you misunderstood. Any extra features that you want should be described in writing. Finally, be sure that the contract includes the total sales price, as well as the date of completion. Take the precaution of having a lawyer read the contract before you sign it.

   The day before you take title (the closing day), make a thorough inspection of the property inside and out. This is your last chance to register any complaints with your builder.

5. *Obtain all important documents.* When you take possession of the property, insist on having the following papers: (1) warranties from all manufacturers for the equipment in the house, (2) a certificate of occupancy, and (3) certificates from the Health Department clearing all the plumbing and sewer installations. If possible, obtain all applicable certificates of code compliance.

Common Complaints of Home Buyers

The U.S. Department of Housing and Urban Development (HUD) lists five common complaints of prospective buyers of existing older homes or new ones. These are:

1. The rooms are too small, particularly the bedrooms.

2. There is inadequate closet and storage space.

3. The laundry facilities are poor.

4. The layout of the house is inconvenient.

5. The kitchen is cramped and too small.

If your prospective home has any of these faults, perhaps you should look for another house instead. A house that is characterized by several of these shortcomings will be more difficult to resell later.

METHODS OF PAYING FOR A HOME

Obviously one could pay for a house in cash, but very few people can afford to do this. Most of the time a down payment of 20 percent is made, with the balance of the purchase price financed by a mortgage on the property. A **home mortgage loan** is a special type of loan for the sole purpose of purchasing residential property. There are five types of home mortgages: the conventional mortgage, the variable rate mortgage, the shared-appreciation mortgage, the FHA-insured mortgage, and the VA-guaranteed mortgage.

Conventional Mortgage

A **conventional real estate mortgage** is one that is not insured by a government agency. The term of the mortgage is 30 years, and the fixed rate of interest is the going rate of interest for long-term loans. Over 80 percent of the conventional home mortgage loans in the United States are provided by savings and loan associations.

Mortgage lenders sometimes charge "points" for making a conventional real estate loan. A **point** is 1 percent of the amount of the loan. For example, a charge of one point on a mortgage of $80,000 would amount to an extra cost of $800 (or 1 percent of $80,000).

If the borrower should want the privilege of paying off a conventional mortgage loan any time during the first five years, a prepayment penalty of 2 percent of the original amount of the loan could be charged. For example, a penalty of $1,600 may be charged on an $80,000 conventional mortgage that is paid off at the end of four years. Therefore, the borrower should determine in advance if the lender imposes this penalty.

Sometimes it is easier to sell a house if the new buyer can assume the balance of an existing loan. Most conventional mortgage loans, however, contain a provision that the mortgage cannot be assumed. Thus, the new buyer has to negotiate an entirely new loan. If the home has an existing loan financed by a federal savings and loan association, the U.S. Supreme Court has ruled that the loan cannot be assumed even though the mortgage document says that it can.

A variation on the conventional 30-year fixed-rate mortgage can be accomplished by inserting a five-year or seven-year *call option*. This option means that the lending institution can state that at the end of five or seven years, the remaining amount of the loan is due and payable.

Variable-Rate Mortgage

A **variable-rate mortgage** permits the lender to vary the interest rate of the loan during the term of the loan. Usually the rate may be raised or lowered by 2 percent in any 12-month period, with the maximum increase or decrease limited to 5 percent for the entire period of the mortgage. The variation is tied to interest currently being earned by six-month Treasury bills, or it can be determined by any one of several other indexes.

Shared-Appreciation Mortgage

A **shared-appreciation mortgage** affords the lender protection from the inroads of inflation. This type of mortgage is accomplished by stipulating in the agreement that the lender is entitled to share in the profits, if any—usually 30 to 40 percent—when the house is sold.

FHA-Insured Mortgage

When a home mortgage loan is described as an **FHA-insured mortgage**, this means that the Federal Housing Administration (FHA), an agency of the U.S. Department of Housing and Urban Development, has insured the loan. Note that the FHA is not in the business of lending the money itself. It simply insures mortgage loans for building, purchasing, or improving homes. The prospective home buyer would still have to apply for a home mortgage loan with a conventional lender such as a bank or a savings and loan association. The lender, in turn, deals with the FHA. If the borrower qualifies, the FHA guarantees to the *mortgagee* (the lender) that in the event of default on the loan by the *mortgagor* (the borrower), it will pay the remaining amount of the loan to the mortgagee after the property has been foreclosed and title has passed to the government.

Government insurance of home mortgages was instituted because many people with low incomes are considered by conventional lenders to be too high a risk. As a result, these people cannot obtain conventional mortgages. To qualify for an FHA-insured mortgage, an individual must have a good credit rating, the necessary cash for the down payment, and a sufficiently steady income to meet the monthly payments that are required. When the application for the insured loan is approved by the FHA, the mortgagee advises the potential home buyer accordingly and the loan is made.

The maximum down payment on an FHA-insured loan is 40 percent of the appraised value, or $36,000, whichever is lower. The FHA fee is 3.8 percent of the loan.

VA-Guaranteed Mortgage

A **VA-guaranteed mortgage** is a home mortgage loan guaranteed by the Veterans Administration and extended to veterans only. The down payment is the same as on an FHA-insured loan. (The Veterans Administration does not require a down payment if the purchase price is less than the appraised value, but the lender usually does.) To qualify for a VA-guaranteed mortgage loan, a veteran must have been honorably discharged and have had 181 days of continuous active duty after January 31, 1955, except that after 1983 the time is extended to two years of continuous duty. If a veteran qualifies, that person is issued a certificate of eligibility, which is presented to the conventional lender.

The federal government, through the FHA and the VA, does not allow conventional lenders to charge either points or prepayment penalties on insured mortgages. Furthermore, the federal government insists that such insured mortgage loans can be assumed by a new owner. For this reason, some conventional lenders prefer not to deal with FHA- or VA-insured loans.

TRANSFER OF TITLE

The process of transferring title to real estate involves the preparation of several documents and the payment of closing costs. This is a complicated process that every real estate buyer and seller should understand. In some states (mainly in the Midwest and the West), a title or abstract company will handle, for a fee, the problems that arise when transferring title to real estate. In most states, an attorney is employed. If the seller uses a real estate agent to handle the sale, the agent will attend to this paperwork.

When the purchase price is agreed upon between buyer and seller and a sales contract is signed, the buyer customarily deposits 10 percent of the eventual down payment. This deposit and the sales contract are placed with the title or abstract company, or the attorney, with instructions to prepare all the necessary documents in order to close the sale. At the same time, a title search is made to ensure that there are no clouds or liens against the property and that the seller actually owns the real estate being transferred and has the right to convey it to someone else.

In the closing process, the seller wants to be sure that she or he will receive the money for the property and will be free thereafter from any obligation in respect to it. On the other hand, the buyer not only wants to have his or her down payment protected but also wants to be sure that he or she is receiving property with a clean title and that the proper financing has been arranged.

When all the necessary papers have been prepared, a closing date is agreed upon. On this date the buyer and seller meet with their respective attorneys and, in some cases, with the lender's attorney as well. The documents that have been drawn up and a statement of the closing costs are presented at this meeting.

Necessary Documents

An imposing array of documents is presented at closing time. These documents are:

1. The **mortgage deed**, which pledges the building and the land as collateral for the mortgage payments.
2. The **promissory note**, which states the total amount of the loan, the monthly payment required, the interest rate, and the due date. This note also states the penalty for any late payment; the prepayment privilege, if any; and the conditions under which the loan may be assumed by another buyer if the property should later be sold to a third party.
3. The *buyer's instructions* to the title or abstract company, or to the attorney, which confirms the sale price and any deductions agreed upon by the buyer.
4. The *seller's instructions* to the title or abstract company, or to the attorney, which confirms the selling price and any deductions agreed upon by the seller.
5. A *notarized deed*, signed by the seller, which transfers the property to the buyer. After the transaction is completed, this deed should be recorded by the buyer in the office of the county recorder. The buyer should keep a certified copy of this deed in a safe place, usually a safe-deposit box.
6. A *copy of the receipted tax bill* from the seller. This receipt proves that the property taxes have been paid for the

year or discloses the amount that is still owed.

7. A *cover note from the insurance broker*, which proves that the property is covered by a stated amount of insurance as of the closing date.

8. A *statement of the amount of rental income*, which is prepared by the seller. This statement is necessary only when rental property is being transferred. It should include a list of the tenants and the dates the rents are due.

9. A **truth-in-lending statement** prepared by the lender, which, among other things, states the annual rate of interest that is being charged by the lender (mortgagee). Truth-in-lending statements are required by federal and state law.

Closing Costs

When transferring title to real estate from one party to another, closing costs are incurred. It is imperative for the real estate buyer to determine in advance which of these closing costs will be borne by the buyer and which will be paid by the seller. On the closing date the buyer must have not only the necessary cash for the down payment but also the money for the closing costs.

The closing costs consist of charges made for all, or most, of the following items:

1. A *survey*, which determines the exact boundaries of the land.

2. *Attorney's fees* charged for the preparation of the deed, the mortgage, and the promissory note, as well as other papers. In those states where a title company is used, these charges are called an *escrow fee*.

3. A *credit report* on the buyer, which is ordered by the lender who wants to be sure that the buyer is a good credit risk. In smaller communities, a credit report is usually not necessary.

4. A *termite inspection report*, which is important in some sections of the country, such as California, but is not required in others. The cost of a termite inspection is usually borne by the seller, and, if termite damage is discovered, it is the seller's responsibility to have the necessary repairs made prior to the closing date and to pay for them.

5. An **origination fee**, which is usually charged by the lender as a small percentage of the loan to cover the lender's expenses.

6. An **appraisal fee**, which is ordered by the lender in order to determine the amount of the loan. If the loan is insured by the FHA or the VA, the amount of this fee is set by law.

7. **Recording fees**, which are charged by local authorities for recording documents such as the deed to the property and the mortgage. These fees are usually small and amount to only a few dollars.

8. *State or local transfer taxes*, depending upon whether or not such taxes are imposed.

9. *Title insurance cost*, which can be a sizable charge of several hundred dollars. This cost is usually borne by the seller.

10. Adjustment of prepaid items or impound accounts. *Prepaid items* are mainly taxes and insurance on the property being conveyed. The seller must pay a prorated share of these costs up to the closing date, after which time they become the obligation of the buyer. If the seller has paid these items for the entire year (which is frequently the case), an adjustment is necessary. Taxes and insurance are called **impound accounts** if the mortgagee requires them to be paid by the month as part of the note agreement.

11. Miscellaneous items, which could include notary fees, inspection fees, and possibly a charge for photographing the property, particularly if it is a sizable income-producing piece of real estate.

TAX ADVANTAGES IN BUYING A HOME

Most people buy a home simply because they want to own one. They don't take into consideration the tax advantages of owning a home as compared with renting. Two important tax advantages for the home owner lie in the full deductibility of property taxes and interest charges on the owner's federal income tax return.

Deductible Property Taxes

Property taxes are assessed against real estate by both the city and the county where the property is situated. These taxes are fully tax deductible, regardless of the reason for purchasing real estate.

Deductible Interest Charges

The interest portion of a mortgage loan is also fully tax deductible. For example, if the interest paid in one year is $3,600, the full amount of $3,600 can be taken as an income tax deduction by the home or real estate owner.

BASICS ABOUT BUYING A CONDOMINIUM

When you purchase a condominium, you buy an individual unit that you own just as you do when buying a detached individual house. You also arrange your own financing and pay your own taxes. The methods of paying for a mortgage, the transfer of title, and the tax advantages are the same for condominiums as for individual detached homes. But there the similarity ends. When you buy a condominium, you become a part of a community that has recreational and other common facilities that are shared and owned by all the condominium owners. This presents not only advantages but also problems.

Documents to Study

In an attempt to solve the problems involved in condominium ownership, various documents are drawn up that have to be signed by all the owners. These documents, which are described below, should be reviewed by the prospective buyer before signing a sales contract.

Enabling declaration. The **enabling declaration** gives authority, through its bylaws, to the board of directors of the home owners' association to regulate and administer the affairs of the condominium project. The bylaws should define the common areas and arrange for each condominium owner to have a vote on the affairs common to all. This is particularly important if some time in the future the bylaws need to be changed or a director removed.

The number of votes each condominium owner has should be carefully determined. Ideally each condominium owner would have one vote. But in most cases the condominiums in the project are not physically alike, so this concept of one condominium-one vote is not feasible.

The bylaws should clearly establish the rights and responsibilities of the condominium owners, both as individuals and as co-owners of the designated common areas. Some of these rights and responsibilities involve the following:

1. Use and maintenance of the common areas, such as a clubhouse, a swimming pool, and tennis courts.
2. Establishment of an operation budget, including a reserve fund.
3. Amount of monthly charges from each condominium owner and the collection of these charges.
4. Amount of fire and liability insurance carried on the common areas.
5. Rules of conduct to promote harmony among the owners.
6. Compliance with state laws.
7. Percentage of the owners' votes that is required when voting to amend the enabling declaration itself or its bylaws.

Subscription and Purchase Agreement. The **subscription and purchase agreement** is primarily a sales contract. This document should be read carefully, preferably by the buyer's attorney. It should describe the individual's interest in the condominium unit and make reference to the enabling declaration.

Regulatory Agreement. A **regulatory agreement** is used only when financing is obtained from the Department of Housing and Urban Development. This document requires that the condominium project meet the regulations under Section 234 of the National Housing Act. It also protects HUD's insured interest in the condominium project.

Information Bulletin. An **information bulletin** gives the buyer an overall, easy-to-understand view of the condominium project. It should not be substituted, however, for an actual reading of the enabling declaration.

Other Questions to Consider

There are several other questions to consider before buying a condominium. These are:

1. Is the condominium project in which you are buying your unit the entire development, or does the developer of the project plan on adding to it by buying more land on which to build more units?
2. Has the developer retained any control over the condominium and, if so, what rights has the developer retained?
3. To what degree is transient residence (renting of the condominium units) permitted in the project?
4. Are there any restrictions on a condominium owner's right to resell? Does the owner have the right to resell his or her unit in the open market, or does the home owners' association have the right of first refusal, requiring the owner to offer it first to the association for a certain period of time?
5. If the condominium project is new, have all municipal building code requirements been met?
6. Can a condominium owner be assessed for additional money in the future, over and above the monthly charges as outlined in the operating budget?

RESIDENTIAL INCOME-PRODUCING PROPERTY

As its name implies, **residential income property** is any piece of residential property that is purchased for either income or profit. In this respect, the real estate buyer's objectives are the same as those of the investor buying securities.

Many of the great family fortunes in the world have been established by investing in real estate. Persons who started with only a few thousand dollars have become multi-millionaires in a few short years, and many more people will become wealthy because they invested their money in real estate. All of them, of course, took what is known as a *businessperson's risk.* There was no guarantee that they would make any money. Many have tried investing in real estate and have lost. But, as we have found out, you have to become an investor and stop saving your money in fixed dollars if you hope to become well-off some day. And certainly you must do so if you want to become wealthy!

Aside from its profit potential, real estate has great attraction as an investment because it is *tangible.* That is, you can see it and walk on it. It is not like a stock investment, which is *intangible* since all you receive for it is a piece of paper—the stock certificate. Land will always be here, and there is only just so much of it. With an expanding population, land has a built-in growth factor since more and more people compete with one another to buy it. Furthermore, land cannot be depreciated for tax purposes on an income tax return. The Internal Revenue Service allows depreciation on buildings (except homes), machinery, furniture, and equipment, but never on land.

BUYING A HOUSE FOR PROFIT

Whenever men and women invest in anything, generally most of them have to start in a small way because they have only a little excess money saved. This is true when buying stocks and bonds, and it is also true when investing in income-producing real estate. Therefore, many people start investing by buying a house as an investment.

When buying a house as an investment, the investor's objective is to look for one that can be bought at the lowest possible price, not a comfortable home in which to live. The investor also wants to buy with the lowest possible down payment and on the best mortgage terms because she or he will be deliberately using leverage. **Leverage** is simply a high-sounding word for buying property mostly with other people's money.

Let us illustrate the use of leverage to increase profits by the following example. Assume that two years ago an investor purchased a house for $80,000 with a down payment of $15,000. Also assume that the balance of the purchase price was financed with a $65,000, 30-year mortgage at 12 percent interest. Finally, assume that today the investor sells the house for $95,000. The calculations for this example are tabulated below.

	Purchase	Sale
Price	$80,000	$95,000
Mortgage	−65,000	−65,000
Equity (down payment)	$15,000	$30,000

In this example, the investor's $15,000 down payment doubled to $30,000 when the house was sold. This means that the investor made a profit of $15,000, which is a 100 percent return on the $15,000 invested. If the investor had paid $80,000 in cash and sold at $95,000, a profit of $15,000 would also have been made. But in this case the return on investment would have been only 18.75 percent ($15,000 ÷ $80,000 = 18.75 percent).

SOURCES OF MORTGAGE FUNDS

Most of the borrowed money with which to buy rental houses comes from conventional mortgages (the FHA insures mortgages on income-producing property, too). Sometimes second mortgages are used as part of the financing.

Conventional Mortgages

Sources of conventional mortgage money for income-producing residential property include insurance companies, private mortgage companies, banks, and savings and loan associations. The rate of interest they charge is normally 1 percent more than that charged for mortgages on owner-occupied homes. The down payment required is also higher, usually 25 percent of the purchase price. If the lender is a savings and loan association, the down payment required is determined by the Federal Home Loan Bank Board, which governs the savings and loan industry.

Second Mortgages

A **second mortgage** is a loan that has second claim against the property if it should be foreclosed. As a consequence, it is a high-risk loan. Therefore, second mortgage interest rates are high, usually 3 percent more than for a first mortgage. Furthermore, a second mortgage is for a short term, usually from three to five years.

When a second mortgage is part of the financing, it is usually arranged through the existing property owner. If the buyer doesn't have enough money for the down payment, the owner-seller is sometimes willing to take back a second mortgage as part of the purchase price. This is called *creative financing* by real estate salespersons and brokers—a phrase coined during a period of time when the country was in a recession. If homeowners wanted to sell, they had to take back part of the purchase price in the form of a second mortgage because most buyers did not have the necessary down payment.

LANDLORD-TENANT RELATIONSHIPS

When investing in residential, income-producing real estate, an investor becomes a landlord and has tenants who occupy the property and pay rent. This situation can create countless problems, for both the landlord and the tenants, unless leases are carefully drawn to include provisions that protect both parties.

Clauses Protecting the Investor-Landlord

Some of the most commonly used clauses in leases that protect the landlord are given below. Note that some of these clauses are used only occasionally.

1. The first and last month's rent must be paid in advance.
2. A security deposit is required (particularly if the house or apartment is furnished). This deposit is refundable if nothing is lost or damaged.
3. A nonrefundable deposit is required for cleaning the premises when the tenant vacates.
4. The assignment or subletting of premises without the written consent of the landlord is prohibited.
5. The landlord is permitted to inspect the premises at reasonable times during the 60-day period prior to termination of the lease.
6. A tax escalation clause is used to permit automatic rent increases if property taxes are increased.

7. The number of persons who are permitted to use the property regularly is limited.
8. Children are prohibited (used occasionally).
9. Animals are prohibited (used occasionally).

Clauses Protecting the Tenant

In the past, the protection of tenants has not been commonly written into a lease. Today there are laws that provide the following clauses for the tenant's protection:

1. The tenant must have *exclusive possession of the premises*. A mere possession to use the premises is a license and not a lease, and a licensee may be evicted by the landlord.
2. Any new owner must honor an existing lease.
3. The landlord may remove the tenant's personal property when the tenant abandons the premises. But the property must be stored for a reasonable period—usually three months.
4. The landlord may not prevent a tenant from moving the latter's personal property out of the premises even if the tenant owes back rent. The landlord is limited to the rights of a creditor only.
5. When a tenant breaks a lease, the landlord may not stand idly by, making no effort to relet the premises. The landlord has a duty to relet and thereby reduce the amount of money that the tenant owes.

COMMERCIAL INCOME-PRODUCING PROPERTY

Investors who do not trust their own judgment to make individual real estate investments can still invest in commercial real estate for the triple objectives of current income, long-term profit, and income tax advantages. These investors can pool their money with many other people and then hire proven experts to invest their money in commercial properties such as apartment houses, shopping centers, and office complexes. This method of investing in real estate is similar to the pooling of mutual fund shareholders' money to buy securities.

Investing in commercial real estate is accomplished by two different methods: (1) by forming real estate limited partnerships and (2) by forming real estate investment trusts (REITs). Each of these methods is discussed below.

REAL ESTATE LIMITED PARTNERSHIPS

A **real estate limited partnership** is a business firm that invests in commercial real estate by using the limited partnership as its legal vehicle. The difference between a general partner and a limited partner (in this case the individual investor) was stated in Chapter 1. Because the difference is important to the limited partner in real estate, the definitions of these types of partners bear repetition.

Unless otherwise specified, each partner in a business enterprise is usually a *general partner* who is a principal and is fully active in the business. A general partner has the authority to act for the partnership within the scope of its activity. A *limited partner* is neither active in the business nor liable for any of its debts. As such, a limited partner cannot lose any more money than the amount that she or he invested in the partnership. This person cannot be assessed for any more money.

In short, the general partners manage the partnership business. The limited partners, as passive investors, are not involved in the day-to-day operations of the partnership.

Various Types

Real estate limited partnerships vary widely as to their investment objectives and the kind of property they acquire. These objectives are stated in the official prospectus. The size of the offering of a limited partnership can vary from a few hundred thousand dollars to 100 million dollars. The location of the properties may be confined to one state or may include many states. The various types of real estate limited partnerships are (1) large public limited partnerships investing in many states; (2) small public limited partnerships investing in one or two states; (3) triple net lease limited partnerships; (4) mini-warehouse limited

partnerships; and (5) private placement limited partnerships. Each of these types is described below.

Large Public Limited Partnerships. Large public limited partnerships invest from ten million to 100 million dollars a year. They buy commercial property (apartment houses, shopping centers, industrial property, and vacant land) located throughout the United States.

Small Public Limited Partnerships. Because of their small size, these limited partnerships raise only one to ten million dollars (or less) a year and buy only a few commercial properties. They confine their investments to the state in which they are domiciled or to one or two states close by.

Triple Net Lease Limited Partnerships. A *triple net lease* **partnership** buys a large commercial building owned and occupied by a big corporation and then leases it back to that same corporation. The name *triple net lease* arises from the fact that the leasing corporation pays for all three of the basic costs: taxes, insurance, and all the operating expenses of the building. Because of this situation, the triple net lease real estate limited partnership is a *nonoperating* limited partnership. That is, it does not manage the property, and its only expense in relation to the building is debt service on the mortgage.

The major objective of a triple net lease limited partnership is income, which is paid quarterly to the limited partners. Part of this income is tax sheltered due to depreciation and interest expenses. There is a long holding period—12 to 15 years—to wait for the effects of inflation and escalation clauses in the lease so that the building can be sold at a profit. The profit is lower than in other types of limited partnerships.

Mini-Warehouse Limited Partnerships. A **mini-warehouse limited partnership** purchases parcels of land and builds mini-warehouses on them. No financing is arranged because the mini-warehouses are constructed for cash, eliminating interim financing costs and later mortgage payments. The mini-warehouses are in demand because apartment house dwellers have small storage space, and so do renters of offices. Since mini-warehouses are inexpensive to construct and they offer storage space at low cost, the income to the limited partner is good in relation to other income investments. In addition, part of this income is tax sheltered due to depreciation on the buildings.

Private Placement Limited Partnerships.

A **private placement limited partnership** invests in commercial income-producing property such as apartment houses, shopping centers, and office complexes. The primary objective of this type of limited partnership is to provide a long-term profit on the investment.

A private placement limited partnership is not a public offering registered with the Securities and Exchange Commission. It is offered under SEC Rule 146 and, as such, can qualify for exemption from registration. In most states, there can be only 35 limited partners in a private placement limited partnership. Since the number of investors is limited, a small amount of money is raised, resulting in the purchase of only one, two, or three properties. This increases the risk to the investor because there is little diversification.

Advantages

The advantages of real estate limited partnerships are described below.

Professional Selection and Management.

Most investors considering a commercial real estate investment do not have the time, experience, or ability to negotiate acquisitions and financing. Nor do they have the knowledge to apply the intensive daily management required for successful investing in income-producing properties, which includes experienced evaluation, acquisition, financing, negotiation, property management, and eventual sale of the properties.

Capital Pooling.

Capital pooling by many investors (in some cases involving thousands who reside all over the United States) provides increased purchasing power for larger properties. In addition, it provides a diversified portfolio by type of property and location that tends to reduce risks and increase profit potential.

Inflation Hedge.

Historically, an inflation hedge is provided by well-selected and well-managed commercial properties. This is because the properties increase in value with time, if for no other reason than the law of supply and demand and yearly inflation.

Income.

Professional real estate investors have always insisted on buying property that has an economic value in the form of net income from rents over and above all operating expenses, including interest and amortization of the mortgage. If the income from rents is insufficient to pay the operating expenses and debt service on the property, the result is *negative cash flow*. Under this condition, the investor will have to pay part of these costs out of his or her own pocket from other income or assets. This situation is not tolerated by the general partners of a real estate limited partnership. Negative cash flow may develop because of adverse economic conditions, but it does not exist at the time the property is purchased.

Tax Benefits.

The tax benefits are provided by a flow-through of the usual tax deductions provided by investment in commercial property, such as depreciation of the building, property taxes, and interest on the mortgage. Quarterly dividends are often completely tax exempt because they are considered to be a return of capital.

Equity Buildup.

The amortization of the mortgage results in an equity buildup because the payments of the principal on the mortgage reduce the balance owed on the loan.

Value-Added Strategy.

Not all real estate limited partnerships apply the principle of

value-added strategy, which states that the real estate owner should add improvements to the property—not just provide ongoing maintenance—to justify raising rents. By selectively improving the properties, occupancies remain high. Deliberately adding value provides greater appreciation than can be obtained from other real estate investments that depend primarily upon the effect of inflation for appreciation. The eventual profit upon sale of the properties will, in the last analysis, be dependent on rent levels as well as on outside factors such as supply and demand. The value-added strategy can also result in a relatively short holding period.

Objections to Investing in Real Estate Limited Partnerships

There are several objections to investing in commercial real estate by using the limited partnership vehicle. These are explained below.

High Costs for the Limited Partner. The average sales charge for a partnership unit is 8 percent, which means that on a $10,000 investment only $9,200 can be invested in the properties. In addition, the general partners are allowed to deduct start-up expenses of the partnership, which can amount to another 2 percent. Finally, the standard charge for intensive property management is 5 percent of the gross rents. Since the general partners are also real estate brokers, they obtain a real estate commission both when the properties are bought and when they are sold.

Businessperson's Risk. There is no assurance that the objectives of the limited partnership will be realized. Instead of income and/or a long-term profit, there could be a loss.

Other People Managing Your Money. Some people don't like other people to manage their money. Win or lose, they would rather do it on their own.

Long Waiting Period Before Properties Are Sold. Some real estate limited partnerships will hold the properties for ten to 12 years. This is too long a time for some people to wait.

Not Liquid Partners. None of the partnership units can be redeemed or sold. Consequently, only long-term excess money can be used for investment in real estate limited partnerships. However, the partnership units can be transferred to another owner, especially in the event of death.

Exclusion of Small Investor. Some limited partnerships allow an investment for as little as $2,000 (particularly for IRA and Keogh accounts), and many allow an investment for as little as $5,000. However, there are minimum financial suitability standards that have to be met by the partners. These standards vary from state to state, but the average standards require that partnership units be sold only to an investor who represents in writing (in the subscription agreement) that he or she has either of the following:

1. A net worth (exclusive of home, furnishings, and automobile) of at least $30,000 plus an annual income of at least $30,000.
2. Irrespective of annual gross income, a net worth of at least $75,000 (exclusive of home, home furnishings, and automobile).

REAL ESTATE INVESTMENT TRUSTS (REITs)

The investor with a small amount of money cannot meet the financial suitability standards of the real estate limited partnerships. This person would also like to be as liquid as she or he would be when owning stocks. For such small investors, the **real estate investment trust (REIT)** (pronounced "reet") exists to purchase and hold income-producing properties of all types and yet have the shares publicly traded. REITs provide a means for the small investor to invest in commercial property for the triple objectives of current income, long-term profit, and income tax advantages through the services of proven professionals.

There are two types of REITs: (1) equity trusts and (2) mortgage trusts. Each of these types is discussed below.

Equity Trusts

The **equity real estate investment trust** invests its customers' money in the ownership of large properties such as apartment houses, shopping centers, commercial and industrial real estate, and large tracts of vacant land.

Brief Background. The concept of the equity real estate trust originated in the middle of the nineteenth century. At that time, Massachusetts law prohibited a corporation from investing in real estate except in the land on which its own offices and factories stood. As a result of this law, an organization that was ruled *not* to be a corporation came into existence and was called the *Boston real estate trust*.

Other similar trusts developed. Soon they became so popular that when they ran out of attractive large investment properties in Boston, they started investing in other big cities across the country. These trusts were set back, however, when a federal court decision in 1936 reversed previous decisions and ruled that the Boston trust was in fact a corporation and therefore had to pay corporation taxes. This ruling made the individual investor in equity trusts subject to double taxation. That is, the trust had to pay a corporation tax, and then the investor had to pay individual income taxes on any distribution of income made by the trust. As a result, equity real estate investment trusts became economically unattractive as an investment.

For a quarter of a century thereafter, the concept of the equity real estate investment trust lay dormant. Then, in 1960, the U.S. Congress recognized the tax inequity faced by equity trusts and passed a law that applied the **conduit theory** to the income distributed by these trusts. According to the conduit theory, as long as the equity trust pays out 95 percent of its investment income to its shareholders, it is simply a conduit through which the income passes and is therefore not subject to corporate taxes. Actually, the conduit theory had already been in effect with respect to mutual funds since the passage of the federal Investment Company Act of 1940.

Protective Provisions for the Small Investor. When passing the law in 1960, Congress not only recognized the tax inequity faced by equity trusts but also legislated comprehensive provisions designed to protect the small investor. These provisions are:

1. To ensure true public ownership of an equity trust, it must have at least 100 shareholders, and no more than 50 percent of its outstanding shares can be owned by five persons or fewer.
2. At least 75 percent of the gross income of the equity trust must come from real estate.
3. An equity trust cannot directly manage any property that it owns. This provision is designed to prevent the small individual shareholder from being victimized by a professional management group. Any group that managed the property could, by clever manipulation, milk it and pay the individual shareholder little or nothing.
4. An equity trust cannot deal exclusively in land development or land sales, for this could result in zero income.
5. An equity trust must have shares that can be freely transferred. This provision is designed to keep the investment liquid. That is, the shareholder can cash out any time as with shares of any other publicly held corporation.

Some Notes of Caution. Despite the protection provided by law, the investor should realize that the success of a REIT rests with its management. The prospective shareholder of a REIT should be sure that the following conditions exist:

1. That no more than 10 percent of the money invested by the shareholders can accrue to the promoters of the REIT. That is, 90 percent of all money received should go into actual investment in real estate properties.
2. That the management has long and successful experience in real estate investments.
3. That management personnel have proven business ability and integrity.
4. That accounting practices of the REIT conform to approved procedures.
5. That leverage—which we have seen to be a very useful tool in pyramiding profit—is used with restraint. The REIT should be allowed to borrow, according to its official prospectus, only a reasonable percentage of the total property values.

Advantages. The equity real estate investment trust has the same tax advantages that are available to the individual taxpayer. This is, the trust takes tax deductions for mortgage interest, property taxes, and depreciation that are so important in minimizing the tax implications of real estate.

Disadvantages. Like all investments, equity real estate investment trusts have disadvantages as well as advantages. Since they must distribute 95 percent of their investment income to their shareholders in order not to be subject to the corporation tax, very little money is left for improvements. Furthermore, some of them have experi-

enced management difficulties. For example, some trusts have purchased properties that were too optimistically appraised. Or some properties have had unusually high vacancies, thus making it difficult for management to meet fixed charges and operating expenses, much less provide a return to the investors.

Mortgage Trusts

The **mortgage real estate investment trust** invests exclusively in mortgages. Instead of buying existing large apartment houses, office buildings, and commercial and residential complexes, mortgage REITs loan money to others who plan to build them.

The best way to evaluate the success of a mortgage REIT is to look at its loan record. If its trend of loan commitments and funds advanced to builders and real estate developers is rising over a period of time, this is favorable because it demonstrates that the trust is generating new mortgages faster than it is retiring old loans.

Unfortunately, mortgage REITs had a dismal record in the first half of the 1970s. They loaned money to big residential and commercial developers who were caught in the squeeze of high interest rates, spiraling costs, and inflation. Many of these developers went bankrupt and handed back to the mortgage REITs partially developed and overfinanced properties that were badly in debt. Some investors in mortgage REITs saw their investment drastically decline in value. Others who wanted to redeem their shares could not. And some investors were unlucky enough not to receive even interest on their money. In the late 1980s, mortgage REITs are suffering the same problems.

SUMMARY

The purchase of a home or a condominium should never be undertaken lightly. For many people it is the largest single investment they will make in their lifetime. If the two tax advantages of ownership were more

widely understood, more people might be inclined to buy a home or condominium instead of renting one.

Real estate is also purchased for income and profit. It has great attraction as an investment because it is a tangible piece of property. When buying income-producing real estate, leverage should be used to increase both income and profit. When leverage is employed, time can be telescoped and wealth accumulated faster than by most other methods.

For those who don't want to trust their own judgment, there are other ways to invest in commercial real estate that provide diversification and professional management. If you can meet the financial suitability standards, the best way to invest is in a real estate limited partnership that meets your objectives. For those with small amounts of money to invest and who need to obtain the liquidity of a common stock, the best way to invest is in a REIT.

5

REVIEW QUESTIONS
SHORT ESSAY

Name _____

Date _____ Points _____

Directions: Answer the following questions according to your instructor's directions.

1. In your own words, define real estate.

_____

_____

_____

2. When buying an existing older home, there are four basic rules to follow. Briefly explain three of them.

a. _____

_____

b. _____

_____

c. _____

_____

3. List four common complaints of home buyers.

a. _____

b. _____

c. _____

d. _____

4. Why are people with low incomes more likely to obtain a home mortgage if they can qualify for a loan with the FHA?

_____

_____

_____

5. Transferring title to property is an involved process. In your opinion, what is the most important document?

_____

_____

_____

6. Why does real estate have such great attraction as an investment, besides its profit potential?

_____

_____

_____

7. When are second mortgages most commonly used?

_____

_____

_____

8. Name the financial suitability standards required by most states for investment in real estate limited partnerships.

_____

_____

9. What are the two major disadvantages of equity real estate investment trusts?

a. _____

b. _____

10. In your own words, define an equity REIT.

_____

_____

_____

_____

Name _____

Date _____ Points _____

5

REVIEW QUESTIONS
MULTIPLE CHOICE

Directions: For each of the following, select the best answer and place the letter that represents it in the Answers column.

ANSWERS

1. The function of the FHA in the home mortgage market is to
   a. loan money.
   b. insure mortgages.
   c. protect veterans from foreclosure.
   d. supply an office where home buyers can make applications for loans. _____
2. The maximum down payment on an FHA-insured loan is
   a. $10,000.
   b. $15,000.
   c. $25,000.
   d. $36,000. _____
3. Transferring title to real estate in most states is arranged by
   a. an abstract company.
   b. a title company.
   c. an attorney.
   d. the individual buyer and seller. _____
4. One of the following is an important tax advantage for a home owner:
   a. depreciation of the building.
   b. depreciation of the land and building.
   c. fully deductible closing costs.
   d. fully deductible property taxes. _____
5. When buying a condominium, the most important document is the
   a. regulatory agreement.
   b. enabling declaration.
   c. information bulletin.
   d. subscription agreement. _____
6. Leverage is defined as
   a. borrowing money.
   b. loaning money.
   c. investing money.
   d. losing money. _____
7. A commonly used clause in rental leases that protects the landlord is
   a. the requirement of a security deposit.
   b. the right to inspect the premises every week.
   c. the right to remove immediately the tenant's personal property when the tenant abandons the premises.
   d. the right to prevent a tenant from moving personal property because the tenant owes back rent. _____

8. An investor's main objective in a real estate private placement limited partnership is
   a. a long-term profit on the investment.
   b. profit.
   c. reliability of the general partners.
   d. capital gain.

9. Real estate professionals employ the principle of
   a. value-added strategy.
   b. investing only in residential property.
   c. investing only in commercial property.
   d. combining ownership and management.

10. In most states, the financial suitability standards for real estate limited partnerships are
    a. $100,000.
    b. $200,000.
    c. $30,000 net worth and $30,000 net income.
    d. $40,000 net worth.

11. The small investor likes real estate investment trusts (REITs) because
    a. there are no financial suitability standards.
    b. they are not liquid like stocks.
    c. they are not publicly traded.
    d. they own only large apartment houses.

12. The equity REITs became popular again in 1960 because
    a. states passed favorable legislation.
    b. the conduit theory was applied to their income.
    c. Congress ruled that they are corporations.
    d. they could directly manage any property they owned.

13. An equity REIT should use leverage
    a. whenever possible to increase profits.
    b. with restraint.
    c. not at all, since it is investing other people's money.
    d. at the rate of 50 percent.

14. It could truthfully be said of mortgage real estate investment trusts that they
    a. invest exclusively in mortgages.
    b. buy property.
    c. loan money to builders and developers.
    d. had an excellent record in the early 1970s.

15. In limited partnerships, the limited partners are
    a. nonpassive investors.
    b. not subject to additional assessments.
    c. actively engaged in the business.
    d. none of the above.

5

REVIEW QUESTIONS
TRUE-FALSE

Name _____

Date _____ Points _____

Directions: Circle T or F to indicate whether each statement is true or false.

1. Every year approximately one million Americans buy a home for the first time.   **T F**

2. The median price of a home in the United States today is over $80,000.   **T F**

3. The total carrying charges of a home should be related to the buyer's income.   **T F**

4. Before buying a new home, a person should check the lot size and setting.   **T F**

5. Over 95 percent of the conventional home mortgage money in the United States is provided by savings and loan associations.   **T F**

6. The U.S. Supreme Court has ruled that loans issued by federal savings and loan institutions may be assumed.   **T F**

7. When buying property, the professional wants a net income.   **T F**

8. In transferring title to property, a title search should always be made.   **T F**

9. In states where an attorney handles the transfer of title to property, an escrow fee must be paid.   **T F**

10. Property taxes and insurance that are paid by the month at the insistence of the lender are called impound accounts.   **T F**

11. When buying a condominium, you don't pay your own taxes.   **T F**

12. You should read the enabling declaration of a condominium project before you sign a sales contract.   **T F**

13. A condominium owner shares the common areas with the other owners.   **T F**

14. A person's objective when buying a home is the same as when buying a house for investment.   **T F**

15. A real estate investor can make money faster by paying cash instead of borrowing.   **T F**

16. Banks are a source of conventional mortgages on income-producing residential property.   T   F

17. Second mortgages are for a short time and have low interest rates.   T   F

18. Landlord-tenant relationships can create countless problems.   T   F

19. A tax escalation clause in a lease allows automatic rent increases if property taxes go up.   T   F

20. Clauses that protect the tenant are included in leases.   T   F

21. A limited partner is fully active in the business of the partnership.   T   F

22. None of the income from a mini-warehouse limited partnership is tax sheltered.   T   F

23. The concept of the equity real estate trust originated within the past 50 years.   T   F

24. A successful mortgage REIT should be able to generate new mortgages faster than it is retiring old loans.   T   F

25. The objectives of a limited partnership are stated in the official prospectus.

5

PROJECT

Name _____

Date _____ Points _____

Mary and Tom Baldwin have received an unexpected windfall. Mary's first cousin died and left $75,000 to Mary as her only living relative. Mary and Tom have decided to invest this money in residential income-producing property.

In this project you are to answer the following questions to help them make the right decisions. (Use the space below and on the back of this page, if necessary.)

1. Should they look for a small house and pay all cash for it? Or should they buy a larger house and use leverage?

2. If they decide to borrow, should they have the seller agree to take back a second mortgage?

3. Since they are buying rental property and will have tenants, what additional information will they need from the seller on the closing date?

CHAPTER 6
OUTLINE

I. **THE AUCTION MARKET**
   A. New York Stock Exchange
      1. A Brief Background
      2. Membership
      3. Listing Requirements
   B. American Stock Exchange
      1. A Brief Background
      2. Listing Requirements
   C. Regional Stock Exchanges
   D. Stock Exchange Trading Procedures
      1. How Stocks Are Traded at the NYSE
      2. Ways of Purchasing Stock
      3. Commodity Futures Trading
      4. Trading in Stock Index Futures
      5. Commissions
   E. Delivery, Registration, and Transfer of Stocks
      1. Confirmation of Transaction
      2. Registration of Stocks
      3. Transfer of Stock

II. **THE OVER-THE-COUNTER (NEGOTIATED) MARKET**
   A. An Overview
   B. Marketing New Issues
      1. Role of the Investment Banker
      2. Methods of Underwriting Securities

6

SECURITIES MARKETS

Stocks and bonds are bought and sold in two types of markets: (1) the auction market and (2) the negotiated market, more commonly known as the over-the-counter (OTC) market. The **auction market** consists of organized stock exchanges, which provide central marketplaces where orders from all over the country to buy or sell securities can be executed in a matter of minutes. These stock exchanges neither buy nor sell securities themselves. They merely provide the place for their members to do so.

The **negotiated market**, or **over-the-counter (OTC) market**, operates outside the organized exchanges and does not provide established locations where business may be transacted. The OTC market is composed of a large number of small broker/dealers who operate computer terminals that enable them to communicate with one another. By this method they can quickly buy or sell.

All stocks and bonds not traded in the auction market are bought and sold in the OTC market. In addition, all new issues and mutual funds are traded in the OTC market. But, despite the larger number of securities that are traded in the OTC market, the auction market is by far the more important of the two.

THE AUCTION MARKET

There are two national stock exchanges and seven regional stock exchanges that comprise the auction market. The two national stock exchanges are the New York Stock Exchange (NYSE), sometimes referred to as the **Big Board**, and the American Stock Exchange (AMEX), formerly called the **Curb Exchange**. Of the seven regional stock exchanges, the best known are the Philadelphia-Baltimore-Washington (PBW) Stock Exchange, based in Philadelphia; the Midwest Stock Exchange, based in Chicago; and the Pacific Stock Exchange, based in San Francisco.

NEW YORK STOCK EXCHANGE

The New York Stock Exchange is the largest and most important security exchange in the world. The securities that are traded on it are referred to as "NYSE-listed." Stocks of the leading business corporations in practically every field of endeavor, which represent the core of our national economy, are listed there. Although the NYSE-listed companies comprise only about .1 percent of all U.S. corporations that file tax reports with the U.S. Treasury, they consistently account for approximately 70 percent of all corporate income in the United States. The 50 leading stocks in market value shown in Table 6-1 are all NYSE-listed. The total market value of these securities at the end of 1987 was $2.2 trillion, and the dividends paid in 1987 rose to a record $84.4 billion.

A Brief Background

When the United States was a young nation, it was in need of vast sums of money to finance industrial expansion. Iron ore and copper had to be discovered and mined, steel mills had to be founded, and railroads and

TABLE 6-1 Fifty Leading Stocks in Market Value (In Millions as of December 31, 1987)

Company	Listed Shares	Market Value
International Business Machines	615.7	$ 71,195
Exxon Corp.	1,812.8	69,338
General Electric	926.6	41,000
American Telephone & Telegraph	1,073.8	29,127
Merck & Co.	151.8	24,067
du Pont de Nemours	240.8	21,039
Morris (Philip)	239.6	20,487
General Motors	320.5	19,668
Dow Chemical	216.1	19,503
Ford Motor	247.8	18,710
Amoco Corp.	269.5	18,626
Eastman Kodak	374.8	18,366
BellSouth Corp.	485.9	17,673
Digital Equipment	130.2	17,574
Mobil Corp.	432.7	16,930
Coca-Cola Co.	415.3	15,833
Minnesota Mining & Manufacturing	236.0	15,193
Atlantic Richfield	217.7	15,078
Hewlett-Packard	258.8	15,077
Wal-Mart Stores	562.5	14,695
Procter & Gamble	169.6	14,479
Johnson & Johnson	191.9	14,413
Chevron Corp.	342.1	13,556
NYNEX Corp.	204.4	13,131
Bell Atlantic	199.7	12,984
Sears, Roebuck	382.8	12,872
American Information Technologies (Ameritech)	146.9	12,432
American Home Products	169.0	12,296
GTE Corp.	339.7	12,061
Bristol-Myers	284.0	11,823
Pacific Telesis	432.1	11,504
Eli Lilly	146.0	11,389
Abbott Laboratories	231.9	11,132
RJR Nabisco	242.6	10,917
Royal Dutch Petroleum	96.3	10,778
American International Group	173.3	10,400
Southwestern Bell	300.9	10,343
Texaco Inc.	274.3	10,252
Anheuser-Busch	301.7	10,070
American Express	434.7	9,943
US WEST	193.2	9,879
PepsiCo, Inc.	287.5	9,596
McDonald's Corp.	208.8	9,188
Westinghouse Electric	183.4	9,122
Schlumberger Ltd.	303.4	8,762
Santa Fe Southern Pacific	189.6	8,721
Dun & Bradstreet Corp.	153.3	8,391
Emerson Electric	239.1	8,368
Waste Management	219.9	8,274
Kellogg Co.	153.7	8,050
Total	16,424.7	$824,305

factories had to be built. Since private financing and the banks could not supply the huge amounts of capital required for industrial expansion, the young, burgeoning companies either offered partial ownership in the form of common stock or sold bonds to willing investors. As a result, the need arose to have a central marketplace where investors could buy and sell stocks and bonds, which represented the money they had invested in these businesses.

On May 17, 1792, a group of 24 far-seeing businesspeople and auctioneers agreed to meet at the same time every day under an old buttonwood tree on Wall Street to handle the public's orders in stock and bonds. The following year they moved their meeting place to the Tontine Coffee House, which had just been built. Thus was born the New York Stock Exchange. Even though its location was changed a dozen times during the first half of the nineteenth century, the NYSE never moved very far away from Wall Street in New York.

Membership

A member of the NYSE is said to hold a "seat" on the exchange. Since 1953, the number of seats at the NYSE has remained constant at 1,366. The record price paid for a seat was $1,150,000 on September 21, 1987; the lowest was $17,000 in 1942. From this you can see that opportunities for holding a seat on the exchange can be quite limited.

About one-half of the 1,366 members are partners or officers of **brokerage houses**, also called **commission houses**, that do business with the general public. These members execute customers' orders to buy and sell securities on the floor of the exchange. The firms they represent receive the commissions from these transactions.

All members of the NYSE are classified according to function as specialists, odd-lot brokers, floor traders, or registered traders. **Specialists** are those whose job is to maintain a fair and orderly market in certain stocks assigned to them, sometimes risking their own capital to do so. **Odd-lot brokers** serve those investors who buy only a few shares at a time instead of the conventional

round-lot trading unit of 100 shares. The function of **floor traders** is to assist the various commission houses in their transactions, for a member who represents a commission house cannot be at two or three trading posts at the same time. The **registered traders** are those who trade strictly for their own accounts.

Listing Requirements

A company can qualify to be listed on the New York Stock Exchange if it meets certain stringent listing requirements. While each case is decided on its own merits, the NYSE generally requires the following minimum qualifications:

1. A demonstrated earning power, under competitive conditions, of $2½ million before federal income taxes for the most recent year and $2 million pretax income for each of the preceding two years.
2. Net tangible assets of $18 million, although the NYSE puts greater emphasis on the aggregate market value of the common stock.
3. A total of $18 million in market value of publicly held common stock.
4. A total of 1,000,000 common shares publicly held.
5. At least 2,000 shareholders, each of whom owns 100 shares or more.

The listing agreement between a company and the NYSE is designed to provide timely disclosure to the public of earnings statements, dividend notices, and other information that might reasonably be expected to affect materially the market for securities. As a matter of general policy, the NYSE has for many years refused to list nonvoting common stocks. That is, all listed common stocks must have the right to vote.

AMERICAN STOCK EXCHANGE

The American Stock Exchange (AMEX) is not as big as the New York Stock Exchange. Its share of the trading volume of all the U.S. exchanges is 9.1 percent. Out of all the securities listed for trading on the AMEX, only a few represent very large companies. For the most part, the companies listed on AMEX are hardly "household" names such as those listed on the Big Board.

Traditionally the AMEX has been a marketplace for fairly new companies. As one former AMEX president aptly said, "It's a marketplace where new chips can grow into blue chips." Of today's largest U.S. corporations, for example, no fewer than 47 were at one time traded on the AMEX. Among them were Cities Service, Dow Chemical, DuPont, Goodyear, Gulf Oil, Procter & Gamble, RCA, and Standard Oil of California. Thus, the major role of the AMEX is to provide a marketplace for stocks of relatively small and new companies in order to help them grow bigger.

A Brief Background

The American Stock Exchange was formed about the time of the gold rush in California in 1849 (the exact year is not known). Until the 1920s it was known as the Curb Exchange because for almost 70 years, transactions took place on the curb at Trinity Place in New York. Its members had to be a robust lot since transactions on the Curb Exchange were executed outside every day despite the vagaries of the weather! Finally, in 1921 the Curb Exchange moved into a building constructed at 86 Trinity Place.

Listing Requirements

The listing requirements of the AMEX are not as stringent as those of the Big Board. However, the AMEX still sets forth strict guidelines that a company must follow to maintain a continued listing of its common-stock issues. The minimum requirements for original listing on the AMEX are:

1. Stockholders' equity of $4 million.
2. A net pretax income of $750,000.
3. The amount of publicly held shares and the number of shareholders to be as follows:
   a. 500,000 shares and 800 owners.
   b. 500,000 shares and 400 owners with an average daily volume of 2,000,000 shares.
   c. 1,000,000 shares and 400 owners.[1]

REGIONAL STOCK EXCHANGES

The seven regional stock exchanges are:

1. Boston Stock Exchange.
2. Philadelphia-Baltimore-Washington Stock Exchange.
3. Cincinnati Stock Exchange.
4. Midwest Stock Exchange.
5. Intermountain Stock Exchange.
6. Spokane Stock Exchange.
7. Pacific Stock Exchange.

The basic function of the regional stock exchanges is to provide a marketplace for the securities of firms that are simply not big enough to qualify for listing on either of the national stock exchanges. Such firms are for the most part of local importance. They are of vital interest to the thousands of investors who reside in the geographic region where these corporations are headquartered.

Listed stocks on the Big Board and the AMEX, however, are also traded on the floors of the regional stock exchanges. Due to the time difference between New York and the rest of the country, one-half of the regional stock exchanges actually stay open after the Big Board and the AMEX have closed for the day.

STOCK EXCHANGE TRADING PROCEDURES

To an investor, the purchase or sale of a security is simplicity itself. A visit or phone call to one's broker to place an order to buy or sell is all that is necessary. In a surprisingly short time the broker can call the investor and quote the exact price at which the order was bought or sold. The machinery by which such a trade is made possible, however, is enormously complex. It includes not only the exchange's far-flung and instantaneous communications network but also a system of operation on the trading floor that functions with amazing speed and precision.

How Stocks Are Traded at the NYSE

Assume that Dr. Isabel Leon, who lives in Columbus, Indiana, wants to buy 100 shares of American Telephone and Telegraph. She contacts her stockbroker and places an order to buy 100 shares of AT&T after finding out that its last trading price was $30. The stockbroker wires the order to the New York office of the firm she or he represents, where it is in turn telephoned to the firm's member on the floor of the exchange. The member immediately hurries over to the post where AT&T is traded and calls out, "How's Telephone?" Someone— usually the specialist in the stock—replies with the current price.

At approximately the same time that Dr. Leon places the order to buy, Carl Edwards, a merchant living in Kalamazoo, Michigan, decides to sell his 100 shares of AT&T. He telephones his stockbroker accordingly. When the order to sell reaches the exchange in New York, another member hurries to the AT&T trading post where the member in charge of Dr. Leon's order happens to be.

At this point both brokers make a split-second decision and exercise the knowledge and skill required to obtain the best price for their customers. Assume that they agree on a price of 30⅛. When Dr. Leon's broker bids out loud, "Thirty and one-eighth" and Mr. Edward's broker replies, "Sold at thirty and one-eighth," the deal is made. Then a computer card is made out and is scanned by an optical reader. Immediately the news that 100 shares of AT&T just sold at 30⅛ is transmitted electronically to 6,246 sales offices of exchange members throughout the 50 states.

Ways of Purchasing Stock

There are many ways in which investors may purchase stock through their stockbrokers. Each of these ways is described below.

Round-Lot Order. As mentioned earlier, the conventional trading unit is for 100 shares, which is a **round-lot order**.

Market Order. When placing a **market order**, the investor instructs the broker to obtain the best price when the order reaches the floor of the exchange. The "best" price may be the last price quoted by the investor's broker, or it may be higher or lower.

Odd-Lot Order. An order for less than 100 shares is an **odd-lot order**. The average investor usually places an odd-lot order because he or she does not have enough money to buy 100 shares. For example, to buy 100 shares of a stock that is selling for $40 requires an investment of $4,000, plus the commission. Most people do not have that much money to invest at one time. But because of the small numbers of shares involved, an odd-lot fee is charged for placing odd-lot orders to buy, as well as to sell.

For a stock that is priced *over $50 a share*, the odd-lot fee is *one-fourth of a point* more than the fee for the round-lot price. For a stock that is priced at *$50 or less a share*, the odd-lot fee is *one-eighth of a point* more than the fee for the round-lot price.

Limit Order. A **limit order** specifies the price at which the stock is to be purchased. For example, if a limit order is placed to buy 100 shares of a stock at $40, the order cannot be placed until this price is quoted. This does not mean, however, that the investor will buy the stock at exactly $40 a share. The actual price may be slightly higher, for there is no guarantee that the exact price of $40 can be obtained when the limit order reaches the floor of the exchange. The limit order merely guarantees the investor that the order will not be placed until the market for the stock reaches the price designated.

Fill or Kill Order. The **fill or kill order** is a special kind of limit order. In this case, again the order is to buy at a certain price. However, if the order to buy at that price cannot be executed, it is to be canceled. In other words, fill the order at the price designated or kill it.

Stop Order. A **stop order** is designed to limit losses or protect profits. Assume that you bought a stock at $50 and it is currently quoted at $80. If you are concerned that the stock may drastically go down in price, you enter a stop order to sell it at $70. If the stock does go down to $70, your stop order immediately becomes a market order to sell. Again, this does not mean that you will get $70 for the stock. It only means that your broker will obtain the best possible price, which could be $70 or a price that is somewhat lower should the stock continue to fall before your order can be executed.

GTC Order. A **good-till-canceled (GTC) order** instructs a broker to buy or sell a stock at a certain price, and this order is good until it is canceled.

MIP Order. An **MIP order** is an order to buy shares under the New York Stock Exchange's *monthly investment plan.* This is a plan that enables the small investor to buy a stock on a monthly or quarterly basis. The least amount that can be invested is $40 per quarter. Under the monthly investment plan, all dividends from the stock purchased are automatically reinvested.

Short Sale. Only speculators engage in short sales. In a **short sale,** you sell stock that you do not own. You do this by borrowing the stock from someone else—usually a broker—and agreeing to sell it back to the same person at a later date. If the price of the stock goes down, you buy the shares that you borrowed at a lower price and make a profit. If the stock goes up in price, however, you will have lost the amount that it has increased in value, plus the interest charges on the loan of the stock.

Buying on Margin. The investor who buys stocks on margin is using leverage in order to buy more shares than she or he would be able to purchase otherwise. **Buying on margin** means paying for only a part of the total price and borrowing the balance from one's broker or a bank under the current margin requirements determined by the Federal Reserve Board.

For example, assume that you want to buy 100 shares of a stock that is selling for $50 a share. Normally this would require a cash outlay of $5,000. If you do not want to pay $5,000 in cash and the current margin requirement is 70 percent, you have to pay in cash only 70 percent of $5,000, or $3,500. This is called a 70 percent margin account.

The amount of margin required by law changes from time to time. It may be 50 percent or 70 percent. Under some circumstances it may be 100 percent, in which case buying on margin would not be possible at all. In addition to federal regulations, the New York Stock Exchange will not permit a margin account to be opened with a member firm unless the customer first deposits at least $2,000 in cash or its equivalent in securities.

Put and Call Options. Puts and calls are *options* to buy or sell stock at some later date. As is the case with any option, if you do not exercise your option to buy or sell the stock by the date specified—usually six months or less—you lose your option money, which is 10 percent of the market price.

A **put** is an option to *sell* a stock at a certain price within a specified time. Assume that you buy a put option of 100 shares of General Motors at $80 a share, with the option expiring in six months. The total market price for the 100 shares is $8,000. However, since you are buying an option to sell the stock six months later, *not* now, you pay only 10 percent of the market price, or $800. If six months later General Motors stock is selling for $60, you buy 100 shares at $60 and then exercise your option to sell at $80, thereby making a gross profit of $20 × 100, or $2,000. To arrive at your net profit, you would have to deduct the following items: the cost of your option, $800; the cost of buying and selling the 100 shares; and the taxes involved.

On the other hand, if the price of General Motors stock had gone up, you would not exercise your put option. All you would have lost was your option money of $800.

A **call** is an option to *buy* a stock at a certain price within a specified date. It is the opposite of a put option. If the price of the stock goes up, you exercise your call option. If the price goes down, you do not. Again, if you do not exercise your option, all you lose is your option money.

Commodity Futures Trading

Trading in *commodity futures* is a form of speculation because you are gambling that the price of a certain commodity (such as corn, wheat, gold, copper, etc.) will go up or down within a stated period of time. You buy a *futures contract*, which fixes the price of the commodity today for delivery, say, three months later. If the price of the commodity, for instance wheat, goes up by the delivery date, you will make money; if it goes down, you will lose money.

Actually, in the above example no wheat changes hands because the purpose of such trading is solely to make money on future price changes. The commodity futures market exists primarily for sound business reasons. Again, using wheat as the example, the farmer, the baker, and the middleman all are interested in stabilizing the price of wheat. This is accomplished by setting the price in advance on the commodity exchanges.

Trading in Stock Index Futures

Trading in *stock index futures* is just like trading in commodity futures except that the item traded is a stock index, such as the Standard & Poor's Index of 500 Common Stocks. Some investors think that this is a better way to invest in the market than buying individual stocks. When buying a certain stock, you and your broker have to make an exhaustive investigation. And even if you buy that stock for sound economic reasons, something unforeseen can happen to that company, such as an unfavorable change in management, an unexpected drop in earnings, etc. But if you are convinced that the broad trend of the market will be up over the next few months, you can buy a futures contract on a stock index instead.

Commissions

On May 1, 1975, the long-established policy of setting the minimum commission that New York Stock Exchange members could charge their customers was ended by an edict of the Securities and Exchange Commission. The investor can now shop among several brokerage houses to obtain the lowest commission rate.

Under the old minimum commission rule, the small investor quite often was carried on the books of the brokers at a loss. When the negotiated commission rule went into effect, it was inevitable that the small investor would pay higher commissions than the big investor. It also became obvious very soon after May 1, 1975, that a negotiated commission on every transaction was virtually impossible. Therefore, after some trial and error, brokerage houses began to establish their own commission schedules. And due to competition, commission schedules among various brokerage houses have become similar in many respects.

The negotiated commission rule of May 1, 1975, resulted in the establishment of firms that offer cut-rate commissions to execute their customers' orders. These brokers are strictly order-takers. They make no attempt to "sell" stocks or to give research information and advice. They offer cut-rate commissions to investors who want a service without any frills, much as gas stations offer a savings to customers who use their self-service islands.

The cut-rate brokers are not for everybody. There will always be those investors who want full service. But for experienced investors who make their own decisions, the cut-rate firms do offer considerable savings in commissions.

DELIVERY, REGISTRATION, AND TRANSFER OF STOCKS

When securites are bought or sold, stockbrokerage firms send a confirmation of the transaction to the customer. In addition, either stock certificates must be registered in the name of the customer on the books of the company or their ownership must be transferred from one customer to another. Each of these procedures is described below.

Confirmation of Transaction

The confirmation slip sent by the stockbrokerage firm to the customer contains the following information:

1. What securities were bought or sold.
2. The number of shares.
3. The price per share.
4. The commission charged.
5. The net amount owed the customer if the transaction was a sale, plus state tax, if any, and the registration fee.
6. The net amount the customer owes the firm if the transaction was a purchase.
7. The trade date and the due date.

A sample confirmation of the sale of 1,000 shares of Tandy Corporation is shown in Figure 6-1.

Trade Date.   The **trade date** is the date on which the transaction takes place. If the transaction is a sale, the firm must pay the customer the new amount of the sale within five business days following the trade date. The customer, on the other hand, must deliver the stock certificate for the shares to the stockbroker within five business days following the trade date. Failure to do so subjects the customer to a premium charge. If the transaction is a purchase, the customer must pay for the stock within five business days following the trade date.

Due Date.   The **due date** is five business days after the trade date. Saturdays and Sundays are not considered business days. Therefore, if the trade date falls on Friday, October 15, the due date becomes Friday, October 22. If the transaction is a sale, the brokerage firm mails a check to the customer on the due date unless the customer instructs the registered representative of the firm to do otherwise. For example, the customer may desire to pick up the check personally or to have the amount held in his or her account.

Registration of Stocks

A **registrar** is a bank whose duty it is to register the stock in the name of the customer on the books of the company. The registrar also maintains an up-to-date list, or register, of all owners of the company's stock, for it is from this list that dividends are mailed to the shareholders. The registration of stocks is important to the customer because of four important dates that are related to a declaration of dividends by the company's board of directors. These dates are:

FIGURE 6-1 Sample Confirmation of Sale

Through the courtesy of
SENTRA SECURITIES CORPORATION
1455 FRAZEE ROAD - 6TH FLOOR
SAN DIEGO, CA. 92108
TEL. 619-296-5885

WE CONFIRM THE FOLLOWING TRANSACTION SUBJECT TO THE AGREEMENT ON THE REVERSE SIDE HEREOF

ACCOUNT NUMBER	TRADE DATE	DATE DUE		PRICE	AMOUNT	INT. OR STATE TAX	POST/REG. FEE	CHARGE OR MARK-UP/DOWN	NET AMOUNT
47K13851	101287	101987	8	51 3/8	1541250		252	8880	1532168

QUANTITY		SECURITY DESCRIPTION		CODE
YOU BOUGHT OR YOU SOLD				
SLD	300	TANDY CORPORATION		

FORM 1099-B SUBSTITUTE
WILL BUY MONEY MKT FUND AS REQUESTED SUBJECT TO FUND REGULATIONS

JOHN BARNES
1532 EDGEWOOD DR
PALO ALTO CA   94303

IF YOU HAVE MOVED OR PLAN TO MOVE, NOTIFY YOUR REGISTERED REPRESENTATIVE OF YOUR NEW ADDRESS

562-26-3012
73429 875382103
0227   30438

AN AFFILIATED CORPORATION OF BROADCORT CAPITAL CORP. TRADES FOR ITS OWN ACCOUNT AS A BLOCK POSITIONER AND/OR ARBITRAGEUR AND AT THE TIME OF YOUR TRANSACTION IT MAY HAVE HAD EITHER A LONG OR SHORT POSITION IN THIS SECURITY WHICH MAY HAVE BEEN PARTIALLY OR COMPLETELY HEDGED. ACCOUNT CARRIED BY BROADCORT CAPITAL CORP., BOX 150 CHURCH STREET STATION, NEW YORK, NY 10008.

PLEASE WRITE YOUR ACCOUNT NUMBER SHOWN ABOVE ON THE FACE OF YOUR CHECK, MONEY ORDER OR CORRESPONDENCE.

BROADCORT CAPITAL CORP. HAS ACTED AS CLEARING AGENT FOR YOUR BROKER. THE SYMBOL EXPLANATION ON THE REVERSE SIDE INDICATES THE CAPACITY IN WHICH YOUR BROKER ACTED.

PAYMENT FOR SECURITIES PURCHASED OR DELIVERY OF SECURITIES SOLD BY YOU ARE DUE ON SETTLEMENT DATE ("DATE DUE" AS INDICATED ABOVE). IF THIS TRANSACTION IS A SALE AND THE SECURITIES ARE NOT ALREADY IN OUR POSSESSION AND DO NOT REPRESENT A SHORT SALE, PLEASE FORWARD THEM IMMEDIATELY TO AVOID POSSIBLE PAYMENT OF PREMIUM ON SECURITIES BORROWED. PLEASE PRESERVE THIS CONFIRMATION FOR INCOME TAX PURPOSES.

A CORPORATION, AFFILIATED WITH BROADCORT CAPITAL CORP. IS A MARKET MAKER AND DEALER FOR ITS OWN ACCOUNT IN ODD LOTS, CONVERTIBLE BONDS, PREFERRED STOCK AND IN TRANSACTIONS EXECUTED ON THE CINCINNATI STOCK EXCHANGE.

1. The *date of declaration* of the dividend by the board of directors.
2. The *date of payment* of the dividends.
3. The **date of record**, which is the date on which all stockholders whose names are registered on the books of the company are entitled to the dividend. The date of record falls between the date of declaration of the dividend and the date of payment. Since a large, publicly held corporation's list of stockholders changes from day to day, it is necessary to declare a date of record so that the registrar will know who is to receive the dividend.
4. The **ex-dividend date**, which is the date on which the stockholders of record will *not* receive the dividend. The ex-dividend date is usually three days before the date of record. It precedes the date of record by a few days in order to allow enough time for stock that was purchased before the ex-dividend date to be recorded in the name of the purchaser by the registrar.

Let us illustrate the importance of the four dates mentioned above. Assume that a dividend is declared by the board of directors on April 1 to be paid May 1 to stockholders of record on April 15. The ex-dividend date would be April 12. Investors who buy the stock on April 11 are entitled to receive the dividend that will be paid on May 1; those who buy the stock on April 12 will not receive the dividend. But those who buy on April 12 will have been sufficiently notified because on that day the stock will be quoted with an "x" following the dividend figure. The "x" means that the stock went ex-dividend that day.

Actually, nobody loses in an ex-dividend situation because the stock's price on the ex-dividend date drops by the amount of the dividend payment. For example, assume that the stock in the above example is quoted at $20.25 a share before the ex-dividend date and the amount of the dividend to be paid is 25¢ a share. The investor who buys one share on April 11 for $20.25 would receive the 25¢ dividend on May 1. The investor who buys one share on April 12, the ex-dividend date, would not receive the dividend but would buy the share for 25¢ less, or $20.00. From an income tax standpoint, it is better to buy the stock ex-dividend and not have to report anything to the IRS until the stock is sold than to receive the dividend and have to pay a tax on it now.

Transfer of Stock

Sometimes a stock that belongs to a registered owner is sold, given away, or inherited. The duty of transferring registration of a stock from one customer to another belongs to the **transfer agent**, the bank that is listed on the face of the stock certificate. The necessary documents required to transfer the stock to the name of someone else can be obtained from the transfer agent.

THE OVER-THE-COUNTER (NEGOTIATED) MARKET

As mentioned earlier in this chapter, all stocks not traded on the exchanges, as well as all new issues and mutual funds, are traded over the counter (OTC). In sheer numbers this is a huge market, four or five times larger than the number of issues traded on the stock exchanges. At the end of 1987, the total market value of these securities was $342.9 billion.[2] Moreover, many stocks that are listed on the exchanges are also traded over the counter in what is called the Third Market. The **Third Market** is largely the result of the buying and selling of huge blocks of listed securities by institutional investors through broker/dealers who are not members of any of the stock exchanges.

The National Association of Securities Dealers Automated Quotations is popularly known by its acronym, NASDAQ (pronounced Naz-dak). As a self-regulating body of the OTC securities business, NASD is more fully discussed in Chapter 9. In this chapter, suffice it to say that NASDAQ has greatly improved conditions in the OTC market by providing instant quotations on unlisted stocks. That is, a registered representative now can obtain the latest quotation on hundreds of OTC stocks by simply punching the OTC button on the same computer that is utilized to obtain prices on listed stocks, and then punching the appropriate stock symbol.

AN OVERVIEW

The individual broker/dealer is the backbone of the over-the-counter securities market. A dealer in securities is a merchant whose commodity consists of stocks and bonds. Some dealers are firms that operate nationwide. Others are very small and local in scope. And there are some who confine their activity to buying and selling among other dealers, thus never dealing with the general public at all.

The OTC (or negotiated) market used to be a mysterious and little known market. Unlike the auction market, the negotiated market never has had, nor does it have today, a central trading place. Quotations in the OTC market not only were difficult to obtain but also were suspect as to their validity regarding the lowest price at which a security could be purchased or sold. Too frequently in the past, these conditions—and the lack of any central source of information—resulted in panic selling of OTC stocks in a bear market. Such panic selling was one of the causes of the very severe market break in OTC stocks in April and May of 1970. All these conditions, however, have changed with the advent of NASDAQ and the computer.

There is no question that the computer has drastically changed business methods of operating many lines of endeavor. This is particularly marked in the operations of the OTC market. Before the advent of the computer, dealers in the OTC market communicated with one another through a vast network of telegraph, teletype, and telephone systems in a language that was all their own. Today they sit in front of computers and obtain the best market price on thousands of OTC stocks by the simple act of pushing a button. They not only find out the best market price but also know who is quoting that price. Thus, as far as the general public is concerned, much of the mystery of OTC operations has been eliminated. This has resulted in greater trading by the average investor in the over-the-counter market.

MARKETING NEW ISSUES

New issues are securities (stock or bonds) that are offered to the public *for the first time*. Since such securities cannot qualify for listing on any of the stock exchanges, they must be offered to the general public through some channel. Such a channel is the **investment banking institution**, more commonly known (albeit misleadingly) as the **investment banker**.

Role of the Investment Banker

The investment banker is *not* a banker in the sense that this term is commonly used. Rather, it is a securities firm that specializes in obtaining external financing for a corporation in the best possible way. The investment banker acts as a middleman between a corporation that needs to raise capital and the investing public. As such it has a dual role. That is, it acts as an adviser to the corporation and serves as a specialist in the distribution, or **underwriting**, of securities.

Investment Banker as an Adviser. As one who is very closely attuned to the existing money market, the investment banker advises its corporate client on the best way to raise capital at a certain point in time. For example, sometimes it might be better for the corporation to raise the needed capital by floating a bond issue. At other times it might be better to offer preferred or common stock. The majority of new issues that come to market are corporate and municipal bonds. In 1987, there were 189 new bond issues, and the largest was worth $1.6 billion.

Investment Banker as a Distributor.
There are two basic ways for an investment
banker to sell a new issue. These are (1) on a
firm commitment basis and (2) on a best
efforts basis.

Under a **firm commitment basis**, the
investment banker agrees to buy the entire
new issue from the corporation at a set price.
Then it offers these stocks or bonds to the
public at a price that allows for a differen-
tial, or *concession,* from which it derives its
gross profit. The investment banker must
continue to offer the securities at this original price until the entire issue is sold.

In large offerings of a new issue, one
investment banking firm is frequently not
willing to assume the risk of selling the
entire issue. Therefore, this firm might form
an **underwriting syndicate** composed of
other investment bankers. Each member of
the syndicate agrees to underwrite a specific
amount of the new issue. In this case, the
organizer of the syndicate is referred to as
the **principal underwriter**.

If the new issue is unusually large, the
underwriting syndicate itself may feel that it
needs further assistance in selling the entire
issue. The syndicate may then ask the help
of other dealers, who become part of what is
known as a **selling group**. Each of the members of the selling group agrees to *sell* a
specified amount of the new issue. The term
"sell" rather than "underwrite" is used because the member of a selling group does not
assume the same liability as the member of
an underwriting syndicate. That is, a syndicate member must purchase any part of its
allotment that may remain unsold, whereas
a selling group member is not obligated to do
likewise. The selling group member may be

penalized for not selling its allotted share,
but that is all.

The other basic way by which an investment banker will sell a new issue is on a best
efforts basis. A **best efforts commitment**
means that if the entire issue is not sold, the
investment banker's offer is withdrawn. The
best efforts commitment is usually given by
an investment banker when money-market
conditions are unfavorable or when the corporation that is seeking new capital is not
well enough known. Under the best efforts
basis, no stock certificates are issued to
those investors who bought part of the issue.
The money is simply refunded to them if the
entire issue is not sold.

Methods of Underwriting Securities

There are three ways of underwriting,
or distributing, securities in the negotiated
market. When the securities are being offered to the public for the first time, as in the
case of new issues, the distribution is known
as a **primary distribution**. The offering is
a **secondary distribution** when it consists
of a large block of securities that have already been issued and are being offered for
redistribution to others. When the securities
are not being offered to the public at all and
are instead offered directly to an institutional investor, such as a large mutual fund,
the distribution is said to be a **private
placement**. A private placement may or
may not involve the services of an investment banker. Frequently, however, the investment banker is not used in the private
placement of securities.

SUMMARY

There are two markets in which securities
are bought and sold: (1) the auction market
provided by the organized stock exchanges
and (2) the negotiated market provided by
relatively small broker/dealers who deal
mainly in over-the-counter stocks. The auction market, which is dominated by the New

York Stock Exchange, is by far the more
important of the two.

In both the auction market and the OTC
market, there are several types of orders
that an investor can place with a broker. The
normal trading unit to be bought or sold at
the market price is 100 shares, or a round

lot. Many investors, however, do not have enough money to buy 100 shares. When they buy fewer than 100 shares, they are subject to an odd-lot fee that is slightly higher than the fee for buying round lots. Some orders are designed to limit losses or to protect profits. Others are speculative in nature, such as short sales, buying on margin, and puts and calls.

The minimum commission rule adopted by the various stock exchanges was abolished by an edict of the Securities and Exchange Commission on May 1, 1975. On that date negotiated commissions went into effect. Yet the new negotiated commission policy has not done much for the small investor. Actually, the large investor can now buy for less, and the experienced investor can go to cut-rate brokers who offer considerable savings in commissions.

It is important for every stock buyer to understand how delivery, registration, and transfer of stocks are effected. It is also important for investors to know what is meant by the ex-dividend date because this information could be valuable from a tax standpoint.

With the advent of NASDAQ and the computer, the securities business has taken much of the mystery out of the over-the-counter market and has made it easy for a broker/dealer in this market to obtain the best price for her or his customers. The use of the computer in the OTC market has increased investor interest in over-the-counter stocks.

ENDNOTES

1. *Requirements for Original Listing* (New York: American Stock Exchange, 1987), 1.

2. *NASDAQ Fact Book* (Washington, DC: National Association of Securities Dealers, Inc., 1988).

6

REVIEW QUESTIONS
SHORT ESSAY

Name _____

Date _____ Points _____

Directions: Answer the following questions according to your instructor's directions.

1.   What is the major difference between the auction market and the OTC market?

   _____

   _____

   _____

   _____

2.   What are the listing requirements of the New York Stock Exchange in terms of (a) the total market value of publicly held shares and (b) the number of public stockholders who must hold 100 shares or more?

   a. _____

   b. _____

3.   The normal order issued to a stockbroker is a market order. What is (a) a limit order, (b) a stop order, and (c) a GTC order?

   a. _____

   _____

   b. _____

   _____

   c. _____

   _____

4.   What is meant by a 50 percent margin account?

   _____

   _____

5. Why do some investors prefer to buy stock index futures rather than individual stocks?

   _____

   _____

   _____

6. What type of investor is interested in cut-rate commission brokers?

   _____

   _____

7. Identify two important dates that appear on a confirmation of transaction.

   a. _____

   b. _____

8. What is the function of a registrar?

   _____

   _____

   _____

9. What is the function of a selling group member?

   _____

   _____

   _____

10. What does an investment banker mean when it offers to sell a new issue on a "best efforts" basis?

   _____

   _____

   _____

   _____

6

REVIEW QUESTIONS
MULTIPLE CHOICE

Name _____

Date _____ Points _____

Directions: For each of the following, select the best answer and place the letter that represents it in the Answers column.

ANSWERS

1. The two major securities markets in the United States are
   a. the auction market and the national stock exchanges.
   b. the auction market and the over-the-counter market.
   c. the New York Stock Exchange and the American Stock Exchange.
   d. the negotiated market and the over-the-counter market.   _____

2. One of the following securities usually is *not* traded over the counter:
   a. mutual fund shares.
   b. stocks not traded on the exchanges.
   c. new issues.
   d. blue-chip stocks.   _____

3. For a firm to be listed on the NYSE, the market value of its publicly held shares must be
   a. $4 million.
   b. $12 million.
   c. $18 million.
   d. $20 million.   _____

4. The NYSE refuses to list
   a. nonvoting stocks.
   b. common stocks.
   c. preferred stocks.
   d. low-dividend-paying stocks.   _____

5. Of the total volume of transactions on the stock exchanges in 1987, the AMEX accounted for approximately
   a. 5 percent.
   b. 10 percent.
   c. 25 percent.
   d. 40 percent.   _____

6. A market order is an order to buy or sell at
   a. the best price.
   b. the last price quoted.
   c. a fixed price.
   d. any price.   _____

7. A limit order
   a. is good until canceled.
   b. specifies the price of the stock.
   c. has no effect on the price of the stock.
   d. buys stock under the MIP plan.   _____

8. MIP orders are placed through
   a. the New York Stock Exchange.
   b. the American Stock Exchange.

  c. the regional exchanges.

  d. individual broker/dealers. _____

 9. Investors engaged in a short sale sell stock that they

  a. do not own.

  b. bought a short time ago.

  c. bought on margin.

  d. bought in odd lots. _____

10. A call is an option to

  a. buy a stock.

  b. sell a stock.

  c. buy a new issue.

  d. open a margin account. _____

11. The negotiated commission rule means that

  a. all investors should always seek cut-rate brokers.

  b. all investors can shop for the best deal.

  c. small investors would always pay lower commissions than big investors.

  d. all stockbrokers should follow a legally established commission schedule. _____

12. A dividend is declared by the board of directors on September 1 to be paid on October 1 to shareholders of record on September 15. On what date would the stock normally go ex-dividend?

  a. September 12.

  b. September 18.

  c. September 27.

  d. October 1. _____

13. The price of a stock on the ex-dividend date will

  a. decrease by the amount of the dividend.

  b. increase by the amount of the dividend.

  c. remain unchanged.

  d. stabilize. _____

14. It is the duty of a transfer agent to

  a. register owners of the company's stock.

  b. transfer registration of stock from one customer to another.

  c. distribute stock dividends.

  d. send confirmations of transactions to customers. _____

15. One of the following is considered to be the backbone of the OTC market:

  a. the registered representative.

  b. the commission house.

  c. the individual broker/dealer.

  d. NASDAQ. _____

6

REVIEW QUESTIONS
TRUE-FALSE

Name _____

Date _____ Points _____

Directions: Circle T or F to indicate whether each statement is true or false.

ANSWERS

1. A stock exchange does not buy or sell securities.   T   F

2. The negotiated market has a central trading place.   T   F

3. Standard & Poor's Index of 500 Common Stocks is a safe way to invest in the stock market.   T   F

4. The lowest price ever paid for a seat on the NYSE was $27,000.   T   F

5. The top 50 firms whose stock is listed on the NYSE had assets of over $800 billion on December 31, 1987.   T   F

6. A floor trader acts as an assistant to the odd-lot dealer on the trading floor of the NYSE.   T   F

7. The listing agreement of the NYSE requires timely disclosure of earnings statements.   T   F

8. Lesser-known firms are traded on the American Stock Exchange.   T   F

9. The AMEX operated on the curb of a street for 70 years.   T   F

10. There are seven regional stock exchanges.   T   F

11. A fill or kill order is a special kind of limit order.   T   F

12. Buying on margin means using leverage.   T   F

13. An investor would exercise a put option if the price of the stock went up.   T   F

14. The policy of minimum commission was ended by the NYSE in 1972.   T   F

15. Under the negotiated commission rule, the small investor is charged less.   T   F

16. Cut-rate commission brokers are not for everyone.   T   F

17. The trade date is the date an investor pays for stock he or she bought.   T   F

18. A registrar maintains an up-to-date list of all owners of a company's stock and transfers registration from one customer to another.   T F

19. The date of record falls between the date of declaration of the dividend and the date of payment of the dividend.   T F

20. The Third Market is composed of new issues.   T F

21. In the past, lack of a central source of information was one of the causes of panic selling of OTC stocks.   T F

22. Due to NASDAQ, a registered representative can obtain quotations for OTC stock as easily as for those listed on the Big Board.   T F

23. An investment banker underwrites new issues.   T F

24. A member of a selling group assumes more liability than a member of an underwriting syndicate.   T F

25. If a corporation offers securities directly to institutional investors, the offering is a secondary distribution.   T F

6

PROJECT

Name _____

Date _____   Points _____

Mary and Tom Baldwin, with their new-found affluence because of Mary's inheritance, have renewed interest in the stock market and are buying stocks again.

In this project you are to answer the following questions in order to make the Baldwins more knowledgeable about securities markets.

1. The Baldwins have taken losses in buying stocks. Their stockbroker says there is no way to limit these losses. Is this true? Why or why not?

2. They have always been confused by the term *ex-dividend*. Explain what is meant by this term. From a tax standpoint, is it better to buy a stock ex-dividend?

3. They are also considering OTC stocks for the first time because they feel that there is more information about OTC stocks today than there used to be. Are they right or wrong? Why?

CHAPTER 7
OUTLINE

I. **THE BALANCE SHEET**
   A. Assets
   B. Liabilities
   C. Stockholders' Equity

II. **THE INCOME STATEMENT**
   A. Gross Sales (or Revenue)
   B. Expenses
   C. Income Before Taxes
   D. Income Taxes
   E. Net Income (or Net Profit)

III. **VALUABLE INFORMATION FROM FINANCIAL STATEMENTS**
   A. Balance Sheet Ratios
   B. Income Statement Ratios
   C. Other Key Ratios

IV. **CONSOLIDATED FINANCIAL STATEMENTS**

7
UNDERSTANDING FINANCIAL STATEMENTS

Corporations publish annual reports for the benefit of their stockholders. The first annual statement was published at the turn of the century. Today federal law requires disclosure of financial information for the protection of investors.

Annual reports consist of financial statements that summarize business activities and provide other useful information about the company. The data presented in a financial statement has to be comprehended before it becomes meaningful. That is what this chapter is about—helping you to understand financial statements.

There are two major parts of an annual report: (1) the balance sheet and (2) the income statement. The **balance sheet** is simply a listing of what is owned and what is owed by a company as of a specific date. It tells you what the company is worth. The **income statement** is a summary of the income and expenses of the company for a specific period of time, usually a year. It tells you whether or not the company is making money. Obviously, both statements are important to an investor. Is the company making money, and is it worth anything? Certainly a prudent investor would like to know the answers to both questions.

THE BALANCE SHEET

The balance sheet lists the assets and liabilities of a business as of a specific date. It shows on the one hand what the business owns (its *assets*) and on the other hand what it owes (its *liabilities*). There is a peculiar thing about a balance sheet. Assets always equal liabilities. How is this done? In a solvent corporation, liabilities are always less than assets. Therefore, the accountant makes up the difference on the liability side of the ledger by calling this amount *stockholders' equity*. The sheet is now in balance. And, of course, this difference is actually a liability of the corporation. If the corporation were dissolved, it would owe this amount to its owners—the stockholders.

The best way to understand a balance sheet is to use an illustration and then show what information can be obtained from it. The balance sheet of the Aztec Corporation for December 31, 1987, is illustrated in Figure 7-1. Note that the balance sheet follows the basic accounting equation: Assets = Liabilities + Stockholders' Equity. Each part of this equation is discussed below.

ASSETS

Assets are what a business owns. They are divided into current assets and fixed assets.

Current Assets

Assets consisting of cash and other assets that a business can reasonably expect to convert to cash within the space of one year are called **current assets**. The other assets (besides cash) are marketable securities, accounts receivable, and inventories.

FIGURE 7-1 A Balance Sheet

Aztec Corporation Balance Sheet
December 31, 1987

Assets

Current assets:		
Cash	$10,000,000	
Marketable securities	2,000,000	
Accounts receivable	12,000,000	
Inventories	25,000,000	
Total current assets		$ 49,000,000
Fixed assets:		
Buildings	$ 75,000,000	
Machinery and equipment	25,000,000	
	100,000,000	
Less accumulated depreciation	25,000,000	$75,000,000
Land		1,000,000
Total fixed assets		76,000,000
Total assets		$125,000,000

Liabilities

Current liabilities:		
Notes payable to banks	$ 1,000,000	
Accounts payable	6,000,000	
Accrued expenses	1,000,000	
Interest on long-term debt	1,000,000	
Income taxes	3,500,000	
Total current liabilities		$ 12,500,000
Long-term liabilities:		
25-year, 4% debentures		25,000,000
Total liabilities		$ 37,500,000

Stockholders' Equity

Capital stock:		
5% preferred stock (par value $100, authorized 60,000 shares)	$ 6,000,000	
Common stock (par value $10, issued 1,800,000 shares)	18,000,000	
Capital surplus	15,500,000	
Total capital stock	$39,500,000	
Retained earnings	48,000,000	
Total stockholders' equity		$ 87,500,000
Total liabilities and stockholders' equity		$125,000,000

Marketable securities are considered temporary investments because they can be converted readily into cash. They are carried on the books of the business either at cost or, if the market value is less than cost, at their market value.

Accounts receivable are debts incurred by customers of the business as the result of buying merchandise (or paying for a service) on time. Credit granted by a business to its better customers is usually for a period of 30, 60, or 90 days, depending on company policy. In preparing a balance sheet, accounts receivable are reduced to allow for those accounts that are considered doubtful and may default.

The items that comprise **inventories** may consist of raw materials, work in process, supplies, and finished goods ready for sale. A problem arises as to which of two methods of evaluating inventories should be used in order to enter the correct dollar amount on the balance sheet.

Under the **first-in, first-out (FIFO)** method of inventory evaluation, the oldest (or first-in) items in the inventory are assumed to be the first ones sold (or first out). If the inventory has gone up in value and the cost is kept low on the balance sheet, the FIFO method would show a higher profit as the result of sales.

On the other hand, under the **last-in, first-out (LIFO)** method of inventory evaluation, the most recently acquired (or last-in) items in the inventory are assumed to be the first ones sold (or first out). The LIFO method results in a higher unit cost being applied to inventories and results in lower profit from sales.

The LIFO method of inventory evaluation has been widely adopted in recent years because it matches current costs against current income. If sales are costed on the basis of the inventory that was most recently acquired, while the first-in inventory is regarded as unsold, a more conservative approach to computing profit is being used by the company. The LIFO method recognizes that inventory currently being sold as a finished product must, after all, be replaced by raw materials at current prices, *not* at the lower prices at which the raw materials might have been purchased some time ago.

Fixed Assets

Assets that are relatively permanent in nature are called **fixed assets**. They normally consist of buildings, equipment and machinery, and land.

Buildings that are owned by corporations are industrial plants or factories, warehouses, and office buildings for the executives and their staffs. When evaluating

buildings on the balance sheet, their original cost is reduced by the amount of depreciation to which they have been subjected over the years. **Depreciation** is a decline in value caused by usage, passage of time, or obsolescence. The amount of annual depreciation is accumulated over the years; hence it is called **accumulated depreciation** on the balance sheet.

Machinery and equipment used in factories, warehouses, and office buildings are subject (like buildings) to depreciation. On the balance sheet, buildings and machinery and equipment are reduced in value by the amount of their accumulated depreciation.

Land normally increases in value with time. Because of this, it is the one fixed asset that cannot be depreciated by IRS rules. Therefore, land is always carried on the balance sheet at its original cost. This presents a problem to the investor, for there is no way of knowing the true value of this valuable fixed asset, particularly if the land has been owned for many years.

LIABILITIES

A business firm's **liabilities** are what it owes to others. They are either current liabilities or long-term liabilities.

Current Liabilities

The **current liabilities** of a company are those obligations that are due and payable within one year. They may consist of notes payable to banks, accounts payable, accrued expenses, interest on long-term debt, and income taxes.

Many corporations continuously borrow money through a line of credit established at a bank in order to finance the purchase of inventories, to meet current operating expenses, or for a variety of other reasons. These short-term obligations to lending institutions are called *notes payable to banks* on the balance sheet.

The amounts that a company owes for goods, services, or supplies obtained on open-book accounts with other businesses are called **accounts payable** on the balance sheet. These are short-term obligations and therefore are considered to be current liabilities.

Those expenses that have been incurred for wages, salaries, and commissions, which have not been paid as of the date of the balance sheet, are classified as **accrued expenses**.

Interest on long-term debt that is due and payable during the current fiscal year is considered to be a current liability.

Income taxes that have not been paid as of the date of the balance sheet are a current liability.

Long-Term Liabilities

Any obligations of a business that are *not* due during the current year are classified as **long-term liabilities**. These may consist of such items as long-term debts in the form of bonds and/or mortgages, notes payable to banks that are due after one year, and other noncurrent liabilities. The long-term liabilities of the Aztec Corporation, as shown in Figure 7-1, consist of $25,000,000 of 25-year, 4 percent debentures.

STOCKHOLDERS' EQUITY

Stockholders' equity is the stockholders' investment in the corporation. It consists of the capitalization of the corporation, capital surplus, and retained earnings.

Capitalization

The **capitalization**, or **capital stock**, of a company is its outstanding common and preferred stock. The balance sheet for the Aztec Corporation (see Figure 7-1) shows that its capitalization consists of 60,000 shares of 5 percent preferred stock at a par value of $100 per share, or a total value of $6,000,000. This $6,000,000 is a liability of the corporation. Aztec's capitalization also includes 1,800,000 shares of common stock at a par value of $10 per share, or a total value of $18,000,000. This $18,000,000 is also owed to its stockholders.

Capital Surplus

Sometimes stockholders pay more into the company than just their purchase of the common and preferred stock. If they do pay an extra amount, this sum is called **capital surplus**. Capital surplus (when it is paid) is considered to be a part of the capitalization of a corporation.

Retained Earnings

That portion of the net earnings not distributed to the stockholders in the form of dividends is called **retained earnings**. For the Aztec Corporation, retained earnings amount to $48,000,000.

The term *capital structure* consists of the total stockholders' equity and the long-term debt. This term is not used often in the investment community. Nevertheless, the investor should be familiar with it. The capital structure of the Aztec Corporation amounts to $112,500,000 ($87,500,000 stockholders' equity + $25,000,000 of 25-year, 4 percent debentures).

THE INCOME STATEMENT

The income statement is a statement of a firm's income and expenses for a specific period of time, usually a year. It is sometimes referred to as a **profit and loss statement**. This statement shows where the money came from, how it was spent, and how much is left. The main parts of an income statement are gross sales (or revenue), expenses, income before taxes, income taxes, and net income (or net profit). The income

statement of the Aztec Corporation is shown in Figure 7-2.

GROSS SALES (OR REVENUE)

If the business is a manufacturing company selling a product, its gross income is called **gross sales** on the income statement. If the business is selling a service, its gross income is called **gross revenue**. For the

FIGURE 7-2 An Income Statement

Aztec Corporation Income Statement
For Year Ended December 31, 1987

Gross sales		$100,000,000
Expenses:		
Cost of goods sold	$74,000,000	
Selling and administrative expenses	14,000,000	
Depreciation expense	4,000,000	
Interest expense	1,000,000	
Total expenses		93,000,000
Income before taxes		$ 7,000,000
Income taxes*		2,380,000
Net Income		$ 4,620,000

*For simplicity, income taxes are computed at 50 percent of income before taxes.

Aztec Corporation, gross sales of $100,000,000 provide the income that enables it to pay its expenses and, it hopes, obtain a profit.

EXPENSES

The total expenses incurred in operating the Aztec Corporation consist of several items, which are discussed below.

Cost of Goods Sold

All the direct expenses that are incurred in manufacturing something for sale comprise **cost of goods sold**. These include the outlay for inventory, wages, and supplies.

Selling and Administrative Expenses

The expenses incurred to run the sales department, to pay salespersons' commissions, and to run the administrative department are classified as **selling and administrative expenses**. These expenses are separated from cost of goods sold because they are not directly involved with the production of the goods. Selling and administrative expenses vary widely from industry to industry.

Depreciation Expense

The item *depreciation* on the balance sheet has already been discussed as a deduction that reduces the value at which fixed assets are carried on the books of the company. Depreciation is an expense item allowed by the Internal Revenue Service. However, depreciation is *not* an out-of-pocket expense, for it is not a cash outlay. It is a bookkeeping item that appears on the income statement to reduce a firm's gross income and, consequently, its income taxes.

Interest Expense

Any interest that a business has to pay during the year appears as an **interest expense** on the income statement. Interest expense can be large or small or nothing, depending upon the company's use of its line of credit at the bank and its outstanding long-term debt.

INCOME BEFORE TAXES

After all expenses, *except* income taxes, have been deducted from gross sales, the amount representing the item *income before taxes* determines whether a business has made a profit for the year. We shall see later that this amount is essential in computing Aztec's pretax profit margin.

INCOME TAXES

Corporate income taxes are assessed against taxable income, which is gross income less the expenses incurred in producing it. These taxes are usually paid on a quarterly basis, although some large corporations pay them by the month.

Effective July 1, 1987, all corporations pay corporate income taxes at the following rates:

15 percent on the first $50,000 of income before taxes;
25 percent on the next $25,000 of income before taxes; and
34 percent on the next $25,000 of income before taxes.

This adds up to $22,250 on the first $100,000 of income before taxes, as computed below:

$50,000 × .15 = $ 7,500
$25,000 × .25 = 6,250
$25,000 × .34 = 8,500
$22,250

On all income above the first $100,000, the rate is 34 percent. In addition, a 5 percent surtax is imposed on corporate taxable income between $100,000 and $335,000. Thus, a corporation with exactly $335,000 of taxable income will, in effect, pay a flat tax of 34 percent on all taxable income, which is $113,900, as computed below:

Tax on the first $100,000 = $ 22,250
Tax on next $235,000, or
$235,000 × .39 = 91,650
Total tax on $335,000 = $113,900

$113,900 ÷ $335,000 = 34%

It therefore follows that any corporation with income in excess of $335,000 will simply ignore the 5 percent surtax and pay a 34 percent rate on its entire income.

NET INCOME (OR NET PROFIT)

The **net income**, or **net profit**, sums up all of the frustrations, triumphs, mistakes, and good judgment of a firm's management during the year. More popularly known as the *bottom line*, net income is the first item investors and stockholders look for when examining an income statement. It is only from a profit that the board of directors can declare a dividend, and it is mainly from net income earned now or in the future that the market price of a stock is determined.

VALUABLE INFORMATION FROM FINANCIAL STATEMENTS

Knowing what dollar amounts go into a balance sheet or an income statement is not enough. In order to evaluate these statements, one must know how to compute some ratios that indicate the financial position of the company. These ratios can be determined from dollar amounts found in the balance sheet, in the income statement, or in both statements taken together. To be meaningful, however, these ratios should be compared with the average for all firms within the same industry. This way an investor can determine if the ratios are good or bad.

BALANCE SHEET RATIOS

Two important ratios that determine a company's ability to meet its short-term obligations are the current ratio and the acid test (or quick) ratio.

Current Ratio

The **current ratio** is obtained by dividing current assets by current liabilities. This ratio indicates whether the company has adequate assets with which to pay its current bills. According to Figure 7-1, for the Aztec Corporation the current ratio is:

$$\frac{\text{Current assets}}{\text{Current liabilities}} = \text{Current ratio}$$

$$\frac{\$49,000,000}{\$12,500,000} = 3.92 \text{ or } 4 \text{ to } 1$$

This is excellent, for a current ratio of 2 to 1 is considered to be adequate.

Acid Test (or Quick) Ratio

The **acid test ratio** is obtained by deducting the inventories from the current assets and dividing the remainder by the current liabilities. It is also called the **quick ratio** because the three assets used in computing this ratio—cash, accounts receivable, and marketable securities—are sometimes referred to as **quick assets**. Inventories are deducted because they are typically the least liquid of the current assets. To many analysts, therefore, the acid test ratio is the real test of a corporation's ability to meet its current bills. For the Aztec Corporation, the acid test ratio is:

$$\frac{\text{Current assets} - \text{Inventory}}{\text{Current liabilities}} = \begin{array}{l}\text{Acid test} \\ \text{(or quick)} \\ \text{ratio}\end{array}$$

$$\frac{\$49,000,000 - \$25,000,000}{\$12,500,000} = \begin{array}{l}1.92 \text{ or} \\ 2 \text{ to } 1\end{array}$$

This is more than satisfactory, for an acid test ratio of 1 to 1 is considered to be good.

INCOME STATEMENT RATIOS

Two ratios that indicate the profitability of the company, or how efficiently the company is being managed, are the pretax profit margin and the post-tax profit margin (or profit margin on sales).

Pretax Profit Margin

The **pretax profit margin** is obtained by dividing income before taxes by sales. If a company is to operate efficiently, the three expenses (selling and administrative expenses, depreciation, and interest expense) should *not* exceed the pretax profit margin. For the Aztec Corporation, the pretax profit margin is:

$$\frac{\text{Income before taxes}}{\text{Sales}} = \begin{array}{l}\text{Pretax profit} \\ \text{margin}\end{array}$$

$$\frac{\$\ \ 7,000,000}{\$100,000,000} = 7\%$$

This pretax profit margin is low. It should be at least twice as much, particularly considering that the three expenses mentioned above amount to $19,000,000.

Post-Tax Profit Margin (or Profit Margin on Sales)

The **post-tax profit margin** is found by dividing net income by sales. This ratio gives the profit per dollar of sales. For the Aztec Corporation, the post-tax profit margin is:

$$\frac{\text{Net income}}{\text{Sales}} = \text{Post-tax profit margin}$$

$$\frac{\$\ 3,500,000}{\$100,000,000} = \begin{array}{l}3.5\%, \text{ or } 3\frac{1}{2}\text{¢ per} \\ \text{dollar of sales}\end{array}$$

This post-tax profit margin is low for a manufacturing company like the Aztec Corporation. On the other hand, it would be high for a supermarket that can operate profitably on 1 percent, or 1¢ per dollar of sales.

OTHER KEY RATIOS

There are some key ratios that can be obtained by consulting other data contained in the company's annual report and comparing them with data on either the balance sheet or the income statement.

Earnings per Share

The **earnings per share (EPS)** of common stock is found by dividing the balance of the net income (after preferred dividends, if any, are paid) by the number of outstanding common shares. Assuming that the Aztec Corporation paid no preferred dividends, its EPS is:

$$\frac{\text{Net income}}{\text{Number of outstanding common shares}} = \frac{\text{Earnings}}{\text{per share}}$$

$$\frac{\$3,500,000}{1,800,000} = \$1.94 \text{ per share}$$

Price-Earnings Ratio

The **price-earnings ratio** (or P/E ratio) is obtained by dividing the current market price of the common stock by its earnings per share. This ratio is important in determining whether the market price of the stock is high or low. Generally speaking, a P/E ratio of 10 to 1 is considered low, while a P/E ratio of 20 or 30 to 1 is considered high. Assuming that the market price of the Aztec Corporation's common stock is $39, its P/E ratio is:

$$\frac{\text{Current market price}}{\text{Earnings per share}} = \frac{\text{Price-earnings}}{\text{ratio}}$$

$$\frac{\$39.00}{\$1.94} = 20 \text{ to } 1$$

On this basis, the Aztec Corporation's stock is selling at a high price.

Dividend Return per Share of Common Stock

The **dividend return per share of common stock** is obtained by dividing the dividend per share by the current market price. On the average, corporations pay out about 50 percent of their net income to the common stockholders, with the balance being retained in the business as surplus or invested for expansion. Assuming that the board of directors of the Aztec Corporation declared one-half of its EPS as a dividend that year, its dividend return per share of common stock is:

$$\frac{\text{Dividend per share}}{\text{Current market price}} = \frac{\text{Dividend}}{\text{return per share}}$$

$$\frac{\$ 0.97}{\$39.00} = 2.48\%$$

This dividend return per share is poor, for it is far less than bank interest.

Times Preferred Dividends Earned

The **times-preferred-dividends-earned ratio** is obtained by dividing net income by total preferred dividends. To the preferred stockholders, this ratio is important because they want to know if the preferred dividend is "safe" and therefore sure to be paid. The Aztec Corporation has 60,000 shares of 5 percent preferred stock outstanding with a par value of $100 a share. On this basis, the dividend owed the preferred stockholders is $300,000 a year ($6,000,000 × .05 = $300,000). Thus, the times preferred dividends earned for the Aztec Corporation is:

$$\frac{\text{Net income}}{\text{Preferred dividends}} = \frac{\text{Times preferred dividends earned}}{}$$

$$\frac{\$3,500,000}{\$ 300,000} = 11.6 \text{ times}$$

With the dividend protected over 11 times what is due them, the preferred stockholders certainly should have no concern about receiving their dividends.

CONSOLIDATED FINANCIAL STATEMENTS

To determine the financial position of the same company over a period of time, one can examine consolidated financial statements such as those shown in Figures 7-3 and 7-4.

Figure 7-3 shows a consolidated balance sheet for the Aztec Corporation for two years (as of December 31, 1986, and December 31, 1987). The Amount column indicates the dollar value of each item. The Percent column expresses each item as a percentage of the total of assets or liabilities and stockholders' equity. The Increase or Decrease

FIGURE 7-3 Consolidated Balance Sheet

Aztec Corporation Consolidated Balance Sheet
December 31, 1987 and 1986

	1987		1986		Increase or Decrease	
	Amount	Percent	Amount	Percent	Amount	Percent
Assets						
Current assets:						
Cash....................	$10,000,000	8.0	$9,600,000	8.0	$400,000	4.2
Marketable securities ...	2,000,000	1.6	1,900,000	1.6	100,000	5.3
Accounts receivable	12,000,000	9.6	11,000,000	9.2	1,000,000	9.1
Inventories	25,000,000	20.0	22,000,000	18.3	3,000,000	13.6
Total current assets...	49,000,000	39.2	44,500,000	37.1	4,500,000	10.1
Fixed assets:						
Buildings and machinery and equipment.......	100,000,000		100,000,000			
Less: Reserves for depreciation	25,000,000		25,500,000		(500,000)	(1.9)
	75,000,000	60.0	74,500,000	62.1	500,000	.7
Land.................	1,000,000	.8	1,000,000	.8		
Total fixed assets.....	76,000,000	60.8	75,500,000	62.9	500,000	.7
Total assets..............	$125,000,000	100.0	$120,000,000	100.0	$5,000,000	4.2
Liabilities						
Current liabilities:						
Notes payable to banks	$1,000,000	.8	$1,000,000	.8		
Accounts payable	6,000,000	4.8	5,000,000	4.2	$1,000,000	20.0
Accrued liabilities	1,000,000	.8	1,000,000	.8		
Interest and long-term debt...............	1,000,000	.8	1,000,000	.8		
Income taxes	3,500,000	2.8	3,000,000	2.5	500,000	16⅔
Total current liabilities	12,500,000	10.0	11,000,000	9.1	1,500,000	13.6
Long-term liabilities:						
25-year, 4% debentures	25,000,000	20.0	26,000,000	21.7	(1,000,000)	(3.8)
Total liabilities............	$37,500,000	30.0	$37,000,000	30.8	$500,000	1.4
Stockholders' Equity						
Capital stock:						
5% preferred stock (par value $100, authorized 60,000 shares).......	$6,000,000	4.8	$6,000,000	5.0		
Common stock (par value $100, issued 1,800,000 shares)....	18,000,000	14.4	18,000,000	15.0		
Capital surplus..........	15,500,000	12.4	15,500,000	12.9		
Total capital stock	39,500,000	31.6	39,500,000	32.9		
Retained earnings........	48,000,000	38.4	43,500,000	36.3	4,500,000	10.4
Total stockholders' equity..	87,500,000	70.0	83,000,000	69.2	4,500,000	5.4
Total liabilities & stockholders' equity	$125,000,000	100.0	$120,000,000	100.0	$5,000,000	4.2

Notes: Figures in parentheses denote a decrease. Discrepancy in percentages is due to rounding.

column shows the amount of change in an item by comparing 1987 with 1986. When comparing periods of time, the earlier period is the base. The Increase or Decrease column converts the amount of change into a percentage of the base year. This consolidated balance sheet shows that there was only a slight improvement in the net worth of the Aztec Corporation.

Figure 7-4 shows a consolidated income statement for the Aztec Corporation for two years (as of December 31, 1986, and

FIGURE 7-4 Consolidated Income Statement

Aztec Corporation Consolidated Income Statement
For Years Ended December 31, 1987 and 1986

	1987		1986		Increase or Decrease	
	Amount	Percent of Gross Sales	Amount	Percent of Gross Sales	Amount	Percent
Gross sales...............	$100,000,000	100.0	$92,000,000	100.0	$8,000,000	8.7
Expenses:						
Cost of goods sold.......	$ 74,000,000	74.0	$69,000,000	75.0	$5,000,000	7.2
Selling and administrative expenses.............	14,000,000	14.0	12,000,000	13.0	2,000,000	16⅔
Depreciation expense....	4,000,000	4.0	4,000,000	4.3	—	
Interest expense	1,000,000	1.0	1,000,000	1.1	—	
Total expenses..........	$ 93,000,000	93.0	$86,000,000	93.4	$7,000,000	8.1
Income before taxes.......	$ 7,000,000	7.0	$ 6,000,000	6.6	$1,000,000	16⅔
Income taxes	3,500,000	3.5	3,000,000	3.3	500,000	16⅔
Net income	$ 3,500,000*	3.5	$ 3,000,000	3.3	$ 500,000	16⅔

Note: Discrepancy in percentages is due to rounding.

*For simplicity, a maximum 50 percent income tax rate was assumed for all of 1987. Actually, the maximum income tax rate was reduced to 43 percent effective halfway through the year, namely on July 1, 1987.

December 31, 1987). This statement shows that there has been no improvement in *cost control* (reducing expenses). As a percentage of gross sales, expenses have remained about the same. The chief cause of the lack of adequate profit for the Aztec Corporation is the excessive selling and administrative expenses. These items must show a drastic improvement before the bottom line (net income) will show a sufficient increase for the stock to become attractive to an investor.

SUMMARY

No one should buy common stock without first obtaining all of the facts. A good part of these facts can be found in a corporation's annual report. Besides other useful information, the two major parts of an annual report are the balance sheet and the income statement. But even these statements are not of much value unless the prospective stock buyer knows how to evaluate them. Knowing how to compute the current ratio and the acid test ratio from the balance sheet will enable an investor to determine if a corporation is able to meet its current bills. Knowing how to compute profit margins from the income statement will disclose to the investor whether a corporation is making money. In the last analysis, the net income, or the bottom line, is the most important item to watch.

If the investor knows how to compare the balance sheet with the income statement, he or she can determine if a corporation is able to meet its annual interest charges and thus avoid legal action by its creditors or even bankruptcy. The investor can also determine if a sufficient return is being earned on the stockholders' investment.

One of the key ratios in determining whether a stock is too high priced is its price-earnings ratio. While this ratio is quoted every business day in *The Wall Street Journal* and the financial pages of many metropolitan daily newspapers, the investor should know how the price-earnings ratio is computed. If income is desired, the prospective stock buyer must know how to compute the percentage yield on the common stock.

Many people like to buy preferred stock for its prior claim on a firm's assets if the corporation should be dissolved and for its higher yield. The preferred stock buyer should know how many times the dividend on the preferred stock has been earned over and above the amount that is actually owed. This ratio is important because it determines if the dividend is "safe" and sure to be paid.

A study of consolidated balance sheets and income statements, not only for this year and last year but also for the last ten years (which are available in many annual reports) is a great help to the investor who is seeking appreciation in a company's stock. These consolidated statements will disclose if a corporation's rate of growth over the years is high enough to interest a prospective stock buyer.

7

REVIEW QUESTIONS
SHORT ESSAY

Name _____

Date _____ Points _____

Directions: Answer the following questions according to your instructor's directions.

1.   What are the two vital questions that a prudent investor would want answered before investing in a company?

   a. _____

   b. _____

2.   In your own words, define current assets.

_____

_____

_____

_____

3.   Why is the LIFO method of inventory evaluation considered more conservative than the FIFO method?

_____

_____

_____

_____

4.   Why is it hard to determine the true value of land when looking at a balance sheet?

_____

_____

_____

_____

5.   In your own words, define the capitalization of a company.

_____

_____

_____

_____

6. What is meant by the term *capital structure?*

_____

_____

_____

_____

7. Why is net income called the true test of management?

_____

_____

_____

_____

8. What is the acid test ratio?

_____

_____

_____

_____

9. What is the formula for obtaining the pretax profit margin?

_____

_____

_____

_____

10. Why is the times-preferred-dividends-earned ratio important information to preferred stockholders?

_____

_____

_____

_____

7

REVIEW QUESTIONS
MULTIPLE CHOICE

Name _____

Date _____ Points _____

Directions: For each of the following, select the best answer and place the letter that represents it in the Answers column.

ANSWERS

1. A balance sheet follows the basic accounting equation
   a. Assets = Liabilities.
   b. Assets = Liabilities − Capitalization.
   c. Assets = Liabilities − Stockholders' equity.
   d. Assets = Liabilities + Stockholders' equity.   _____
2. Marketable securities are part of the
   a. capital structure.
   b. stockholders' equity.
   c. current assets.
   d. long-term liabilities.   _____
3. Accounts receivable are
   a. debts incurred by the corporation's customers.
   b. notes due from banks.
   c. mortgages held by the corporation.
   d. overdue debts of the corporation.   _____
4. Depreciation is termed "accumulated depreciation" on a balance sheet because
   a. machines and equipment become worn out or obsolete.
   b. the rate of depreciation allowed by the IRS depends on the type of building.
   c. it is not an out-of-pocket expense.
   d. the amount of annual depreciation is accumulated over the years.   _____
5. Land is carried on the balance sheet
   a. as capitalization.
   b. at its original cost.
   c. with an allowance for accumulated depreciation.
   d. at its present market value.   _____
6. Current liabilities are obligations of a corporation due and payable in
   a. one year.
   b. two years.
   c. five years.
   d. ten years.   _____
7. Accounts payable are a
   a. current liability.
   b. current asset.
   c. long-term liability.
   d. part of capital stock.   _____

8. Part of a corporation's long-term liability is
   a. accrued expenses.
   b. notes payable to banks.
   c. income taxes.
   d. debentures.   _____

9. Depreciation is *not*
   a. an out-of-pocket expense.
   b. deductible under IRS rules.
   c. a bookkeeping item.
   d. a decrease in the value of fixed assets.   _____

10. Current ratio is computed by dividing
    a. current assets minus inventories by current liabilities.
    b. current assets by current liabilities.
    c. current liabilities by current assets.
    d. current assets by liabilities and stockholders' equity.   _____

11. One of the following indicates the profitability of a company:
    a. pretax profit margin.
    b. current ratio.
    c. acid test ratio.
    d. times-interest-earned ratio.

12. Fixed assets normally consist of
    a. buildings, equipment, and machinery.
    b. buildings, equipment and machinery, and land.
    c. buildings and machinery.
    d. buildings and land.   _____

13. A company has a net income of $22,000,000. Its capitalization
    includes 6,000,000 common shares. Its earnings per share are
    a. $3.66.
    b. $5.66.
    c. $18.44.
    d. $27.27.   _____

14. A company's stock is quoted in *The Wall Street Journal* at $30 per
    share. Its quarterly dividend is 30¢ per share. The dividend return
    per share is
    a. 1.0 percent.
    b. 2.5 percent.
    c. 3.0 percent.
    d. 4.0 percent.   _____

15. A company has 60,000 shares of 10 percent preferred stock
    outstanding with a par value of $100 per share. Its net income is
    $4,800,000. The preferred dividend was earned
    a. 2.0 times.
    b. 4.0 times.
    c. 8.0 times.
    d. 12.5 times.   _____

7	

REVIEW QUESTIONS
TRUE-FALSE

Name _____

Date _____ Points _____

Directions: Circle T or F to indicate whether each statement is true or false.

1. The first annual statement was published at the turn of the century. **T F**

2. A balance sheet lists only what a corporation owns. **T F**

3. An income statement discloses whether or not a company is making money. **T F**

4. Accounts receivable are seldom reduced on the balance sheet. **T F**

5. The FIFO method of inventory evaluation gives a low cost to items sold and therefore results in a higher profit from sales. **T F**

6. Depreciation is accumulated over the years and is called accumulated depreciation on the balance sheet. **T F**

7. Land is depreciated as are other fixed assets. **T F**

8. Income taxes are long-term liabilities. **T F**

9. Many businesses continuously borrow money from banks. **T F**

10. Capital structure consists of the total stockholders' equity and long-term debt. **T F**

11. A manufacturing company's gross income is called *gross revenue* on an income statement. **T F**

12. Cost of goods sold includes the outlay for inventories, wages, and supplies. **T F**

13. Selling and administrative expenses do not vary much from industry to industry. **T F**

14. The net income of a firm determines the market price of its stock. **T F**

15. A company is in a good financial position for the year if its current ratio is 2 to 1. **T F**

16. Accounts receivable are not considered in determining the acid test ratio. **T F**

17. Inventory is subtracted from current assets in determining the quick ratio. **T F**

18. Pretax profit margin is income before taxes divided by inventory. **T F**

19. Post-tax profit margin is the same as profit margin on sales. **T F**

20. An acid test ratio and a quick ratio describe the same method of evaluation. **T F**

21. On average, American corporations pay out 50 percent of their net earnings to their shareholders in the form of dividends. **T F**

22. A price-earnings ratio of 10 to 1 is considered high. **T F**

23. Corporations normally do not pay out all of their net income to their stockholders in the form of dividends. **T F**

24. The times-preferred-dividends-earned ratio is found by dividing net income before taxes by preferred dividends. **T F**

25. When comparing periods of time on a consolidated balance sheet, the latest period is the base. **T F**

7

PROJECT

Mary and Tom Baldwin are not satisfied with their stockbroker's explanations about financial statements. They feel they need to know more about annual reports. They have obtained the consolidated balance sheet of the ABC Corporation, a firm in which they are interested, for the years 1986 and 1987. That balance sheet is illustrated in Figure 7-5. In addition, the Baldwins have the following information from the income statements of the ABC Corporation:

1. The net income per share for 1987 was $3.00, compared with $1.50 for 1986.
2. The dividend for 1987 was $1.00, and the current market price of the common stock is $30.00.

In this project you are to provide them with the answers to the following questions about the ABC Corporation.

1. What is the current ratio? Is it adequate?
2. What is the acid test ratio? Is it satisfactory?
3. What is the dividend yield?
4. What is the P/E ratio?
5. Based on your answers to the above questions, would you recommend that they purchase the stock?

FIGURE 7-5

The ABC Corporation Consolidated Balance Sheet
December 31, 1987 and December 31, 1986

	1987	1986
Assets		
Current assets:		
Cash	$ 5,890,000	$ 5,187,000
Temporary investments	34,799,000	16,700,000
Receivables	32,474,000	18,238,000
Inventories:		
Raw materials	27,263,000	17,270,000
Work-in-process and finished products	7,329,000	13,591,000
Prepaid expenses, etc.	1,417,000	1,425,000
Total current assets	109,172,000	72,411,000
Property, plant, and equipment, at cost:		
Land...	3,164,000	3,061,000
Buildings and improvements	31,315,000	28,247,000
Machinery and equipment	9,439,000	8,737,000
Idle facilities, less reserves for depreciation...................	4,617,000	5,559,000
Total property, plant and equipment	48,535,000	45,604,000
Less: Reserves for depreciation	(13,693,000)	(11,404,000)
Total fixed assets	34,842,000	34,200,000
Total assets	$144,014,000	$106,611,000
Liabilities and Shareholders' Equity		
Current liabilities:		
Accounts payable	$ 41,608,000	$ 18,201,000
Employee compensation and benefits.......................	5,174,000	3,092,000
Federal and state taxes on income........................	5,268,000	3,672,000
Other	5,772,000	2,461,000
Total current liabilities	57,822,000	27,426,000
Shareholders' equity:		
Common stock, $1 par value, authorized 75,000,000 shares,		
outstanding 11,370,000 shares stated at	11,470,000*	11,470,000
Capital surplus..	28,001,000	28,001,000
Retained earnings	46,721,000	39,714,000
Total shareholders' equity................................	86,192,000	79,185,000
Total liabilities and shareholders' equity	$144,014,000	$106,611,000

*100,000 shares were reacquired by the company, but under California corporate law the *par value* of these 100,000 shares had to be shown in the balance sheet.

CHAPTER 8
OUTLINE

I. **BASIC TAX RATES AND CLASSIFICATION OF INCOME**

II. **CAPITAL GAINS AND LOSSES**
   A. Tax Treatment of Capital Gains
   B. Tax Treatment of Capital Losses
   C. Avoiding or Deferring a Capital Gain

III. **HOW INCOME FROM INVESTMENTS IS TAXED**
   A. Taxation of Income from Stocks and Bonds
   B. Taxation of Income from Stock Dividends
   C. Taxation of Income from Stock Rights
   D. Taxation of Income from Mutual Funds
   E. Taxation of Income from Real Estate

IV. **TAX-DEFERRED RETIREMENT PLANS**
   A. Individual Retirement Account (IRA)
   B. Keogh Plan
   C. Other Qualified Retirement Plans

V. **FEDERAL ESTATE AND GIFT TAXES**
   A. Estates of Unmarried Decedents
   B. Estates of Married Decedents
   C. Gift Tax Rules

VI. **STATE INHERITANCE AND GIFT TAXES**

8

TAXES AND THE INDIVIDUAL INVESTOR

Taxes are important in financial planning. Since a comprehensive discussion of income taxes is not within the scope of this text, this chapter will be confined to essential topics with which every investor should be familiar.

BASIC TAX RATES AND CLASSIFICATION OF INCOME

Before a meaningful discussion of income taxes can be presented, basic tax rates for individuals must be understood. Beginning with the year 1988, the basic rates for married (filing jointly) and unmarried taxpayers are as follows:

Married Filing Jointly		Unmarried	
Taxable Income	Rate	Taxable Income	Rate
0 – $29,750	15%	0 – $17,850	15%
Over $29,750	28%	Over $17,850	28%

In addition, for a married couple filing jointly, there is a 5 percent surtax on taxable income between $71,900 and $149,250. For an unmarried taxpayer, the 5 percent surtax applies to taxable income between $43,150 and $89,560. Once these upper levels of income are reached, the effect of the surtax is to tax all income at the 28 percent rate. (Note: After 1988 the tax rates are indexed for inflation.)

For tax purposes, income is divided into three classes: (1) portfolio income, (2) passive income, and (3) other income. **Portfolio income** is gross income from dividends, interest, annuities, and royalties that are not derived in the ordinary course of a trade or business.

Passive income is income from a business or partnership in which the investor does not *materially participate* in the conduct of that trade or business. A taxpayer materially participates in an activity if he or she is involved in the operations of the business on a regular, continuous, and substantial basis. For example, an interest in a limited partnership is not an activity in which a taxpayer materially participates. As such, the taxpayer is considered to be a passive investor; the activity, a passive activity.

Other income is income from wages, salaries, commissions, self-employment, and *pass-through entities* such as S corporations, REITs (real estate investment trusts), and mutual funds.

CAPITAL GAINS AND LOSSES

Capital gains and losses are reported on Schedule D when the federal income tax return is filed. (Schedule D is illustrated in Figure 8-1 on pages 189–190.) A **capital gain** is a profit obtained by selling a capital asset that an investor bought, held for a

certain period of time (currently six months or longer), and later sold. For income tax purposes, any property that is not used in the operation of a trade or business is considered a **capital asset**. Examples of capital assets are stocks, bonds, mutual funds, and

FIGURE 8-1 Schedule D (page 1)

SCHEDULE D ·	**Capital Gains and Losses**	OMB No. 1545-0074
(Form 1040)	**(And Reconciliation of Forms 1099-B)**	**1988**
	▶ Attach to Form 1040. ▶ See Instructions for Schedule D (Form 1040).	
Department of the Treasury Internal Revenue Service	For Paperwork Reduction Act Notice, see Form 1040 Instructions.	Attachment Sequence No. **12**

Name(s) as shown on Form 1040	Your social security number

1 Report here the total sales of stocks, bonds, etc., reported for 1988 to you on Form(s) 1099-B or on equivalent substitute statement(s). If this amount differs from the total of lines 2b and 9b, column (d), attach a statement explaining the difference. See the Instructions for line 1 for examples . . . . . | **1**

Part I Short-Term Capital Gains and Losses—Assets Held One Year or Less (6 months or less if acquired before 1/1/88)

(a) Description of property (Example, 100 shares 7% preferred of "Z" Co.)	(b) Date acquired (Mo., day, yr.)	(c) Date sold (Mo., day, yr.)	(d) Sales price (see Instructions)	(e) Cost or other basis (see Instructions)	(f) LOSS If (e) is more than (d), subtract (d) from (e)	(g) GAIN If (d) is more than (e), subtract (e) from (d)
2a Stocks, Bonds, and Other Securities (Include all Form 1099-B transactions. See Instructions.)						

2b Total (add column (d)) . . . . **2b▶**

2c Other Transactions (Include Real Estate Transactions From Forms 1099-S)

3 Short-term gain from sale or exchange of your home from Form 2119, line 8a or 14 . | **3**
4 Short-term gain from installment sales from Form 6252, line 22 or 30 . . . . . | **4**
5 Net short-term gain or (loss) from partnerships, S corporations, and fiduciaries . | **5**
6 Short-term capital loss carryover . . . . | **6**
7 Add all of the transactions on lines 2a and 2c and lines 3 through 6 in columns (f) and (g) . | **7** ( ) |
8 Net short-term gain or (loss), combine columns (f) and (g) of line 7 . . . . | **8**

Part II Long-Term Capital Gains and Losses—Assets Held More Than One Year (more than 6 months if acquired before 1/1/88)

9a Stocks, Bonds, and Other Securities (Include all Form 1099-B transactions. See Instructions.)

9b Total (add column (d)) . . . . **9b▶**

9c Other Transactions (Include Real Estate Transactions From Forms 1099-S)

10 Long-term gain from sale or exchange of your home from Form 2119, line 8a, 10, or 14 . | **10**
11 Long-term gain from installment sales from Form 6252, line 22 or 30 . . . . . | **11**
12 Net long-term gain or (loss) from partnerships, S corporations, and fiduciaries . | **12**
13 Capital gain distributions . . . . | **13**
14 Enter gain from Form 4797, line 7 or 9 . . . . | **14**
15 Long-term capital loss carryover . . . . | **15**
16 Add all of the transactions on lines 9a and 9c and lines 10 through 15 in columns (f) and (g) . . | **16** ( ) |
17 Net long-term gain or (loss), combine columns (f) and (g) of line 16 . . . . | **17**

Schedule D (Form 1040) 1988

FIGURE 8-1 Schedule D (page 2)

Schedule D (Form 1040) 1988 | Attachment Sequence No. **12** | Page **2**

Name(s) as shown on Form 1040. (Do not enter name and social security number if shown on other side.) | Your social security number

Part III	**Summary of Parts I and II**

18 Combine lines 8 and 17, and enter the net gain or (loss) here. If result is a gain, also enter the gain on Form 1040, line 13 . . . . | **18**

19 If line 18 is a (loss), enter here and as a (loss) on Form 1040, line 13, the **smaller** of:

  a The (loss) on line 18; **or**

  b ($3,000) or, if married filing a separate return, ($1,500) . . . . | **19** ( )

  Note: When figuring which amount is **smaller,** treat them as if they were positive numbers.

Part IV	**Computation of Capital Loss Carryovers From 1988 to 1989**

(Complete this part if the loss on line 18 is more than the loss on line 19.)

20 Enter the loss shown on line 8; if none, enter zero and skip lines 21 through 24. . . . . | **20**

21 Enter gain shown on line 17. If that line is blank or shows a loss, enter zero . . . . . . | **21**

22 Subtract line 21 from line 20 . . . . | **22**

23 Enter the **smaller** of line 19 or 22 . . . . | **23**

24 Subtract line 23 from line 22. This is your **short-term capital loss carryover from 1988 to 1989** . . | **24**

25 Enter loss from line 17; if none, enter zero and skip lines 26 through 29 . . . . | **25**

26 Enter gain shown on line 8. If that line is blank or shows a loss, enter zero . . . . . . | **26**

27 Subtract line 26 from line 25 . . . . | **27**

28 Subtract line 23 from line 19. (**Note:** If you skipped lines 21 through 24, enter the amount from line 19.) | **28**

29 Subtract line 28 from line 27. This is your **long-term capital loss carryover from 1988 to 1989** . . . | **29**

Part V	**Complete This Part Only If You Elect Out of the Installment Method and Report a Note or Other Obligation at Less Than Full Face Value**

30 Check here if you elect out of the installment method . . . . ▶ ☐

31 Enter the face amount of the note or other obligation . . . . ▶ . . . .

32 Enter the percentage of valuation of the note or other obligation . . . . ▶

Part VI	**Reconciliation of Forms 1099-B for Bartering Transactions**	Amount of bartering income from Form 1099-B or equivalent statement reported on form or schedule
	(Complete this part if you received one or more Form(s) 1099-B or an equivalent substitute statement(s) reporting bartering income.)	

33 Form 1040, line 22 . . . . | **33**

34 Schedule C (Form 1040) . . . . | **34**

35 Schedule D (Form 1040) . . . . | **35**

36 Schedule E (Form 1040) . . . . | **36**

37 Schedule F (Form 1040) . . . . | **37**

38 Other (identify) (if not taxable, indicate reason—attach additional sheets if necessary) ▶ . . . .

. . . .

. . . .

. . . . | **38**

39 Total (add lines 33 through 38) . . . . | **39**

Note: The amount on line 39 should be the same as the total bartering income on all Forms 1099-B and equivalent statements received.

real estate. A **capital loss** is a loss incurred by selling a capital asset.

TAX TREATMENT OF CAPITAL GAINS

Prior to passage of the Tax Reform Act of 1986 (TRA 1986), a *long-term capital gain* had a preferential tax treatment in that 60 percent of it was nontaxable. This nontaxable percentage was called the *capital gain deduction*. Today, no such preferential tax treatment exists. A long-term capital gain is treated as any other income and is fully taxable. After TRA 1986, the only purpose of calculating long-term and short-term gains and losses is to determine the limit on capital losses.

TAX TREATMENT OF CAPITAL LOSSES

Capital losses are still allowed in full against capital gains, if any. Losses that exceed gains can be deducted, to a maximum of $3,000 in any one calendar year. Any excess losses above the $3,000 limit may be carried forward indefinitely.

Capital losses from passive activities (primarily real estate and limited partnerships) receive special treatment under the Internal Revenue Code. Passive losses cannot be balanced against other income or portfolio income. They can only be offset against passive income. Under TRA 1986, passive losses are subject to the following transition rules:

1. Passive losses that cannot be deducted from passive income can be partially deducted. The amount of the loss that may be deducted is 20 percent in 1989 and 10 percent in 1990. After 1990, the deductible amount is zero.
2. Passive losses that cannot be deducted from passive income because most of the losses do not come under

the partial deduction rule in (1) above can be carried forward indefinitely.
3. Passive losses that are still not used under (1) and (2) above can be used to offset capital gains when the assets in the passive activity are sold. A word of caution: This rule cannot be used until *all of the assets in the passive activity are sold.*

Passive Losses on Rental Real Estate

In addition, real estate that is personally owned is entitled to an exemption from the passive loss limitation rules. A special $25,000 loss offset against nonpassive income applies to individuals who *actively participate* in their rental real estate activity during the year. (For married taxpayers filing separately and living apart at all times during the year, the loss offset is $12,500.) This offset allows qualifying taxpayers to use up to $25,000 of otherwise unallowable passive losses to offset other income or portfolio income.

To illustrate, assume that Richard Hayashi has other income of $80,000 from his salary, $10,000 in passive income from a limited partnership, and a $25,000 loss from rental real estate in which he actively participates. Mr. Hayashi's $25,000 rental real estate loss will be used first to offset his $10,000 passive income. The remaining $15,000 of this loss can be used to reduce his otherwise fully reportable salary of $80,000, thus reducing it to a taxable income of $65,000. So, even though the rental loss is from a passive activity, Mr. Hayashi can offset his $25,000 loss.

Investors should not confuse active participation with material participation, which was previously defined as regular, continuous, and substantial involvement in the business operations. A taxpayer who *actively participates* is involved in the business activity in a significant sense, such as making management decisions or arranging for others to provide services such as repairs. Relevant management decisions include approval of tenants, rental terms, capital expenditures, and other similar decisions. It is not necessary for the investor to live in the same state where the property is located as long as she or he can satisfy the criteria for active participation.

If the taxpayer's ownership interest is less than 10 percent of the value of the real estate activity at any time during the tax year, the taxpayer cannot be treated as one who actively participates.

Phase-Out Rule on Rental Real Estate

The $25,000 offset for rental real estate activities is reduced by 50 percent of the amount by which an individual's adjusted gross income exceeds $100,000 a year. Thus, generally speaking, for a taxpayer with an adjusted gross income of $150,000 or more, there is no relief from the passive activity loss rules, since 50 percent of the $50,000 that exceeds $100,000 is $25,000.

AVOIDING OR DEFERRING A CAPITAL GAIN

There are four conditions under which a property transaction will not incur a reportable capital gain for the taxpayer. These conditions are explained below.

Sale of a Principal Residence

If you sell your home and buy a new one, you can defer the capital gain if you meet the following three tests:

1. *Principal residence test*. You must have used your old home as your principal residence.
2. *Time test*. You must buy or build your new home and use it within two years before or after you sell your old home. Caution: The IRS is very strict on this time test.
3. *Investment test*. You must buy or build your new home at a cost that is at least equal to the amount you received from the sale of your old home. If the replacement property costs less, part or all of the gain is taxable. If you

exchange houses as your principal residence, the trade is considered to be a sale of your old home and a purchase of the new one. If you make an even exchange or pay more cash to buy the new home, there is no capital gain. If you receive cash in addition to the proceeds from the sale of your old house, you generally realize taxable gain.

For example, assume that you sold your old home for $158,000. You exchange it for a new home that costs $161,000, and you also receive $5,000 in cash. Since you invested $161,000 in your new home, your capital gain is $5,000 (the cash you received). If you should later sell your new home, its cost basis is $158,000 (or $161,000 less the $3,000 untaxed gain).

Sale of a Principal Residence by a Person 55 Years of Age or Older

A home owner who sells a principal residence will not incur a capital gain on the first $125,000 of profit if the following conditions are met:

1. The home owner must be 55 years of age *before* the date of the sale. It is not sufficient that the home owner turns 55 sometime during the year of the sale. If the sellers of a principal residence are married, only one spouse has to be 55 years old.
2. The home owner must have used the house as a principal residence for three of the past five years.
3. This exemption may be used only once in a lifetime. If the sellers of the principal residence are married, neither spouse may have used the exemption in the past.

Exchange of Property

A property may be exchanged for another property without capital gain being incurred, provided both properties are of like kind and were held for investment or business purposes.

Involuntary Conversion

An **involuntary conversion** occurs when property is taken by a government (federal, state, or local) under its **right of eminent domain**. A government might exercise this right to build a highway or a school, for instance. The property owner does not incur a capital gain if the money received for the involuntarily converted property is used to buy similar property. If the involuntarily converted property was residential, the owner must buy replacement residential property. If the involuntarily converted property was used for business, the owner must buy property that is similar to or related in service or use.

HOW INCOME FROM INVESTMENTS IS TAXED

Income from investments in stocks, bonds, mutual funds, and real estate is taxed in different ways.

TAXATION OF INCOME FROM STOCKS AND BONDS

Dividends from stocks and interest income from bonds are taxed at ordinary income rates. If the dividends and/or interest are less than $400, they are reported on IRS form 1040 on the lines specified by the instructions on that form. If either dividends or interest exceeds $400, it has to be listed on Schedule B according to the instructions contained therein. Schedule B, which is illustrated in Figure 8-2, is another IRS form that must be attached to form 1040.

TAXATION OF INCOME FROM STOCK DIVIDENDS

In Chapter 2 you learned that sometimes a corporation will declare a stock dividend instead of a cash dividend. Stock dividends, which are distributions by a corporation of its own stock to its shareholders, are not taxable *when received*. In effect, stock dividends reduce the cost basis of all the shares owned by the shareholder. However, if the shares are subsequently sold, the difference between the reduced cost basis and the sale price must be treated by the shareholder as a capital gain (or loss).

For example, assume that you own 100 shares of the XYZ Corporation that cost you $20 each for a total of $2,000. If the XYZ Corporation subsequently issues a 50 percent stock dividend, this means that you now own 150 shares instead of 100. The additional 50 shares do not constitute taxable income. However, the cost basis of all 150 shares is reduced from $20 a share to $13.33 a share ($2,000 ÷ 150). If you subsequently sell the shares, the price you must use to determine your capital gain (or loss) is $13.33.

TAXATION OF INCOME FROM STOCK RIGHTS

In Chapter 2 you also learned that sometimes stock rights are issued to stockholders when a corporation wants to raise money via a new stock issue. For instance, one stock right might be given to buy one new share for each ten shares already held by a stockholder. These stock rights have a value in the market, and they may or may not be exercised by the stockholder. At the time the stock rights are received, they are nontaxable. However, if the rights are exercised or sold, the stockholder must know how to compute the cost basis of the rights as well as the cost basis of the new and old shares.

The value of one right is computed by the following formula:

$$\text{One right} = \frac{\text{Market value of stock less subscription price}}{\text{Number of rights required to purchase one share plus 1}}$$

For example, assume that you own 100 shares of the ACE Corporation that you

FIGURE 8-2 Schedule B

Schedules A&B (Form 1040) 1988   OMB No. 1545-0074   Page **2**

Name(s) as shown on Form 1040. (Do not enter name and social security number if shown on other side.)	Your social security number

Schedule B—Interest and Dividend Income

Attachment
Sequence No. **08**

Part I
Interest
Income

(See
Instructions on
pages 10 and 26.)

If you received more than $400 in taxable interest income, you must complete Part I and Part III and list ALL interest received. You must report all interest on Form 1040, even if you are not required to complete Part I and Part III. If you received, as a nominee, interest that actually belongs to another person, or you received or paid accrued interest on securities transferred between interest payment dates, see page 27.

Interest Income		Amount	
1 Interest income from seller-financed mortgages. (See Instructions and list name of payer.) ▶	**1**		
2 Other interest income (list name of payer) ▶................................			
--			
--			
--			
--	**2**		
--			
--			
--			
--			
--			
3 Add the amounts on lines 1 and 2. Enter the total here and on Form 1040, line 8a. ▶	**3**		

Note: If you received a Form 1099–INT or Form 1099–OID from a brokerage firm, list the firm's name as the payer and enter the total interest shown on that form.

Part II
Dividend
Income

(See
Instructions on
pages 11 and
27.)

If you received more than $400 in gross dividends and/or other distributions on stock, complete Part II and Part III. You must report all taxable dividends on Form 1040, even if you are not required to complete Part II and Part III. If you received, as a nominee, dividends that actually belong to another person, see page 27.

Dividend Income		Amount	
4 Dividend income (list name of payer—include on this line capital gain distributions, nontaxable distributions, etc.) ▶ ------------------------------			
--			
--			
--			
--	**4**		
--			
--			
--			
--			
--			

Note: If you received a Form 1099-DIV from a brokerage firm, list the firm's name as the payer and enter the total dividends shown on that form.

5 Add the amounts on line 4. Enter the total here	**5**		
6 Capital gain distributions. Enter here and on line 13, Schedule D.*	**6**		
7 Nontaxable distributions. (See Schedule D Instructions for adjustment to basis.)	**7**		
8 Add the amounts on lines 6 and 7. Enter the total here	**8**		
9 Subtract line 8 from line 5. Enter the result here and on Form 1040, line 9 . . . ▶	**9**		

If you received capital gain distributions but do not need Schedule D to report any other gains or losses, enter your capital gain distributions on Form 1040, line 14.

Part III
Foreign
Accounts
and
Foreign
Trusts

(See
Instructions
on page 27.)

If you received more than $400 of interest or dividends, OR if you had a foreign account or were a grantor of, or a transferor to, a foreign trust, you must answer both questions in Part III.

	Yes	No
10 At any time during the tax year, did you have an interest in or a signature or other authority over a financial account in a foreign country (such as a bank account, securities account, or other financial account)? (See page 27 of the Instructions for exceptions and filing requirements for Form TD F 90-22.1.)		
If "Yes," enter the name of the foreign country ▶		
11 Were you the grantor of, or transferor to, a foreign trust which existed during the current tax year, whether or not you have any beneficial interest in it? If "Yes," you may have to file Form 3520, 3520-A, or 926 . . .		

For Paperwork Reduction Act Notice, see Form 1040 Instructions.   **Schedule B (Form 1040) 1988** bought at $22 a share for a total of $2,200. Also assume that the current market price of ACE stock is $30 and that the corporation issues you ten stock rights that entitle you to purchase ten additional shares of ACE stock at a subscription price per share of $26. According to the formula given above, the value of one right is $2, computed as follows:

$$\frac{\$30 - \$26}{1 + 1} = \frac{\$4}{2} = \$2 \text{ (value of one right)}$$

Thus, if you sell the ten rights, the cost basis that you must use to determine your capital gain (or loss) is $2 per right, or $20 for all ten rights.

On the other hand, if you decide to purchase new shares when exercising your rights, the cost bases of both the new and the old shares are computed in different ways. The cost basis of the new stock is equal to the subscription price plus the value of one right ($26 + $2), or $28 per share. The cost basis of the 100 shares of the old stock is reduced by the cost basis of the ten rights to $2,180 (or $2,200 − $20).

TAXATION OF INCOME FROM MUTUAL FUNDS

Subchapter M of the Internal Revenue Code states that as long as a mutual fund distributes 95 percent of its dividend income to its shareholders, it may be considered as a conduit, or pipeline, through which the dividends are passed to the shareholders. The effect of this regulation is to exempt mutual fund corporations from payment of corporation taxes on their dividend income. This exemption is granted only to investment companies registered with the SEC under the federal Investment Company Act of 1940.

The dividends that are passed through to the mutual fund shareholders are classified as portfolio income and are fully taxable.

Withdrawal Plan Distributions

In Chapter 4 you learned that a mutual fund shareholder on a systematic withdrawal plan receives a check monthly or quarterly from the fund for selling some of her or his shares. The shareholder must know whether the shares were sold at a long-term gain or a long-term loss. The amount of gain (or loss) is determined by a computer, using the *average cost* of the shares in the shareholder's account.

TAXATION OF INCOME FROM REAL ESTATE

In Chapter 5 you learned that property taxes and interest on the mortgage are tax deductible for the real estate owner. If real estate is sold, the gain (or loss) is subject to the rules concerning capital gains and losses.

Depreciation is a loss in value of an asset due to deterioration, obsolescence, or use. Depreciation may be taken as a deduction over a period of years on the improvements and buildings on *income-producing property*.

It is important to realize that depreciation, when taken, is not a cash outlay. It is simply a bookkeeping entry for income tax purposes. Also, it can never be taken as a tax deduction on one's home or on land at any time, no matter how the land may be used (such as erecting a commercial building on it).

Just how much depreciation can be taken changes from time to time according to the dictates of Congress. At the time of this writing, depreciation can be taken for 27½ years on residential income property and for 31½ years on nonresidential income property. Thus, on residential income property a deduction can be taken on the cost basis of the property at the rate of 3.637 percent a year (3.637 percent × 27.5 = 100.01 percent).

Depreciation is a bigger tax deduction than most people realize because it is taken against *the entire value of the property, not just the amount of the property owner's down payment*. As a result of this inherent advantage, income-producing property that is actually operated at a profit can often be shown as operating at a loss on the owner's income tax return.

For example, assume that an investor bought an old apartment house for $200,000 with a down payment of 25 percent and financed the balance of the purchase price with a $150,000 mortgage at 10 percent. Assume also that the gross rental income is $30,000 and that operating expenses are $10,000. The net loss is calculated as follows:

Gross rental income	$30,000
Less operating expenses	10,000
Income after operating expenses	$20,000
Less interest on the mortgage	
(10% × $150,000)	15,000
Net income	$ 5,000

Less depreciation (3.637%	
of $200,000)	7,274
Net loss	($ 2,274)

The above example demonstrates how a net income of $5,000 actually turned into a net loss because of the $7,274 depreciation deduction. The net income of $5,000 was cash in the investor's pocket because depreciation is not an out-of-pocket expense. Ideally the investor should put this money aside every year so that some day, when the apartment house wears out, he or she will have the money available to buy or build a new structure. In reality, however, no real estate owner sets this money aside. The depreciation deduction means income to the investor, and it is excluded income as far as federal income tax returns are concerned.

TAX-DEFERRED RETIREMENT PLANS

The Internal Revenue Service provides incentives for all people who have earned income to set aside part of their earnings in several types of tax-deferred plans for their eventual retirement. Two of the most popular plans are the individual retirement account (IRA) and the Keogh plan. While both plans are easy to set up, there are rules and penalties that govern them. Other retirement plans will also be discussed in this section.

INDIVIDUAL RETIREMENT ACCOUNT (IRA)

The **individual retirement account (IRA)** is a plan for employees. If you are an employee who is not covered by a qualified retirement plan where you work, you may set up your own IRA. You can open an IRA as easily as you can open a bank account. All thrift institutions, mutual funds, and brokerage houses have prepared forms that you can fill in and sign.

The maximum amount that you can put into an IRA in one taxable year is $2,000, or 100 percent of your total compensation, whichever is less. The money may be invested in almost any place you choose— banks, savings and loan associations, mutual funds, stocks, bonds, or real estate. However, you may *not* invest it in insurance or *collectibles*, which include works of art, antiques, gold and silver, precious stones, rare stamps, and coins, except gold coins issued by the U.S. Treasury.

Advantages of the IRA

Assume that you are 35 years old and plan to retire at age 65. If you put the maximum of $2,000 a year into an IRA at an annual return of 12 percent, you would amass a nest egg of $540,585 after 30 years. Without this tax shelter, every year you would have to pay taxes on both the $2,000 and the yearly return from it.

Putting Money into an IRA

When you have an IRA, you are not committed to invest $2,000 every year. You may put in amounts less than $2,000 in any one year, or nothing. The funds that you have previously contributed to this account will continue to accumulate tax-deferred earnings.

In addition, if you want to invest the maximum of $2,000, you don't have to make this investment in one lump sum. You can invest the $2,000 in installments, even beyond December 31 of the year. The deadline for investing in the IRA is the due date, with extensions, for filing that year's income tax return (normally April 15 of the following year). If for some reason you should make an excess contribution to the account, there is no penalty as long as you withdraw the excess before the date for filing your income tax return.

Restrictions on Qualifying for an IRA

There are two restrictions on qualifying for an IRA. First, are you covered by a qualified plan at work? Second, how much is your adjusted gross income? A *qualified plan* is one that is approved by the Internal Revenue Service.

If you are covered by a qualified plan at work and your combined adjusted gross income (AGI) is $50,000 when filing a joint return (or $35,000 if single), you cannot open an IRA. If both spouses work and only one is covered by a qualified plan at work, the restriction still applies.

There are two exceptions to this broad rule. First, if you are married and you and your spouse's combined AGI is $40,000 or less ($25,000 or less if single), you may open an IRA even though you are covered by a qualified plan at work. Second, you are allowed a partial deduction if your income rises above the lower limit but does not reach the higher limit of $50,000 for married couples filing jointly or $35,000 for singles. In effect, the normal $2,000 deduction is reduced by 10 percent for each $1,000 that the taxpayer's income is above the lower limit.

To illustrate, assume a married couple filing jointly has an AGI of $45,000. The partial deduction allowed is computed as follows:

$45,000 adjusted gross income
− 40,000 lower limit
$ 5,000 amount over the lower limit

$5 \times 10\% = 50\%$
$50\% \times$ normal $2,000 deduction = $1,000 partial deduction

Withdrawing Money from an IRA

Since an IRA is your own tax-deferred retirement plan, there are penalties for withdrawals before age 59½ (except for death or total and permanent disability). There is a nondeductible penalty of 10 percent, and the amount withdrawn is subject to ordinary income tax rates.

The Internal Revenue Service limits the time period in which you may defer your taxes on an IRA. You *must* start receiving distributions from an IRA no later than April 1 of the calendar year following the year in which you reach age 70½. Distributions may be in a lump sum or may extend over a span of years based on your life expectancy or the combined life expectancy of you and any beneficiary.

The penalty for failure to make the required withdrawal from an IRA is severe. It is a nondeductible excise tax of 50 percent of the *underpayment* (the amount not withdrawn), unless you can convince the Internal Revenue Service that you had reasonable cause for not making the withdrawal.

Taxation of IRA Withdrawals

There are no special tax breaks for withdrawals from an IRA. Whether you take the amount in a lump sum or on a periodic basis, the amount is fully taxable at ordinary income tax rates.

KEOGH PLAN

A **Keogh plan** is a retirement plan that can be set up if you have self-employment income from personal services rendered. There are other pension devices for a Keogh plan, but the most common one is a profit-sharing plan that is opened by an owner, called an *owner-employee*. A Keogh plan is similar to an IRA in that the contribution is fully deductible and compounds tax free. A Keogh plan is also subject to penalty for early withdrawal before age 59½, and distributions must start the year after the owner-employee is 70½.

A formula limits the amount that an owner-employee can contribute to a Keogh plan. It works like this: The *maximum* yearly contribution is 15 percent of earned income, or $200,000—whichever is less. To determine this reduction, add the number 1 to the 15 percent rate, which becomes 1.15 percent; then subtract 1.15 percent from 15 percent, resulting in 13.85 percent. For instance, if your earned income is $50,000, you may contribute $6,925 (or $50,000 × 13.85 percent). No *minimum* contribution is mandated.

The simplest way to set up a Keogh plan is to join a master plan that is already approved by the IRS and administered by a bank, an insurance company, or a mutual fund. But even though you adopt this method, you must submit an annual information return using IRS form 5500EZ that is due by July 31 of the following year.

If you want to establish a Keogh plan for your unincorporated business and you have employees, you must include in your plan any employee who has three or more years of service. This means that you must weigh your tax savings against the added cost of paying for the coverage of your eligible employees. For this reason, many self-employed persons do not set up Keogh plans because there is no tax advantage for them to do so.

OTHER QUALIFIED RETIREMENT PLANS

Other qualified retirement plans are those established by an employer for the tax benefit of the employees. They can be either pension plans or profit-sharing plans. A pension plan is more often established by an older, profitable company that can commit itself to paying into a plan *every year*. A profit-sharing plan is not obligatory and will contribute to the retirement plan in any one year only if there are profits; therefore, the profit-sharing plan is more likely to be chosen by a young company. Contributions by both the employer and the employees, as well as the earnings on these contributions, are tax-deferred.

Since pension plans and profit-sharing plans are qualified plans, they are subject to the same general rules applicable to IRAs and Keogh plans, such as penalty for early redemption before age 59½ and mandatory distributions at age 70½, with lump-sum distributions allowed to be rolled over tax free into an IRA. There are several different kinds of these plans. Each one is briefly discussed below.

401(k) Plan

If you are employed by a company that has a profit-sharing or a stock bonus plan, it can give you additional tax-sheltered pay through a plan called the **401(k)**. Such a plan allows employees to contribute tax-deferred amounts up to $7,000 a year through salary deduction. (Note: Starting in 1988, the $7,000 contribution limit may be increased by an adjustment for inflation.) These contributions are placed in a trust account. In some 401(k) plans, the employer also makes contributions. In such cases, the amount contributed by the employer is also tax deferred but is subject to the Social Security tax.

Income on a 401(k) account, as with all qualified plans, accumulates tax deferred. The employee may not withdraw funds attributable solely to elective salary-reduction contributions (not earnings) until age 59½. If they are withdrawn before that time, except for separation from service, disability, or demonstration of financial hardship, the premature withdrawal is subject to a penalty for early withdrawal.

Employee Stock Ownership Plan (ESOP)

In an **employee stock ownership plan, (ESOP)**, the company contributes its own stock instead of cash. The purpose of the ESOP, as with all qualified plans, is to benefit the employees by giving them a tax deferral. By contributing company stock instead of cash, a business is able to conserve its cash and still receive a 34 percent deduction by not having to pay a corporate tax on its contributions of stock.

There are questions to be raised about ESOPs. For example, will the contributed stock increase in value? Will the employees work harder because they are now stockholders? And how will management educate its employees on stockholders' risks and benefits?

One way to reduce the investment risk is not to have all of the amount that is credited to each individual employee's account invested in the company's stock. Older employees must be allowed to diversify their accounts by having part of their money invested elsewhere. The ESOP must contain the provision that when an employee reaches age 55 with ten years of service, he or she must be given the option of being able to invest 25 percent of the value of the account someplace else; at age 60 with ten years of service, the employee must be given the option of investing 50 percent of the value of the account someplace else. In addition, the ESOP must provide the employee with three different investment options (regarding where he or she might invest) besides the company's stock.

Tax-Sheltered Annuity (TSA)

If you are employed by a tax-exempt educational, religious, or charitable organization, you may be able to purchase a **tax-sheltered annuity (TSA)** through a payroll-deduction plan. A tax-sheltered annuity allows contributions to it, as well as earnings, to be tax deferred until annuity payments begin, usually at retirement. TSAs are widely used by schoolteachers.

The *total* tax-sheltered contribution is generally 20 percent of pay, multiplied by years of service, minus tax-free contributions made in prior years. The amount that may be contributed *annually* is 25 percent of pay, or $9,500, whichever is less. (Note: The $9,500 limitation remains in effect until the $7,000 limitation on 401(k) contributions is increased by inflation adjustments, starting in 1988, to more than $9,500. At that time TSA contributions may be increased.)

A TSA may be invested in shares of mutual funds, and a distribution from it may be rolled over into an IRA. TSAs are subject to the same general restrictions as are other qualified plans.

Simplified Employee Pension (SEP) Plan

A **simplified employee pension (SEP)** plan allows an employer to contribute and deduct for an employee's IRA account more money than would be allowable under IRA rules. The employer may contribute up to 15 percent of the employee's compensation or $30,000, whichever is less.

Only a qualifying small company may offer a SEP. The company cannot have more than 25 employees in the preceding tax year. In addition, if a salary-deduction plan is offered, at least 50 percent of the employees must accept it. Also, the deferral percentage for highly compensated employees cannot exceed 125 percent of the average contribution of the regular employees.

The employer's contribution is exempted from taxes (prior to 1987 it was not). Also, an employee over age 70½ may still participate in a SEP but may not make a contribution to his or her personal IRA.

FEDERAL ESTATE AND GIFT TAXES

Upon a person's death, all of his or her assets—whether real or personal and wherever situated—comprise that decedent's estate. If the decedent's estate exceeds $600,000, the federal government imposes an estate tax. Those who wish to reduce this obligation may do so by making annual gifts during their lifetime. However, if an annual gift exceeds a certain amount prescribed by law, then it too is subject to tax.

Under the Internal Revenue Code, estate taxes and gift taxes share a common table and a common rate, called a *unified tax rate schedule*, which is displayed in Table 8-1. When the estate has been appraised, the estate tax is first determined by finding this sum in the column labeled Taxable Amount. Then the tentative tax is determined from the last three columns. This amount is called a tentative tax because the actual tax is found by deducting the credit at the bottom of the table. For example, if the deceased died in 1986 and left a net estate of $500,000, the tentative tax would be $155,800, but this amount would be reduced by $155,800, which is the amount of the credit at the

bottom of the table. Therefore, the estate tax would be zero ($155,800 − $155,800 = 0).

When the amount of the estate is between $500,000 and $750,000 (for example, $600,000), the computation is not as easy. The formula for this amount is shown in the middle of the table. But once again, by taking the credit, the estate tax is zero.

ESTATES OF UNMARRIED DECEDENTS

To illustrate, assume that an estate of an unmarried decedent is appraised at

TABLE 8-1 New Rate Schedule for Federal Estate and Gift Taxes

Estate and Gift Taxes, Unified Tax Rate Schedule

If the Taxable Amount Is:		Tentative Tax Is:		
From	*To*	Tax on Amount in *First Column*	*+ %*	*On Excess over*
$ —	$ 10,000	$ —	18	$ —
10,000	20,000	1,800	20	10,000
20,000	40,000	3,800	22	20,000
40,000	60,000	8,200	24	40,000
60,000	80,000	13,000	26	60,000
80,000	100,000	18,200	28	80,000
100,000	150,000	23,800	30	100,000
150,000	250,000	38,800	32	150,000
250,000	500,000	70,800	34	250,000
500,000	750,000	155,800	37	500,000
750,000	1,000,000	248,300	39	750,000
1,000,000	1,250,000	345,800	41	1,000,000
1,250,000	1,500,000	448,300	43	1,250,000
1,500,000	2,000,000	555,800	45	1,500,000
2,000,000	2,500,000	780,800	49	2,000,000
2,500,000	and over	1,025,800	50	2,500,000

Note: $155,800 + ($600,000 − $500,000) × 37 percent = $192,800.

Unified Credit for Estate and Gift Taxes

Year	Amount of Credit	Amount of Exemption Equivalent
1983	$ 79,300	$275,000
1984	96,300	325,000
1985	121,800	400,000
1986	155,800	500,000
1987 and thereafter	192,800	600,000

$750,000. According to Table 8-1, the tentative amount of the estate tax is $248,300, reduced by the amount of the unified credit of $192,800. This results in an estate tax of $55,500 ($248,300 − $192,800 = $55,500).

Let's take another example. Assume that an estate is appraised at $1,200,000. The amount of the estate tax is computed as follows:

Appraised Estate	Tentative Tax
$1,000,000	$345,800
$200,000 excess at 41 percent	+ 82,000
Tentative tax	427,800
Unified credit	− 192,800
Estate tax	$235,000

ESTATES OF MARRIED DECEDENTS

In the examples given above for an estate of $1,200,000, it was assumed that the decedent was single.

If the $1,200,000 were owned by a married couple, there would be no estate tax upon the first death. This is because each spouse would own only half of the estate, or $600,000, which is exempt. But if the deceased spouse left his or her half to the surviving spouse, that person would then be single and possessed of the entire $1,200,000 and would be taxed for $235,000.

A married couple would like to avoid this tax, especially if they have children, rather than pay this sum to the Internal Revenue Service. To accomplish this, married persons with an estate of this size should each create a trust. Each trust would leave half of the combined estate to the children, with lifetime income to the survivor. Then, when the second spouse died, the trust estate of $600,000 would go tax free to the children, and so would the survivor's estate of $600,000 (because of the $600,000 exemption), resulting in a zero estate tax on the entire $1,200,000.

The Tax Reform Act of 1986 also allows a spouse to give any amount during his or her lifetime to the other spouse without paying a gift tax.

GIFT TAX RULES

Every person can give $10,000 a year under the **annual exclusion rule**, completely exempt from gift taxes, to as many people as that person desires, whether or not they are relatives. If a spouse joins in the gift, the husband and wife may give $20,000 a year to as many people as they like. For example, assume that a married couple filing a joint return has three children. If both spouses join in the gift, they may give $20,000 a year, gift tax free, to each of their three children, for a total of $60,000 a year. If they continue to do this every year for ten years, they will have given away $600,000 completely free of estate and gift taxes.

The $10,000 annual exclusion is subject to the **present interest rule**, which states that if a gift is made under the annual exclusion, the donee must have right to the ownership benefits now. For example, if the gift consists of stock that pays dividends, the donor cannot retain the right to receive the dividends. If the donor should retain the right to the dividends, this would be a gift of a future interest.

A **taxable gift** is a gift deliberately made in excess of the $10,000 annual exclusion. In that event, the gift is subject to the gift tax at the time of the donation, or it must be included in the estate appraisal upon the death of the donor. Well-to-do people make taxable gifts for several reasons:

1. The income from a taxable gift is taxed in the probably lower income tax bracket of younger heirs, provided the heirs are 14 years of age or older.
2. If the gift appreciates in value, the appreciated value is not subject to estate taxes, for it is no longer in the donor's estate.
3. The donor has the opportunity to observe how well the younger heirs manage the asset that constitutes the gift.

STATE INHERITANCE AND GIFT TAXES

State inheritance and gift taxes can no longer be ignored because they have seriously escalated in recent years. These taxes are imposed by most states. Since tax laws vary from state to state, it is impossible to discuss in this text the exemptions and rates with regard to these taxes. The investor who is seriously concerned with planning for these taxes has no alternative but to consult the law in his or her particular state of domicile.

A state inheritance tax is a true inheritance tax, for it is imposed on the individual heirs, not on the estate of the deceased. As a general rule, both the amount that is exempt and the rate of the inheritance tax depend upon the heir's relationship to the deceased.

Heirs that receive the most favorable treatment are surviving spouses and minor children. As the relationship of an heir to the deceased grows more remote, the exemption granted becomes less and the tax rate increases. Although states move slowly, it is anticipated that they will increase the exemptions granted in their inheritance tax laws to conform with the federal estate tax law.

States that impose an inheritance tax usually have a gift tax as well. Some states have always recognized the annual exclusion. Other states do not. Once again, heirs have to find out what the gift tax law is in their particular state.

SUMMARY

No one should pay more in income taxes than the law demands. Under our income tax system of individual self-assessment and voluntary compliance, it is up to the individual taxpayer to take all of the deductions allowed under the law. These deductions make for a significant difference between gross income and the taxable income on which taxes are actually paid. This variation is inherent in our income tax system. After recovery of the expenses and capital consumed in earning income, and after setting aside a basic sum for personal expenditures of the taxpayers and their families, only net income is subject to the income tax.

There are four conditions under which a taxpayer can reduce capital gains taxes or even not pay them at all. The most important of these conditions involve selling a home, with special rules relating to the taxpayer who is age 55 or older.

Investment income from securities is taxed. The investor should realize that a stock dividend (as opposed to a regular cash dividend) is not taxed when received; it is taxed only when sold. When receiving stock rights, it is important to know how to compute the cost bases of both the new and the old shares and to realize that stock rights have a small value that can be sold to someone else if the shareholder does not want to exercise them.

The dividends and realized capital gains from mutual funds are taxed. If a systematic withdrawal plan is being used by a shareholder, the mutual fund company will provide a year-end statement using the average cost basis of the shares. This statement will disclose whether the shares sold during the year to receive a monthly or quarterly check were sold at a profit or a loss.

Depreciation is a big tax deduction for people who own income-producing property. It is a bigger tax deduction than most people realize because depreciation can be taken against the entire value of the property, not just on the amount of the property owner's down payment or equity.

When a property owner dies, that person's estate is subject to the combined federal estate and gift tax schedule, but only if the appraised estate exceeds $600,000. If a married couple's estate is a large one, the estate tax can be reduced to zero on an estate valued up to $1,200,000 by the judicious use of a trust.

<table>
<tr><td>**8**</td><td>Name _____</td></tr>
</table>

REVIEW QUESTIONS
SHORT ESSAY

Name _____

Date _____ Points _____

Directions: Answer the following questions according to your instructor's directions.

1. What is the maximum amount that is taxed (a) at the 15 percent rate and (b) at the 28 percent rate?

   a. _____

   b. _____

2. At what dollar level is all income taxed at 28 percent?

   _____

3. Define a capital gain.

   _____

   _____

4. What are the three classes of income?

   a. _____

   b. _____

   c. _____

5. What is considered to be a capital asset?

   _____

   _____

   _____

6. What is the dollar amount of a loss that can be deducted by a taxpayer in any one year?

   _____

7. Against what kind of income can passive losses be balanced?

   _____

8. When does an investor *materially participate* in the management of real estate?

    _____

    _____

    _____

9. When an investor personally invests in real estate, under what conditions can that person offset $25,000 in losses against other income?

    _____

    _____

    _____

10. An owner aged 55 sells his or her principal residence after living in it for three years. How much of the profit is a capital gain?

    _____

<table>
<tr><td>

8
</td><td>
Name _____
</td></tr>
<tr><td>

REVIEW QUESTIONS
MULTIPLE CHOICE
</td><td>
Date _____ Points _____
</td></tr>
</table>

Directions: For each of the following, select the best answer and place the letter that represents it in the Answers column.

ANSWERS

1. Passive losses can be balanced against
   a. other income.
   b. passive income.
   c. no other income.
   d. portfolio income.   _____
2. The $25,000 offset for rental real estate activities is phased out when adjusted gross income is
   a. $25,000.
   b. $50,000.
   c. $75,000.
   d. $100,000.   _____
3. When you trade a home and receive cash, you generally
   a. realize a gain.
   b. realize a loss.
   c. realize neither a gain nor a loss.
   d. none of the above.   _____
4. To be exempt from the capital gains tax on the first $125,000 of profit from selling a residential home
   a. the home owner must be 50 years old before the sale.
   b. the home owner must be 55 years old after the sale.
   c. both spouses must be 55 years of age.
   d. none of the above.   _____
5. The depreciation deduction for real estate may be taken on
   a. the amount of the down payment.
   b. the amount of the mortgage.
   c. the full value of the property.
   d. none of the above.   _____
6. As an owner-employee setting up a Keogh plan, you must include
   a. all of your employees.
   b. none of them.
   c. only those who are 21 years of age.
   d. none of the above.   _____
7. A 401(k) plan permits employees to contribute up to
   a. $7,000 a year.
   b. $30,000 a year.
   c. $2,000 a year.
   d. $10,000 a year.   _____
8. In an employee stock ownership plan (ESOP), the
   a. employer contributes the cash.
   b. employer contributes the company stock.
   c. employees buy the company stock.
   d. employees have no say in the matter.   _____

9. In tax-sheltered annuities, the maximum amount that can be contributed is
    a. $7,500.
    b. $8,500.
    c. $9,500, which can never be changed.
    d. $9,500, which can be increased when certain conditions are met.   _____

10. The exemption equivalent of the unified credit under the federal estate and gift tax laws is
    a. $600,000.
    b. $200,000.
    c. $182,800.
    d. none of the above.   _____

11. Under the federal gift tax rules, the maximum amount that a spouse may give to the other spouse is
    a. $600,000.
    b. $1,200,000.
    c. an unlimited amount.
    d. none of the above.   _____

12. Taxable gifts include
    a. gifts over $10,000 to any one person in any one year.
    b. gifts that can be subject to the gift tax.
    c. gifts that can be included in the donor's estate.
    d. all of the above.   _____

13. The present interest rule for gifts states
    a. that the donee must enjoy ownership benefits now.
    b. that the donor can retain the income from the gift but must let the donee have ownership of the gift now.
    c. that the donor's present interest cannot be forfeited.
    d. none of the above.   _____

14. State inheritance tax laws
    a. vary from state to state.
    b. are the same for most states.
    c. make no distinction among heirs.
    d. do not exist in most states.   _____

15. The *exemption equivalent* refers to
    a. the annual exclusion rule.
    b. the $10,000 exemption for gift taxes.
    c. the amount that is exempt from the federal estate tax.
    d. none of the above.   _____

8
REVIEW QUESTIONS
TRUE-FALSE

Name _____

Date _____ Points _____

Directions: Circle T or F to indicate whether each statement is true or false.

ANSWERS

1. Taxes play an important role in any financial planning by the individual investor.

    T   F

2. For income tax purposes, any property that is used in the operation of a trade or business is considered a capital asset.

    T   F

3. The maximum tax rate is 28 percent.

    T   F

4. *Other income* is all income except portfolio income and passive income.

    T   F

5. For federal income tax purposes, losses must be balanced against gains.

    T   F

6. The text lists four classifications of income.

    T   F

7. The text explains five different conditions under which a taxpayer can eliminate a capital gain.

    T   F

8. If you sell your home and buy another one for the same price within two years, you can defer any capital gain.

    T   F

9. You have to start receiving distributions from a qualified retirement plan when you reach age 70½.

    T   F

10. You may roll over a lump-sum distribution from a qualified retirement plan into an IRA.

    T   F

11. Dividends from stocks and interest income from bonds are not taxed at ordinary income rates.

    T   F

12. Mutual fund shareholders on a systematic withdrawal plan must know the average cost of their shares for income tax purposes.

    T   F

13. A depreciation deduction can be taken on an individual's home.

    T   F

14. For tax purposes, income-producing property that operates at a profit often can be shown as operating at a loss due to depreciation.

    T   F

15. Most investors put the depreciation deduction money aside for future improvements.

    T   F

16. A spousal IRA should be used when available.   **T F**

17. There are no special tax breaks on distributions from an IRA.   **T F**

18. There is a limit to the amount that an owner-employee can contribute to a Keogh plan.   **T F**

19. Some well-to-do people donate assets during their lifetime to obtain a tax advantage.   **T F**

20. There are no drawbacks to the establishment of an employee stock ownership plan.   **T F**

21. You may leave your entire estate to a surviving spouse entirely free of estate and gift taxes.   **T F**

22. Because of the combined rate schedule for estate and gift taxes, no incentives remain for making taxable gifts.   **T F**

23. A nontaxable gift must be one of a present interest.   **T F**

24. You may give your spouse property and it will not constitute a gift.   **T F**

25. State inheritance taxes are least favorable to widows and minor children.   **T F**

8

PROJECT

Name ———————————————

Date ——————— Points ———————

Mary and Tom Baldwin have become well to do in their later years due to their successful business, Mary's inheritance, and careful, sound investing. When they retired their assets were worth $1,000,000. Both children are happily married, and each has a child. Tom and Mary each have a will that leaves the entire estate to the survivor.

Mary and Tom have become concerned about the death taxes that will have to be paid on their estate. They want to know how big a death tax problem they have and the best way to reduce it. You are to provide them with suggested answers to the following questions. (Use the space below and on the back, if necessary.)

1. How much will the federal estate tax be when Tom dies?

2. How much will the federal estate tax be when Mary, as the surviving spouse, dies and leaves the estate to their children?

3. Because of the answers to questions 1 and 2, how much of the estate will go for federal estate taxes?

4. What is one way to reduce these taxes without incurring a gift tax, assuming that Tom and Mary live many years?

CHAPTER 9
OUTLINE

I. **LAWS PROTECTING THE INVESTOR**
   A. Securities Act of 1933
   B. Securities Exchange Act of 1934
   C. Investment Advisers Act of 1940
   D. Investment Company Act of 1940
   E. Statement of Policy of the SEC
   F. State Securities Laws

II. **REGULATIONS CONTROLLING CREDIT IN PURCHASING SECURITIES**
   A. Regulation T
   B. Regulation U

III. **NATIONAL ASSOCIATION OF SECURITIES DEALERS, INC.**
   A. Brief History
   B. Function of the NASD
   C. Membership Requirements
   D. Organization of the NASD
   E. Duties of the District Business Conduct Committees
   F. Some Rules of Fair Practice
   G. Uniform Practice Code
   H. Annual Statement of Financial Condition
   I. NASD Rules for Investors

9

REGULATION OF THE SECURITIES INDUSTRY

Prior to the stock market crash of 1929, there was very little regulation of the securities industry. Lack of information, unfair practices, and price manipulation were commonplace. And all too often, outright fraud existed. In this chapter you will learn about laws that protect the investor, regulations that control the use of credit in the purchase of securities, and the self-imposed regulations of the National Association of Securities Dealers, Inc.

LAWS PROTECTING THE INVESTOR

When individuals purchased securities prior to 1933, the rule was "let the buyer beware." It was up to investors to see, to the best of their ability, that they were not being cheated. Starting in 1933, Congress passed laws to protect investors and to punish people who attempted to deceive or defraud those who in good faith made investments in the marketplace. As a result of these laws, which are briefly described below, the rule changed from "let the buyer beware" to "let the seller beware."

SECURITIES ACT OF 1933

The Securities Act of 1933 has rightly been called the *full disclosure law*. Its express purpose is "to provide full and fair disclosure of the character of securities sold in interstate and foreign commerce and to prevent fraud in the sale thereof." This act accomplishes its objective by requiring a company to:

1. File with the federal government a **registration statement**, which contains all the details about the *new* securities that it proposes to offer to the public.
2. Prepare a **prospectus**, which is a digest of the registration statement, to be issued and given to a prospective

purchaser either before or at the time of the sale.

SECURITIES EXCHANGE ACT OF 1934

Despite the fact that the Securities Act of 1933 was a milestone in federal securities regulation, it was limited in scope because it dealt only with *new* issues. Neither the vast number of securities that were already in the hands of the public nor broker/dealers and the exchanges who executed transactions in these securities were regulated by the 1933 act. It therefore became apparent to Congress, almost immediately after the passage of the 1933 act, that additional legislation was required. Hence Congress passed the Securities Exchange Act of 1934.

The major reforms brought about by the Securities Exchange Act of 1934 were:

1. It regulated trading in already outstanding securities both on the national exchanges and in the over-the-counter market.
2. It required the registration of all national securities exchanges and all brokers and dealers.
3. It gave the Federal Reserve Board (FED) complete control over the

amount and nature of credit that could be extended to security buyers.

4. It established the Securities and Exchange Commission (SEC), which is composed of five members appointed by the president of the United States, by and with the advice and consent of the U.S. Senate. As the watchdog of the securities industry, the SEC is empowered to make investigations and to bring civil and criminal actions against persons who willfully violate either the Securities Exchange Act of 1934 or the Securities Act of 1933.

5. It prohibited manipulative practices that are designed to make money for those in the securities business at the expense of the general public. Some of these practices involve false appearance of active trading in a security, false and misleading statements, false changes of ownership, the "pegging" or "fixing" of prices, excessive prices that are not fairly related to the market, false representation to a customer, taking secret profits, failure to disclose control of a market in a security, and excessive *churning* of a customer's account (the frequent buying and selling of securities for the sole purpose of generating commissions).

INVESTMENT ADVISERS ACT OF 1940

Under the Investment Advisers Act of 1940, individual investment counselors and investment counseling firms are required to register with the SEC. Unfortunately, this act does not adequately protect the investor. Almost anyone with limited investment experience who is willing to fill out an application form and pay a $150 fee can obtain a license from the SEC to act as an investment adviser and charge investors for his or her advice. This lack of strict qualification for investment advisers is not well known, even among members of the securities industry.

Fortunately for the investing public, most registered investment advisers have excellent backgrounds and are well equipped to give sound advice. At this writing, however, both Congress and the SEC are sufficiently concerned about the problem of lack of strict qualification for investment advisers to warrant saying that this area of the law should be considerably strengthened in the near future.

INVESTMENT COMPANY ACT OF 1940

A void in the law governing securities was filled by the passage of the Investment Company Act of 1940, which regulates investment companies. By 1940 there were about 70 mutual funds with total assets approaching $500 million. To prevent the speculative abuses and management manipulation that resulted in losses by the public between 1929 and 1935, Congress felt (in 1940) that an industry of this size warranted federal regulation. This was a fortunate decision for the investing public because the growth of investment companies in the intervening years has been phenomenal. Today there are over 2,300 mutual funds with assets approaching $70 billion, representing 54.7 million shareholders. Dividends and capital gains distributions increased from $3.2 billion in 1981 to over $54 billion in 1987.

The Investment Company Act of 1940 provides for the registration and regulation of companies primarily engaged in the business of investing, reinvesting, owning, holding, or trading in securities. Among its major provisions are the following:

1. It requires full disclosure of the financial condition and investment policies of investment companies.
2. It prohibits investment companies from changing the nature of their business or their investment policies without the shareholders' approval.

3. It requires bank custodianship of investment companies' assets.

4. It requires management contracts to be submitted to security holders for approval.

5. It prohibits underwriters, investment bankers, and brokers from constituting more than a minority of the directors of investment companies. It also prohibits transactions between such companies and their officers, directors, and affiliates except with the approval of the SEC.

6. It states that investment companies are subject to the Securities Act of 1933 because they continuously offer new shares to the public. Therefore, when offering their shares, investment companies must issue prospectuses, which must be periodically updated to conform to SEC requirements.

The Investment Company Act of 1940 was amended in 1970. The amendments dealt with management fees, sales charges, contractual plans, and many other areas of mutual fund operations. (See Chapter 4, pages 96–97, in regard to the 1970 amendments that affect contractual plans.)

STATEMENT OF POLICY OF THE SEC

As mutual funds became increasingly popular, and as more and more sales representatives offered them to the public, abuses inevitably developed in the sale of investment company shares. To correct these abuses, the Securities and Exchange Commission issued in 1950 (as amended in 1957) its now famous *Statement of Policy*, which established ethical standards in three areas: (1) sales literature, (2) sales practices, and (3) advertising.

Sales Literature

The *Statement of Policy* defines **sales literature** as *any communication* in writing, on radio, or on television used by an issuer, underwriter, or dealer to induce the purchase of shares of an investment company. Communications among issuers, underwriters, and dealers were also ruled to be sales literature if the communications were to be passed on orally or in written form to prospective purchasers of mutual funds. This meant that sales bulletins that were issued to sales representatives, as well as other information, came within the scope of the *Statement of Policy*. As a result of this sweeping definition of sales literature, abuses in sales literature distributed by mutual funds and their sales representatives were abruptly and effectively stopped.

Sales Practices

The term *sales practices* involves the use of sales aids. Prior to the issuance of the SEC's *Statement of Policy*, the use of sales aids of every description was widespread in the sale of investment company shares. For example, one mutual fund salesperson formerly carried with him a pocket-size replica of a coffin. Inside the coffin was a dollar bill. In trying to make a sale, he would open the lid of the coffin and say, "Unless your dollar is invested in mutual fund shares, it's dead!" Of course, very few sales representatives of investment companies went to this extreme. Nonetheless, there were many violations of ethical sales practices. After the issuance of the *Statement of Policy*, no sales aids could be used that did not have the prior approval of the SEC.

Advertising

Abuses in advertising mutual funds were also prevalent prior to the issuance of the *Statement of Policy*. After 1950, any advertising copy had to be submitted within three days of its use to the SEC or the National Association of Securities Dealers, Inc. (NASD). If the advertising copy did not conform to the SEC's *Statement of Policy*, it could not be used again.

STATE SECURITIES LAWS

The first state to adopt a securities law was Kansas. This was in 1911. Because Kansas declared that in its state the blue sky was not going to be the limit when offering securities for sale, state laws since then have come to be known as **blue sky laws.**

Within a few years, as many as half of the states had followed Kansas' leadership and adopted similar laws. With the passage of time, however, the wide variety in state requirements for registration became a problem to underwriters when selling new issues on a nationwide basis. In 1929 a Uniform State Securities Act was approved by the Conference of Commissioners on Uniform State Laws and by the American Bar Association. This act, however, was superseded by a new Uniform State Securities Act that was approved in 1956.

Two uniform state laws that should be discussed here are (1) the prudent man rule, and (2) the state Uniform Gifts to Minor Act.

Prudent Man Rule

The **prudent man rule** sets forth broad principles by which fiduciaries can invest money that has been entrusted to their care. A **fiduciary** is simply one who is empowered by law to invest for someone else, usually an incompetent adult or a minor child. The prudent man rule states in part:

> All that can be required of a trustee is that he shall conduct himself faithfully and exercise a sound discretion. He is to observe how men of prudence, discretion, and intelligence manage their own affairs, not in regard to speculation but in regard to the permanent disposition of their funds, considering the probable income, as well as the probable safety, of the capital to be invested.[1]

Fiduciaries do invest in common stocks and in mutual funds. Therefore, a court order in a state that observes the prudent man rule automatically allows a fiduciary to invest in securities (stocks, bonds, and mutual funds).

Uniform Gifts to Minors Act

Most states have adopted the Uniform Gifts to Minors Act. Under this act, gifts of almost any kind of property (securities, real estate, cash) may be given to minors and placed under the control of a custodian. Normally the donor and the custodian should not be one and the same person. If they are, the gift would be taxed in the donor's estate. This would defeat one of the purposes of making a gift to a minor, which is to exclude the gift from the donor's estate and thus reduce any estate taxes for which the donor's estate may be liable.

Under the Uniform Gifts to Minors Act, making a gift to a minor is accomplished by placing the gift in the name of the custodian for the benefit of the minor. For example, a gift of money to a minor registered in the name of a custodian bank would read as follows:

> (Name of bank) as custodian for (name of minor), a minor, under the (name of state) Uniform Gifts to Minors Act.

If the gift is a registered security, the donor registers the security in the same manner. If the security is unregistered, it must be delivered by the donor to the custodian, accompanied by a written statement signed by the donor. The custodian must acknowledge receipt of the security.

Under the Uniform Gifts to Minors Act, when a minor's property is held by a custodian, the custodian has discretionary power to use the property for the minor's "support, maintenance, education, and benefit." This means that the custodian may withdraw any part or all of the account without prior approval of the probate court.

REGULATIONS CONTROLLING CREDIT IN PURCHASING SECURITIES

In Chapter 6 you learned that a purchaser of stocks can use credit to pay for part of her or his investment by opening a margin account. Many investors purchase securities in this manner. About 40 percent of securities accounts are margin accounts. These accounts, however, are subject to the margin requirements set by the FED, as explained on page 151 in Chapter 6.

As mentioned earlier in this chapter, the Securities Exchange Act of 1934 granted the FED complete control over the use of credit when buying securities. The two regulations set forth by the FED governing the purchase and sale of securities are Regulation T and Regulation U, which are discussed below.

REGULATION T

Regulation T governs the use of credit between a broker/dealer and a customer in the buying and selling of securities.

Use of Credit in a Purchase

When a customer buys a security for cash, the broker/dealer may extend credit for only seven days (or five full business days). If the customer fails to pay for the securities within seven days, the broker/dealer must cancel the transaction, except under the following conditions:

1. When the amount of money owed is less than $500.
2. When additional time is required for shipment of the securities.
3. When the transaction is a cash-on-delivery sale.

If none of the above exceptions applies and payment has not been made within five full business days after the trading date, the customer's account must be frozen for 90 days. Except for a cash trade, no other transaction may be made with this customer during that time.

If the customer purchases the security on margin, the margin requirements of the FED that prevail at the time must be observed. Furthermore, if, for instance, the purchaser has an 80 percent margin account, he or she must have an equity of at least 80 percent every time an additional security is purchased.

Use of Credit in a Sale

When a customer sells a security, that person may extend credit to the broker/dealer for seven days (or five full business days). The money due the customer cannot be held for a longer period.

REGULATION U

Regulation U governs the amount of credit that a bank may extend to a customer who wishes to purchase stocks or bonds on margin. A bank must observe the same FED margin requirements as a broker/dealer. Furthermore, a bank may not extend loans for purchases of securities that are not listed on the national stock exchanges or for purchases of mutual funds.

NATIONAL ASSOCIATION OF SECURITIES DEALERS, INC.

The National Association of Securities Dealers, Inc. (NASD) was formed in order to *self-regulate* the over-the-counter securities business. It is *not* an organization imposed upon this industry by the federal government through the SEC or by the Securities Exchange Act of 1934.

Why should you, the individual investor, want to know something about the work and the regulations of the NASD? For one thing, it will give you more confidence in

dealing with the registered representative of a NASD member. You will understand how strictly this individual and the employer whom he or she represents are regulated; how carefully the representative is chosen; and, after having been chosen, how closely the representative is supervised. Furthermore, you will know what recourse you would have under the regulations if a member firm of the NASD commits unfair practices.

BRIEF HISTORY

The first attempt to achieve self-regulation of the over-the-counter market was made in 1933 under the Investment Bankers Code, which was authorized by the National Recovery Administration (NRA). When the NRA was declared unconstitutional in 1935, a large segment of the industry recognized the need for legislation in order to maintain its self-imposed standards. At the suggestion of the SEC, the Code Committee continued to exist and cooperated with the SEC in seeking legislative authority. There were many conferences, not only with the Code Committee but also among other representative associations of the securities and investment banking business.

Finally, on January 18, 1938, the proposed legislation was introduced in the U.S. Senate by Senator Francis T. Maloney of Connecticut. Five months later, the Maloney Act (provided for under Section 15A of the Securities Exchange Act of 1934) became law. However, it was not until August 7, 1939, that the registration statement of the NASD received approval from the SEC.

In one of his speeches, Senator Maloney stated why he thought his amendment to the Securities Exchange Act of 1934 was necessary:

There can be no large group of people engaged in any industry enjoying potentialities for profit which does not attract the careless or the greedy few who bring discredit upon the entire group unless prevented by regulation from so doing. It is with this problem of imposing proper standards of business conduct that we have all been wrestling for years. The machinery of the securities business is delicate. It can be dislocated either by corruption from within or by unwise and burdensome regulation from without. Our task is to prevent the former without risk of the latter. The Maloney Act provides a formula designed to accomplish this result. The formula is predicated upon the principle that corruption from within, so far

as possible, should be prevented from *within*, and that external restraints should be rendered unnecessary as a result of the exercise of self-restraint.[2]

FUNCTION OF THE NASD

The NASD seeks to prevent by self-regulation unfair practices and fraud in the over-the-counter securities market. Its purposes are clearly stated in its articles of incorporation. These are:

1. To promote through cooperative effort the investment banking and securities business.
2. To standardize its principles and practices.
3. To promote therein high standards of commercial honor.
4. To encourage and promote among members observance of federal and state securities laws.
5. To provide a medium through which its membership may be enabled to confer, consult, and cooperate with government and other agencies in the solution of problems affecting investors, the public, and the investment banking and securities business.
6. To adopt, administer, and enforce rules of fair practice.
7. To prevent fraudulent and manipulative acts and practices.
8. To promote just and equitable principles of trade for the protection of investors.
9. To promote self-discipline among members.
10. To investigate and adjust grievances between the public and members and among members themselves.

In order to achieve self-regulation, the NASD requires registration of all brokers and dealers, as well as the licensing of all sales representatives.

MEMBERSHIP REQUIREMENTS

Any broker or dealer authorized to transact any investment banking or securities business under the laws of any state and/or the laws of the United States is eligible for membership in the NASD. Membership entitles the member (who may be an individual but is generally a firm) to participate in the investment banking and over-the-counter securities business on a preferential basis, to distribute new issues that have been underwritten by NASD members, and to distribute investment company (mutual fund) shares that are sponsored by NASD members.

The requirements for membership in the NASD that are discussed below concern the net capital rule, the financial principal, and the registered representatives of NASD members.

Net Capital Rule

Every member shall have and maintain a net capital of not less than $25,000 and shall not permit its aggregate indebtedness to all other persons to exceed 1,500 percent of this amount. However, a member may have and maintain a net capital of not less than $5,000 provided that all of the following conditions are met:

1. The member promptly transmits all funds and delivers all securities received in connection with its activities as a broker or dealer.
2. The member does not hold funds or securities for customers.
3. The member does not owe money or securities to customers.

A monthly statement showing that the net capital requirement is being maintained must be submitted to the NASD by the financial principal of the member firm.

Financial Principal

To become a financial principal, one must pass Parts 1 and 2 of a two-part qualification examination for principals and pay an examination fee of $50. The duties of the financial principal of a member firm include the actual preparation and/or approval of financial statements and supporting schedules as well as the preparation and submission of monthly statements regarding the maintenance of the net capital rule mentioned above. The NASD also requires that every broker and dealer making application for admission to membership must identify which individual will act as the financial principal.

Registered Representatives

All persons associated with a NASD member who are designated as its representatives must be registered and pass a qualification examination for registered representatives before their registration can become effective. This examination must be taken and passed by all designated representatives—whether they are full-time or part-time personnel—of a member firm. This requirement ensures that each representative will have a basic knowledge of the securities business and of the rules and regulations of the NASD.

ORGANIZATION OF THE NASD

The management and administration of the affairs of the NASD is vested in a board of governors composed of 27 members.

For administrative purposes, the NASD is divided into 13 districts. Each district has a district business conduct committee, which functions as an agent of the board of governors in executing NASD policy. Members of these district committees are chosen from local leaders of the investment community and serve without pay. The chairpersons of the 13 district committees comprise an advisory council, which meets with the board of governors once a year, or more often, to discuss problems, policies, and actions to be taken.

The NASD maintains a national executive office in Washington, DC, as well as an office in each of its 13 districts. A permanent district secretary is assigned to each district.

DUTIES OF THE DISTRICT BUSINESS CONDUCT COMMITTEES

It is the duty of the district business conduct committee in each of the 13 district offices to enforce the bylaws and rules of fair practice of the NASD. Along with the district secretary, each district business conduct committee is responsible for the following:

1. To review all examination reports submitted by NASD examiners in the district.
2. To investigate all complaints against members, as well as persons associated with a member, who appear to have violated the NASD's bylaws and rules of fair practice.
3. To conduct disciplinary proceedings in accordance with the NASD's code of procedure for handling trade practice complaints.
4. To render decisions and impose penalties where appropriate.

The Maloney Act, which amended the Securities Exchange Act of 1934, provides that the SEC may review any disciplinary action imposed by the NASD through a decision of one of its district business conduct committees. Furthermore, the SEC may abrogate any rule of the NASD, disapprove any change in the NASD's rules, and suspend or revoke the NASD's registration with the SEC if it fails to enforce compliance with its own rules.

SOME RULES OF FAIR PRACTICE

The NASD lists 28 rules of fair practice. In this chapter, only those rules that are of significance to the individual investor will be discussed.

Fair Dealings with Customers

When recommending to a customer the purchase, sale, or exchange of any security, a member shall have reasonable grounds for believing that the recommendation is suitable for such customer, based on facts disclosed by the customer as to her or his other security holdings, financial situation, and needs.

Discretionary Accounts

In a **discretionary account**, an investor gives a stockbroker the authority to exercise judgment in buying and selling securities without prior consultation. Discretionary power in such an account must be given by prior written authorization from the customer, and it must be accepted in writing by a designated representative of the NASD member who is authorized to accept it. No member vested with any discretionary power in a customer's account shall effect transactions of purchase or sale that are excessive in size or frequency in light of the financial resources and character of such account.

Use of Fraudulent Devices

No member shall induce the purchase or sale of any security by means of a manipulative, deceptive, or fraudulent device or contrivance.

Partial Payment Sales

No member shall make a transaction for any customer in which payment for the security is to be made over a period of time in installments. Regulation T of the FED must be adhered to at all times.

Disclosure of Financial Condition

A member shall make available for inspection by any bona fide regular customer, upon request, the information relative to such member's financial condition as disclosed in its most recent balance sheet, which is prepared as required by state or federal securities laws. In this case the term *customer* means any person who, in the regular course of the member's business, has cash or securities in the possession of such member.

Investment Companies

No member shall offer to sell any investment company security except at the effective public offering price described in the current prospectus of the issuing company. No member shall withhold placing customers' orders for any mutual fund security so as to make a profit as a result of such withholding. If a customer changes his or her mind and tenders investment company shares for redemption to the underwriter within seven business days of their purchase, the sales load paid shall be refunded to the customer.

Supervision

Each member shall establish, maintain, and enforce written procedures that will enable the NASD to supervise properly the activities of its registered representatives so as to ensure compliance with applicable securities laws, rules, regulations, and statements of policy as well as rules of the NASD.

The best way to demonstrate how strictly and constantly the ethical conduct of NASD members and their registered representatives is supervised under the rules of fair practice is to cite three examples of actions actually taken by a district business conduct committee of the NASD. The first example took place on June 15, 1987. The committee barred a representative from associating with any member of the NASD in any capacity and imposed a fine of $25,000 for violation of Article 111, Section 1 of the Rules of Fair Practice. These sanctions were based on findings that the representative had received checks from customers and failed to remit the checks to the employer-member, converting the funds instead to the representative's own use.

The second example took place on June 29, 1987. The committee suspended a representative from associating with any member of the NASD for 15 business days and fined him $10,000. These sanctions were imposed because the representative effected transactions in the accounts of customers without the customers' prior knowledge or authorization.

Finally, the third example took place on August 11, 1987. The committee barred a representative from associating with any member of the NASD in any capacity and fined that person $100,000. These sanctions were based on findings that the representative induced the purchase of limited partnership interests by means of fraudulent devices.

From these three examples, it can be seen that the investment community is carefully supervised and that the sanctions for violating the Rules of Fair Practice are severe. It should be noted in the interest of fairness that any sanctions imposed by the committee may be appealed to the SEC.

Margin Accounts

Any member who effects a security transaction for a customer in a margin account must obtain from the customer, no later than the settlement date, sufficient margin in an amount consistent with the credit provisions of the FED. Every margin account shall have a minimum equity deposit of $2,000.

UNIFORM PRACTICE CODE

The bylaws of the NASD authorize the board of governors to adopt a Uniform Practice Code in order to make trading techniques that are employed in the securities business uniform throughout the industry. Some important provisions of this code are discussed below.

Opening an Account

When an investor *first* opens an account with a stockbroker, that investor cannot buy a security without paying cash or sell a security without delivering it. This is simply sound business practice. However, neither failure to deliver the securities sold nor failure to pay for securities purchased cancels the contract. A customer is held accountable for her or his part of the contract.

Good Delivery of Stocks

A customer who is selling stock must provide **good delivery**. This means that the stocks must be delivered in such a condition that a transfer agent will be able to transfer the stock certificates to a new owner without additional legal requirements.

There are many cases in which a delivery of stocks cannot be considered to be "good delivery." For example, a stock certificate that is signed and delivered by a person who soon after dies is *not* good delivery. It does not matter whether the deceased who signed the certificate is the owner, a trustee, a guardian, an executor, an administrator, an assignee, a receiver in bankruptcy, an agent, or an attorney—a delivery under the above conditions is not valid.

Let us take another example. Assume that a stock certificate contains only the name of your spouse. If the law in your state limits the right of a married person to sell securities, to effect good delivery the stock certificate must be signed by both you and your spouse even though only the name of your spouse is on the face of the certificate. In addition, both signatures must be guaranteed by a bank or a stockbrokerage firm. If the certificate is endorsed by your spouse alone and delivered to the stockbroker, the delivery is not good.

Good Delivery of Bonds

The good delivery of bonds involves a different set of rules since bonds create a debtor-creditor relationship between the issuer and the holder. When delivery of a fully registered bond is made between the record date and the next interest payment date, the full amount of the interest has to be added to the market value of the bond and paid to the seller. As mentioned in Chapter 3, such a bond is said to be traded "and interest." A fully registered bond is said to be **trading flat** when its interest payments are in default. When this condition exists, a due bill for the amount of the interest that is in arrears should be given by the seller.

In the case of a coupon bond—whether it is a partly registered bond or a bearer bond—all the unpaid coupons must be securely attached to constitute good delivery. Otherwise the new owner of the bond would

be unable to collect the interest when it became due.

It is therefore obvious that whenever a customer has any question about good delivery of the securities being sold, the matter should be discussed with his or her stockbroker. If the broker does not know the answer, the question should be cleared with the operations officer of the brokerage firm involved before any securities are surrendered.

ANNUAL STATEMENT OF FINANCIAL CONDITION

The Securities Act of 1933 and the Securities Exchange Act of 1934, along with the Investment Company Act of 1940, authorize the SEC to adopt regulations to implement the broad purpose of the law. Any regulation issued by the SEC becomes part of the law and has to be observed.

One of these SEC regulations that is of particular importance to the investor concerns the **annual statement of financial condition,** which must be submitted to the SEC by every member of the NASD. This annual statement is completed on a form designated by the SEC. It must be submitted in duplicate and filed with the regional office of the SEC within 45 days of its completion, although a maximum extension of no more than 90 days is permitted. It is understood that the information in this annual statement will not be kept confidential and that the statement must be made available to the public on demand.

NASD RULES FOR INVESTORS

In its pamphlet titled *The NASD: What It Is, What It Does to Protect the Public,* the NASD lists ten simple rules for an investor to follow. These are:

1. Think before buying.
2. Deal only with a securities firm you know.
3. Beware of securities offered on the telephone from any firm or salesperson you do not know.

4. Guard against all high-pressure sales talks.
5. Beware of promises of quick, spectacular price rises.
6. Be sure you understand the risk of loss as well as the prospect of gain.
7. Get the facts—do not buy on tips or rumors.
8. Request the person offering securities over the telephone to mail to you written information about the corporation, its operations, net profit, management, financial position, and future prospects. Save all such information for future reference.
9. If you do not understand the written information, consult a person who does.
10. Give at least as much thought when purchasing securities as you would when acquiring any valuable property.

SUMMARY

Many good laws have been passed by Congress and the various states to protect the securities investor. At the federal level, the first law passed was the Securities Act of 1933, which has been rightfully called the *full disclosure law*. The federal Securities Exchange Act of 1934, among other things, required the registration of the national securities exchanges and all brokers and dealers, including their sales representatives. It also established the SEC—the watchdog of the securities industry—and provided for self-regulation of the over-the-counter securities market and the investment banking fraternity through the establishment of the NASD. Finally, to provide much-needed regulation of investment companies, the federal Investment Company Act of 1940 was passed. This act was further strengthened by the SEC's famous *Statement of Policy*, which regulates the use of sales literature, sales aids, and advertising in the offering of mutual fund shares.

Various states have also passed their own "blue sky" laws to protect the investor. By enacting uniform state laws, the states have succeeded in standardizing regulations, particularly in the registration of new securities for sale. Among the uniform state laws are the prudent man rule, which allows fiduciaries to invest in stocks, bonds, and mutual funds, and the Uniform Gifts to Minors Act, which enables adults to make gifts of cash, real estate, or securities to minors without having to resort to intricate court procedures.

Control of credit in buying securities was wisely turned over to the FED by the Securities Exchange Act of 1934. This body is best equipped to make decisions about changing margin requirements from time to time.

For the most part, the securities investor is well protected from manipulation, unfair practices, and outright fraud that might be committed by unscrupulous individuals engaged in the securities business. Certainly the individual investor cannot be protected from personal mistakes. Since the careless and the greedy will always be with us, the individual investor should not rely solely upon the law for protection. The individual should observe how others manage their own investments with prudence, discretion, and intelligence by considering the probable income, as well as the probable safety, of any capital invested.

ENDNOTES

1. *Harvard College v. Armory*, Massachusetts State Supreme Court.

2. *The NASD: What It Is, What It Does to Protect the Public* (Washington, DC: National Association of Securities Dealers, Inc., 1959), 3–4.

9
REVIEW QUESTIONS
SHORT ESSAY

Name _____

Date _____ Points _____

Directions: Answer the following questions according to your instructor's directions.

1.   Why has the Securities Act of 1933 been called the "full disclosure law"?

_____

_____

_____

_____

2.   What securities come under the Securities Exchange Act of 1934?

_____

_____

3.   The federal Investment Company Act of 1940 governs mutual funds. List three of the investment restrictions under which funds must operate.

   a.   _____

   b.   _____

   c.   _____

4.   What constitutes sales literature as defined in the SEC's *Statement of Policy?*

_____

_____

_____

5.   What is the purpose of Regulation U?

_____

_____

_____

6. What is the function of the NASD?

    _____

    _____

    _____

7. What is the net capital rule?

    _____

    _____

    _____

8. How does a member of the NASD determine that a security is suitable for a customer?

    _____

    _____

    _____

9. What is the purpose of the Uniform Practice Code?

    _____

    _____

    _____

10. List four NASD rules for investors to follow.

    a. _____

        _____

    b. _____

        _____

    c. _____

        _____

    d. _____

        _____

REVIEW QUESTIONS
MULTIPLE CHOICE

Name _____

Date _____ Points _____

Directions: For each of the following, select the best answer and place the letter that represents it in the Answers column.

ANSWERS

1. After 1933, the rule that prevailed in the securities industry was
   a. let the buyer beware.
   b. let the seller beware.
   c. every man for himself.
   d. the devil take the hindmost.   _____

2. The Investment Company Act of 1940 regulates
   a. mutual funds.
   b. the over-the-counter market.
   c. the national stock exchanges.
   d. the new issues market.   _____

3. The SEC's *Statement of Policy* regulates the use of sales literature, sales aids, and advertising in the sale of
   a. listed securities.
   b. new issues.
   c. over-the-counter stocks.
   d. investment company shares.   _____

4. Uniform state security laws were passed because
   a. the SEC prohibits federal regulation.
   b. widely varying state requirements made it difficult to sell securities nationwide.
   c. blue sky laws became unenforceable.
   d. investors wanted uniform laws.   _____

5. A fiduciary is a
   a. person who manages money.
   b. financial adviser.
   c. broker or dealer who advises clients in a fiduciary capacity.
   d. person who is empowered by law to invest for someone else.   _____

6. The Uniform Gifts to Minors Act allows
   a. donors to take an estate tax exemption if they are also the custodians.
   b. custodians to use the property for the support or education of the minor.
   c. donors to give securities to minors only if the securities are unregistered.
   d. probate courts to grant approval for custodians to withdraw part or all of the account.   _____

7. A broker's customer bought a certain stock for $2,000 but did not pay for it. Two weeks later the same customer wanted to buy another stock. Under Regulation T, the broker was required to
   a. demand a deposit of 25 percent of the purchase price.
   b. give the customer an extension in time.
   c. freeze the account for 90 days.
   d. deal with the customer at her or his own risk.   _____

8. If the FED's margin requirement is 70 percent, the
   a. customer must at all times have an equity in his or her account of at least 70 percent of the market value.
   b. customer must have an equity equal to 70 percent every time she or he makes a purchase.
   c. broker may loan up to 70 percent of the equity in the customer's account.
   d. customer must liquidate his or her account if the equity falls below 70 percent. _____

9. The first attempt to achieve self-regulation of the over-the-counter securities market was made in
   a. 1933.
   b. 1934.
   c. 1938.
   d. 1940. _____

10. Eligibility to act as a financial principal of an NASD member is determined by
   a. a qualification examination for registered representatives.
   b. a qualification examination for principals.
   c. authorization to transact any investment banking or securities business by state or federal law.
   d. the board of governors. _____

11. Enforcement of the bylaws of the NASD is handled by the
   a. district business conduct committees.
   b. board of governors.
   c. permanent district secretary.
   d. SEC. _____

12. To open a discretionary account, a customer must
   a. give instructions to the broker for all purchases or sales.
   b. submit a report on her or his financial situation.
   c. give prior written authorization.
   d. have an equity of at least 50 percent when making a purchase. _____

13. Every margin account must have a minimum equity deposit of
   a. $2,000.
   b. $4,000.
   c. $7,000.
   d. $8,000. _____

14. Good delivery of stocks means that the
   a. stocks will be in good physical condition when delivered.
   b. stocks will be delivered in good time, which is seven days.
   c. transfer agent will not demand additional legal requirements.
   d. broker will certify delivery. _____

15. A bond that is traded "and interest" means that the interest
   a. must be paid to the seller.
   b. must be paid to the buyer.
   c. payments are in default.
   d. must be added to the broker's commission. _____

9

REVIEW QUESTIONS
TRUE-FALSE

Name _____

Date _____ Points _____

Directions: Circle T or F to indicate whether each statement is true or false.

ANSWERS

1. The Securities Act of 1933 was limited in scope because it dealt
    only with new issues.   T   F

2. "Pegging" or "fixing" prices was made unlawful by the Securities
    Act of 1933.   T   F

3. "Churning" of a customer's account means that frequent
    transactions are made for the sole purpose of generating
    commissions.   T   F

4. The Investment Advisers Act of 1940 does a good job of protecting
    the investor.   T   F

5. Investment companies are not subject to the Securities Act of 1933
    because they are regulated under the Investment Company Act of
    1940.   T   F

6. The Investment Company Act of 1940 was amended 30 years later.   T   F

7. The use of sales aids in the sale of mutual funds requires prior
    approval of the SEC.   T   F

8. Missouri was the first state to adopt a securities law.   T   F

9. Prudent people do not invest in securities.   T   F

10. Approximately 60 percent of securities accounts are margin
    accounts.   T   F

11. Regulation T does not apply when the amount of money owed is less
    than $500.   T   F

12. A bank may loan money to a customer to buy investment company
    shares.   T   F

13. The NASD is not an organization imposed on the securities
    industry by the federal government.   T   F

14. One function of the NASD is to promote through cooperative effort
    the investment banking and securities business.   T   F

15. Under certain conditions the net capital requirement of a broker
    need be only $5,000.   T   F

16. Every NASD member must tell the NASD district office which individual in the firm will act as a financial principal. **T F**

17. Part-time sales personnel do not have to pass a qualification examination with the NASD. **T F**

18. The district business conduct committees conduct disciplinary proceedings for handling trade practice complaints. **T F**

19. The SEC may abrogate any rule of the NASD. **T F**

20. Installment buying is permitted in security transactions. **T F**

21. When an investor who has just opened an account with a stockbroker fails to pay for securities purchased through the broker, the contract is canceled. **T F**

22. A certificate signed by a person who soon after dies constitutes good delivery as long as the broker knew the person. **T F**

23. Regulations issued by the SEC have the effect of law. **T F**

24. The annual statement of financial condition that an NASD member must submit to the SEC must be made available to the public upon demand. **T F**

25. An investor should always request written information about a corporation when considering buying its securities. **T F**

APPENDIX
Sources of Investment Information

Throughout this text you have been advised to obtain the facts before investing. This advice applies particularly to stocks and bonds. It has already been pointed out that a corporation's annual report is an excellent source of information. If you are interested in a particular company, all you have to do is write or telephone the corporation's home office and it will be glad to send you its annual report free of charge.

There are a host of sources of investment information, but only some can be considered here. These sources consist of (1) reference manuals and corporation records provided by investment advisory services, (2) financial publications, and (3) information booklets.

REFERENCE MANUALS AND CORPORATION RECORDS

The major investment advisory services that provide reference manuals and corporation records are:

1. Moody's Investors Service, Inc.
   99 Church Street
   New York, NY 10007
2. Standard & Poor's Corporation
   25 Broadway
   New York, NY 10004

These companies issue a great number of publications, bulletins, and reports. Most large brokerage houses subscribe to one or another of their basic services. Some of these basic services are described below.

Moody's *Manuals*

Consisting of several reference volumes, Moody's *Manuals* contain the financial history and full investment data for a period of years for thousands of companies and government institutions. These volumes are prepared annually according to the following classifications:

1. Banks and finance companies.
2. Industrials.
3. Municipals and governments.
4. Public utilities.
5. Transportation.

Standard & Poor's *Stock Records*

This is a quarterly publication that provides basic financial and business information on over 1,000 stocks with high investor interest. For each stock, the record provides the following information:

1. Capsule stock information, showing where the stock is traded and its exchange symbol, as well as the approximate yield afforded by the indicated dividend based on a recent price.
2. Standard & Poor's comment on the intrinsic investment grade of the stock.
3. A long-term price chart of the stock.
4. The current outlook for the company.
5. Interim earnings.
6. Important developments.
7. Ten-year comparative statistics and P/E ratios for the stock.

Figure 1 is an example of a typical page from Standard & Poor's *Stock Records* (Spring 1988 edition).

Standard & Poor's *Corporation Records*

Consisting of six volumes, Standard & Poor's *Corporation Records* are continuous and alphabetical, regardless of field. These volumes also provide comprehensive coverage of almost all important corporate issuers of securities, both listed and unlisted issues. Each volume is divided into three sections: a yellow index, blue pages, and white pages. The yellow index gives the following vital and basic information about a company:

FIGURE 1 A Page from Standard & Poor's *Stock Records*

Fleetwood Enterprises   903E

NYSE Symbol FLE Options on ASE (Feb-May-Aug-Nov) In S&P 500

Price	Range	P–E Ratio	Dividend	Yield	S&P Ranking	Beta
Mar. 16'89	1989					
30	30⁵/₈–24⁵/₈	10	0.64	2.1%	B+	1.40

Summary

Fleetwood is the leading manufacturer of recreational vehicles and manufactured housing. Sales and earnings are extremely sensitive to cyclical economic fluctuations and especially to the level of interest rates. The long-term outlook is enhanced by FLE's growing market share in both of its major product groups and its strong financial position.

Current Outlook

Earnings for the fiscal year ending April 30, 1990 are projected at $3.25 a share, compared with the $3.15 estimated for 1988-9.

The $0.16 quarterly dividend is likely to be raised in 1989.

Recreational vehicle sales should continue strong in fiscal 1989-90 unless the general economy begins to weaken. Manufactured housing sales may begin to slip because of rising mortgage interest rates, but FLE should continue to gain market share. Margins and earnings should improve somewhat on the higher recreational vehicle sales.

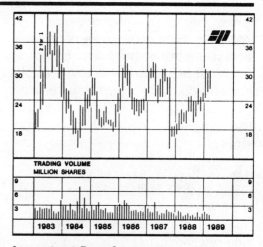

Revenues¹ (Million $)

Quarter:	1989-90	1988-9	1987-8	1986-7
Jul.	---	427	362	314
Oct.	---	419	360	304
Jan.	---	347	309	292
Apr.	---	---	374	349
	---	---	1,406	1,259

Sales for the nine months ended January 29, 1989 rose 15%, year to year, primarily reflecting a 17% gain in recreational vehicle sales. Manufactured housing sales were up 8.3%. Margins widened, and pretax earnings climbed 57%. After taxes at 37.8%, versus 38.5%, net income was up 59%. Share earnings were $2.29, compared with $1.43.

Common Share Earnings ($)

Quarter:	1989-90	1988-9	1987-8	1986-7
Jul.	E0.90	0.83	0.61	0.43
Oct.	E0.90	0.92	0.47	0.37
Jan.	E0.60	0.54	0.35	0.37
Apr.	E0.85	E0.86	0.65	0.53
	E3.25	E3.15	2.08	1.70

Important Developments

Mar. '89— FLE said that fiscal 1988-9 third quarter manufactured housing sales were $126.7 million, up 18% from $106.9 million the year before. Recreational vehicle sales were $213.1 million, up 6.2% from $200.6 million a year earlier.

Nov. '88— The company adopted a "poison pill" stock purchase rights plan as an anti-takeover move, but emphasized that the action was not taken in response to any actual or perceived takeover threat.

May '88— FLE said that its share of the manufactured housing market had risen to 14.8% in 1987, from 14.3% the year before, more than its two closest competitors combined. The year saw declining sales for the industry as a whole.

Next earnings report expected in late May.

Per Share Data ($)

Yr. End Apr. 30	1989	1988	1987	1986	1985	1984	1983	1982	1981	1980
Tangible Bk. Val.	NA	15.02	13.56	12.37	11.10	9.25	6.85	4.87	4.78	4.93
Earnings	NA	2.08	1.70	1.69	2.29	2.71	1.33	0.41	0.11	d0.38
Dividends	0.64	0.60	0.52	0.44	0.36	0.30	0.27	0.26	0.26	0.26
Payout Ratio	NA	28%	31%	26%	16%	11%	21%	64%	239%	NM
Calendar Years	1988	1987	1986	1985	1984	1983	1982	1981	1980	1979
Prices—High	26⁵/₈	32	33¹/₂	28³/₄	30³/₄	41⁷/₈	20⁵/₈	7¹/₂	4⁷/₈	6¹/₂
Low	17	14	20³/₄	17¹/₂	14¹/₈	18	5¹/₄	4¹/₈	2⁵/₈	3¹/₂
P/E Ratio—	NA	15-7	20-12	17-10	13-6	15-7	16-4	18-10	45-23	NM

Data as orig. reptd. Adj. for stk. div(s). of 100% Apr. 1983. 1. Sales prior to 1988-9. E-Estimated. NA-Not Available. NM-Not Meaningful.

Source: From Standard & Poor's *Stock Records*, Spring 1989 edition. Standard & Poor's Corporation, 345 Hudson St., New York, NY 10014.

1. Capitalization.
2. Corporate background.
3. Number of employees.
4. Names of executives and directors.
5. Stock data.
6. Earnings and finances from the last two annual reports of the company.

The blue pages furnish information about subsidiary companies, and the white pages provide information about the parent company.

Standard & Poor's *Stock Guide*

If Standard & Poor's *Corporation Records* are too involved for you or provide too much information for you to digest, Standard & Poor's monthly *Stock Guide* will give you a great deal of information about a company on just one line across two facing pages. This amazing amount of information consists of the following:

1. The ticker symbol for the stock.
2. The name of the issue and the market (or markets) on which it is traded.
3. Dividend ranking.
4. Par value.
5. The number of institutions that own the stock and their total holdings in thousands of shares.
6. The company's principal business.
7. The price range since 1971 broken down into the high and the low for the previous two years.
8. The previous month's high, low, and last stock quotation.
9. The percentage dividend yield.
10. The P/E ratio.
11. The length of time during which some dividends have been paid each year.
12. The dividend record.
13. The firm's financial position, from which the current ratio and the quick ratio can be computed.
14. The firm's capitalization.
15. Earnings per share for the past five years.
16. Interim earnings or remarks.

Figure 2 on pages 232–233 shows a sample two-page spread from Standard & Poor's *Stock Guide* for July 1988.

The information in Standard & Poor's *Stock Guide* is complete enough that the average registered representative seldom turns to Standard & Poor's *Corporation Records* but refers instead to the monthly *Stock Guide* to refresh his or her memory about a particular company. If you want to keep informed, you would be wise to obtain an up-to-date *Stock Guide* every six months or so. You don't need to obtain a new one every month. If you need more up-to-date information than that provided in your latest issue, you can obtain it from your stockbroker, who always has the latest month's issue.

FINANCIAL PUBLICATIONS

Among the most widely read general financial publications are:

1. *The Wall Street Journal.*
2. *Barron's Financial Weekly.*
3. *Business Week.*
4. *Forbes.*
5. *Fortune.*
6. *Commercial and Financial Chronicle.*

For those interested in mutual funds, the bible of the mutual fund industry is *Wiesenberger Services Investment Companies*, which can be purchased directly from Wiesenberger Financial Services, Inc., One Penn Plaza, New York, NY 10019.

Every major industry publishes a trade magazine that gives the latest developments that affect its own particular segment of the national economy. Some of these trade publications are:

1. *Automotive News.*
2. *Iron Age.*
3. *Food Industries.*

Finally, government data are available from the Department of Commerce, the Federal Reserve Board, and the Department of Labor. Some of the major government publications most widely used are:

FIGURE 2 A Sample Two-Page Spread from Standard & Poor's *Stock Guide* (page 1)

98 **Gan-Gen** Standard & Poor's Corporation

¶S&P 500 •Options Index	Ticker Symbol	Name of Issue (Call Price of Pfd. Stocks)	Market	Com. Rank. & Pfd. Rating	Par Val.	Inst.Hold Cos	Inst.Hold Shs. (000)	Principal Business	Price Range 1971-86 High	1971-86 Low	1987 High	1987 Low	1988 High	1988 Low	Jun. Sales in 100s	June, 1988 Last Sale Or Bid High	Low	Last	%Div. Yield	P-E Ratio
¶ 1•[1]	GCI	**Gannett Co**	NY,B,M,P,Ph	A+	1	559	109480	Newspapers: TV/radio:adv	43 9/16	3⅝	56¼	26	39⅞	29¼	81043	33⅝	30⅞	32	3.1	14
2	GTOS	**Gantos Inc**	OTC	NR	1¢	17	1043	Woman's apparel stores	26½	13½	23⅜	10	14½	10¼	6810	11¾	10¼	11¾B	...	14
¶ 3•[2]	GPS	**Gap Inc**	NY,B,M,P,Ph	A–	5¢	134	12773	Apparel specialty stores	45⅞	⅞	77⅞	16	32½	18½	51330	32½	24	31	1.6	13
4	GAN	**Garan Inc**	AS	B	1	20	1344	Knitted/woven apparel	33	3¾	28¾	13¾	22½	14½	163	22½	20⅝	22½	3.6	13
5	GACO	**GardenAmerica Corp**	OTC	NR	No	26	1496	Mfr automatic watering sys	20	10	18¾	7¾	17¾	9¼	2412	17¾	14¾	17¼B	...	18
6	GART	**Gartner Group**[51]	OTC	NR	1¢	23	719	Mkts research reports/svcs	12⅝	9½	17	5¾	22¼	6½	22073	22¼	12¾	22¼B	...	38
7	GWAY	**Gateway Commun'n**	OTC	NR	No	10	299	Mfr data commun network sys	17	2	12½	2⅛	4⅜	2½	3494	3½	2¾	3B	...	d
8	GMSIE	**Gateway Medical Sys**	OTC	NR	10¢	4	98	Own,operate hospitals	27½	½	5	¼	⅝	¼	899	⅜	¼	¼B	...	d
9	GMT	**GATX Corp**	NY,B,M,P,Ph	B–	62½¢	86	7250	Railcar leas'g/equip financ'g	65	20½	50¾	33⅜	49⅝	37	1372	48¾	46⅜	48¾	3.7	11
10	Pr	**$2.50 cm Cv Pfd (63)vtg**	NY,M	NR	1	2	25	tank terminals, shipping	80	28½	62¾	45	60	46	4	60	59⅛	60⅞B	4.1	..
11	GCR	**Gaylord Container'A'**	AS	NR	1¢	..	....	Mfr paper packaging prod	....	....	....	....	21⅛	20½	8993	21⅛	20½	20⅝	...	12
12	GOI	**Gearhart Ind**[52]	NY,B,M,P,Ph	↓C	50¢	38	5373	Oil wireline svs & equip	60¾	⅞	4	½	1½	⅝	13448	⅞	⅝	¾	...	d
13	GEC	**GEICO Corp**	NY,B,M,P	A–	1	112	11900	Direct writer of auto insur	105½	2⅛	136¾	90⅛	129¼	101½	1114	127½	122¾	127¼	1.3	14
14	GSC	**Gelman Sciences**	AS	B–	10¢	10	394	Lab health devices: filters	20	1	16¼	6½	11¾	7⅝	928	11¾	8⅞	11	...	33
15	GNL	**Gemco Nat'l**	AS	C	50¢	6	420	Distributes headwear, gloves	11¾	⅛	3⅝	1⅜	3	2⅜	358	2⅝	2⅜	2⅜	...	15
16	GEMH	**Gemcraft Inc**[53]	OTC	NR	10¢	15	857	Single-family home builder	17¾	5¾	9¾	⅞	1¾	1	1355	1⅜	1	1B	...	d
17	GMI	**Gemini II**	NY,M	NR	1	13	2897	Dual purpose investment co	13	9⅜	17½	9¼	13⅛	10	4724	13⅛	11	12¾	...	..
18	Pr	**cm Income share,vtg**	NY	NR	1	5	64	Com-cap gains:Pfd-income	14⅜	10	15	9¾	13⅝	11¾	1448	13⅜	12¾	13	†8.9	..
19	GCOR	**Gencor Indus**	OTC	NR	10¢	8	194	Mfrs ind'l combustion sys	18¼	1⅞	21	4	10	5½	470	7¾	6½	7¼B	...	22
20•[2]	GY	**GenCorp**	NY,B,C,M,P,Ph	B	10¢	99	23243	Tires, plastics, chemicals:TV	28⅛	2⅝	40	19⅞	23⅜	16½	30058	20¼	18	19½	3.1	10
¶21•[3]	GNE	**Genentech, Inc**	NY,M,P	B–	2¢	246	19538	Health care pr-gene splic'g	49⅜	4⅜	65¼	26	47½	25	106707	29¾	25	27	...	25
22	GAM	**Gen'l Amer Investors**	NY,M	NR	1	27	702	Medium sized closed end	24	6⅞	22	11½	16	13¼	2227	16	14½	15⅞	2.2	..
23	GA	**General Automation**	AS	C	10¢	8	385	Multi-user microcomputers	25¾	1½	6⅝	1⅝	2⅜	1⅜	2312	1⅞	1⅜	1½	...	d
24	GBND	**General Binding**	OTC	B	12½¢	29	2509	Mfr business machines & sup	16½	3⅛	15¾	7⅞	26	13¾	6583	26	18½	25½B	1.1	22
25	GBLD	**Gen'l Building Prod**	OTC	NR	5¢	10	290	Mkt lumber/build'g supplies	....	....	12¾	4	6½	4¼	1662	6	5	5½B	...	16
26	GCER	**General Ceramics**	OTC	B+	1	17	491	Mfr electronic ceramics	21¾	¼	25½	9	13	9¾	1547	10½	9¾	10¼B	1.0	10
¶27	GCN	**General Cinema**	NY,B,M,P	A+	1	193	32357	Soft drinks:theatre chain	29½	⅜	31¾	13¾	20⅞	15¾	29216	20⅞	18¾	19⅝	1.8	15
28	Pr A	**Ser[60]A cm Cv Stk(NC)**	NY,M	NR	1	9	3080	TV & radio stations	28½	6⅜	31⅛	14	21	15¾	83	21	18½	19B	2.1	..
29	GDC	**Gen'l DataComm Ind**	NY,B,M,P	B	10¢	32	4304	Data communic'n netwk/eq	21	⅛	14¼	3⅜	4⅝	3	3383	3⅝	3⅛	3⅜	...	d
30	GDV	**General Development**	NY,M,P,Ph	NR	1	47	4736	Dev communities in Florida	25¼	9⅞	26⅝	8⅛	19½	10⅜	5771	14¾	12⅝	13⅝	...	6
31	GDIC	**General Devices**	OTC	C	1¢	1	27	Engr & tech svs: personnel	7½	1/16	1⅝	⅜	⅝	½	163	½	½	½B	...	d
¶32•[4]	GD	**General Dynamics**	NY,B,C,M,P,Ph,Mo	B+	1	269	18052	Aerospace: sub mfr: bldg mtl	89¼	2¾	79	42⅝	59	46¾	16726	55½	52½	53	1.9	5
¶33•[2]	GE	**General Electric**	NY,B,C,M,P,Ph	A+	63¢	1357	423170	Consumer/ind'l prod,broad'cst	44⅜	7½	66⅜	39	47⅞	38⅜	322590	44½	41¾	43⅞	3.2	12
34	GNU	**G.E.,Americus(Unit[62])**	AS,M,Ph	NR	No	16	3681	Unit Trust for Gen'l Electr	....	....	131½	81	91	78	287	87	83	83½B	3.3	..
35	GNS	**Score**	AS,Ph,M	NR	No	6	225	Capital appreciation	....	....	49	12¾	17¾	6½	2368	8¾	7⅞	8¼	...	..
36	GNP	**Prime**	AS,M,Ph	NR	No	16	348	divd income pay'g component	....	....	89	64	81	71	244	81	75½	78½	3.5	..
37	JOB	**Gen'l Employ Enterpr**	AS	C	No	2	26	Personnel placement service	9¾	¾	3¼	1⅝	2	1⅝	45	1⅞	1⅝	1⅝	...	d
38	GED	**Gen'l Energy Dev Ltd**[63]	NY,M	NR	No	...	....	Oil & gas explor,dev,prod'n	20	3⅛	5⅝	2	3½	2⅛	1760	3½	2½	3⅛	12.8	..
39	GHO	**General Homes**	NY,M	C	1¢	16	1196	Builds single-family homes	19½	4¾	10⅛	1½	2¼	1½	919	1¾	1½	1½	...	d
40	GH	**General Host**	NY,B,M,P,Ph	B	1	66	6849	Specialty retailer:food prod	25⅝	⅝	16¼	6⅝	11¾	8	8416	11¾	10½	11⅜	2.5	4
41	GHW	**General Housewares**	NY,B,M,Ph	B–	33⅓¢	19	909	Mfr cookware & giftware	29¾	¼	13	5¾	9⅜	7¼	698	9⅜	7⅝	9	2.7	17
¶42•[5]	GRL	**General Instrument**	NY,B,C,M,P,Ph	B	1	246	25571	Electronic components & sys	66⅞	1⅜	47⅞	18⅝	40	26⅝	52405	40	35½	37¾	1.3	13
43	GMCC	**General Magnaplate**	OTC	B+	No	4	16	Corrosion/wear-proof coating	16¾	¼	7¾	5	13¾	6¾	23	12½	9½	9½B	1.1	10
44	GMW	**General Microwave**[68]	AS	B+	1¢	...	....	Electron measure/control eq	18¼	⅜	14⅝	5	6¼	5⅛	204	6¼	5⅝	5⅞B	...	9
¶45•[1]	GIS	**General Mills**	NY,B,C,M,P,Ph	A	75¢	473	52342	Consumer foods,apparel,toys	47⅜	7	62⅛	40¾	52¾	43⅛	53287	49	45⅝	46⅞	4.0	14

Uniform Footnote Explanations—See Page 1. Other: [1]P:Cycle 1. [2]CBOE:Cycle 3. [3]CBOE,P:Cycle 1. [4]CBOE:Cycle 2. [5]Ph:Cycle 3. [51]Saatchi & Saatchi offer,$22.50 to Jul 20. [52]Plan vote on Halliburton acq,0.03575 com. [53]First Texas Svgs plans acq,$1.50 cash. [54]Excl 2.93M conv restricted stk. [55]©$0.21,'88. [56]©$1.71,'87. [57]Fiscal Jul,'85 & prior. [58]11 Mo Jun'86. [59]®$0.11,'87. [60]Divd rt $0.03 plus amt pd on com. [61]Pfd in M$. [62]Rep 2 com shrs of G.E.. [63]Inst hldg not available due to buyback. [64]100% non-taxable,'87. [65]19 Wk Dec'84. [66]®$0.49,'87. [67]®$1.88,'88. [68]Inst.hldg not available.

1. *Statistical Abstract of the United States.*
2. *Survey of Current Business.*
3. *Business Statistics.*
4. *U.S. Industrial Outlook.*
5. *Business Conditions Digest.*

The above publications and several others may be obtained from the Superintendent of Documents at the U.S. Government Printing Office, Washington, DC 20402.

INFORMATION BOOKLETS

There are also many booklets that can be obtained either at a small cost or free of charge. Some of these booklets and their respective sources are given below.

1. The New York Stock Exchange Information Bureau, 11 Wall Street Station, New York, NY 10005, provides the *New York Stock Exchange Fact Book* and an information kit that contains the following booklets:
   a. *Understanding Stocks and Bonds.*
   b. *Capital Markets.*
   c. *Understanding Financial Statements.*
   d. *A Glossary.*
2. The American Stock Exchange, 86 Trinity Place, New York, NY 10006, publishes the *Requirements for Original Listing.*
3. The National Association of Securities Dealers, Inc., 1735 K Street, N.W., Washington, DC 20006, publishes the *NASDAQ Fact Book.*
4. The Investment Company Institute, 1775 K Street, N.W., Washington, DC 20006, annually updates a publication called *Mutual Fund Fact Book.*

FIGURE 2 (page 2)

Common and Preferred Stocks

Splits ◆	Cash Divs. Ea.Yr.	Dividends			Total $			Financial Position Mil-$				Capitalization			Earnings $ Per Shr.							Interim Earnings			
		Latest Payment		Ex. Div.	So Far 1988	Ind. Rate	Paid 1987	Cash& Equiv.	Curr. Assets	Curr. Liab.	Balance Sheet Date	Lg Trm Debt Mil-$	Shs. 000		Years End	1984	1985	1986	1987	1988	Last 12 Mos.	Period	$ Per Shr.		Index
Index	Since	Per$	Date										Pfd.	Com.									1987	1988	
1◆	1929	Q0.25	7-1-88	6-6	0.75	1.00	0.92	26.9	601.	475.	12-27-87	1094		161967	Dc	1.40	1.58	1.71	1.98	E2.30	2.11	3 Mo Mar	0.33	0.46	1
2		None Since Public			....	Nil	....	1.17	44.0	23.5	1-31-88	9.69		5264	Ja	D0.23	0.69	0.90	△0.95		0.86	3 Mo Apr	△0.14	0.05	2
3◆	1976	Q0.12½	6-13-88	5-27	0.37½	0.50	0.50	32.1	259.	129.	1-30-88	12.0		35826	Ja	0.36	0.81	1.93	P1.95	E2.35	1.62	3 Mo Apr	0.45	0.12	3
4	1963	Q0.20	5-31-88	5-18	0.50	0.80	0.60	16.5	63.9	15.8	12-31-87	7.96		2611	Sp	3.63	1.71	0.96	0.81		1.71	6 Mo Mar	0.25	1.15	4
5	....	None Since Public			....	Nil	....	....	29.7	21.6	12-31-87	15.1		2947	Sp	0.61	0.94	1.05	0.89		0.97	6 Mo Mar	0.40	△0.48	5
6	....	None Since Public			....	Nil	....	8.67	25.0	16.1	3-31-88			3344	Mr	*0.12	*0.41	0.52	0.59		0.59				6
7◆	....	None Since Public			....	Nil	....	2.01	5.80	0.84	12-31-87	0.02		4523	Dc	d0.02	*0.16	0.33	0.11		d0.01	3 Mo Mar	0.14	0.02	7
8◆	....	None Paid			....	Nil	....	0.56	86.1	106.	1-31-88	10.2	1	8975	Ap	d0.72	△d0.24	*0.05	d0.27		d0.49	9 Mo Jan	*0.06	d0.16	8
9	1919	Q0.45	6-30-88	6-9	0.90	1.80	1.50	Equity per shr $24.74			12-31-87	1221	132	8797	Dc	2.37	■d3.80	2.40	3.64	E4.30	3.85	3 Mo Mar	0.80	1.01	9
10	1969	Q0.62½	6-1-88	5-10	1.25	2.50	2.50	Conv into 1.25 shares common				....	132		Dc	n/a	n/a	n/a	n/a		....				10
11	....	None Since Public			....	Nil	....	5.00	128.	121.	p12-27-87	p422.		±*15300	Sp				p0.65		1.79	3 Mo Dec△pd0.55		p0.59	11
12	....	0.10	5-20-85	5-3	....	Nil	....	90.8	234.	410.	1-31-88	18.0	880	39991	Ja	0.66	■d8.44	d11.13	d0.54		0.39	3 Mo Mar	△1.78	△2.01	12
13	1977	Q0.41	6-30-88	5-31	0.82	1.64	1.36	Equity per shr $39.03			12-31-87	169.		p15549	Dc	△5.11	△4.21	*6.91	△9.01	E9.25	9.24	3 Mo Mar	0.14	0.30	13
14	....	None Paid			....	Nil	....	0.55	26.1	10.5	12-31-87	15.5		2338	Jl	■0.66	0.30	d0.29	0.17		0.33	3 Mo Mar	0.14	0.30	14
15	....	0.12	3-7-70	2-17	....	Nil	....	1.92	13.5	6.45	12-31-87	3.22		2782	Dc	0.05	d2.14	*d0.86	*0.16		0.16	3 Mo Mar	*0.05	*0.05	15
16	....	None Since Public			....	Nil	....	Equity per shr $1.45			9-30-87	100.		4917	Dc	0.28	1.21	0.42	Pd2.94		d3.48	3 Mo Mar	d1.30	d1.84	16
17	1988	0.04	3-2-87	1-27	....	Nil	0.04	Net Asset Val $16.89			6-24-88		10921	10921	Dc		§11.47	§13.87	§12.98			To redeem 1-31-97,$9.30			17
18	1985	0.20	6-1-88	4-26	†0.96	1.16	†1.23	Net Asset Val $9.60			6-24-88		10921		Dc		§9.83	§9.73	§9.39		0.33	3 Mo Mar	0.43	0.53	18
19◆	....	None Paid			....	Nil	....	0.43	20.8	9.93	9-30-87	9.90		±1532	Dc	0.42	0.80	0.03	P0.23	E2.00	7.78	3 Mo May	3.28	1.19	19
20◆	1937	Q0.15	5-31-88	4-26	0.30	0.60	0.50	35.0	555.	362.	2-29-88	681.		31730	Nv	0.11	1.12	1.94	9.87						20
21◆	....	$$0.01	2-10-88	1-21	$$0.01	*0.35	$$0.70	158.	315.	82.8	12-31-87	168.		⁵⁴78740	Dc	0.04	0.09	■d5.08	0.50	E1.10↓	0.62	3 Mo Mar	0.06	0.18	21
22	1939							Net Asset Val $19.26			6-24-88			15894	Dc	§16.72	§20.63	§19.29	§16.76						22
23	....	None Paid			....	Nil	....	2.46	24.2	16.7	9-30-87	1.03		5456	Je	*d1.27	§²d2.98	§d2.85	*⁵⁹0.12		d0.39	9 Mo Mar	*d0.01	△d0.52	23
24◆	1975	0.06	6-20-88	5-17	0.12	0.28	0.195	19.1	103.	49.3	12-31-87	5.13		±10749	Dc	0.58	0.33	0.33	±1.01		1.16	6 Mo Mar	*0.16	0.31	24
25	....	None Since Public			....	Nil	....	1.45	20.8	6.95	8-31-87	0.76		4017	Nv	0.18	0.33	0.67	P0.58		0.34	6 Mo May	0.29	0.05	25
26	1983	0.10	1-4-88	12-1	0.10	0.10	0.09	11.6	21.5	2.59	12-27-87	3.56		3254	Dc	0.63	0.87	1.13	1.18	E1.00	0.44	9 Mo Mar	0.88	0.14	26
27◆	1953	Q0.09	7-29-88	7-12	0.27	0.36	0.31½	67.8	734.	449.	1-31-88	★963.	4820	†68474	Dc	△**0.97	●1.16	●1.71	●0.94	E1.28†	●1.38	6 Mo Apr	*0.43	*0.87	27
28◆	1982	Q0.09¾	7-29-88	7-14	0.29¼	0.39	0.34½	Cv into com shr/shr.					4863		Oc			b1.56	b1.94						28
29◆	....	None Since Public			....	Nil	....	1.21	104.	31.0	12-31-87	26.9		14324	Sp	0.80	0.71	0.26	0.05		d0.86	6 Mo Mar	0.21	d0.70	29
30	....	None Since Public			....	Nil	....	Equity per shr $13.78			12-31-87	★482.	⁶¹★25	8598	Dc	p3.05	p3.01	2.67	2.60		2.36	3 Mo Mar	0.65	*0.41	30
31	....	None Paid			....	Nil	....	0.22	6.97	4.30	12-31-87	3.56		2721	Dc	*0.12	d0.21	*0.35	0.17		d0.25	3 Mo Mar	d0.06	d0.14	31
32	1979	Q0.25	8-19-88	7-13	0.75	1.00	1.00	178.	3034	2106	12-31-87	★628.		41925	Dc	8.08	9.05	d1.23	10.26	E10.40	10.33	3 Mo Mar	2.45	2.52	32
33◆	1899	Q0.35	7-25-88	6-7	1.05	1.40	1.29	2692	15739	12671	12-31-87	4491		902953	Dc	2.51	2.56	2.73	□△2.33	E3.65	2.78	3 Mo Mar	△0.35	0.80	33
34	1987	Q0.68¾	8-3-88	6-7	2.06¼	2.75	1.29½	Net Asset Val $88.25			12-31-87			4607	Dc				§8.25			Expires 5-11-92			34
35	....	None Since Public			....	Nil	....								Dc										35
36	1987	Q0.68¾	8-3-88	6-7	2.06¼	2.75	1.29½	Termination claim $140							Dc										36
37	....	0.05	12-20-85	12-4	....	Nil	....	1.17	2.68	1.41	12-31-87	0.68		1447	Sp	0.33	0.10	d0.18	d0.04		d0.06	6 Mo Mar	d0.08	d0.10	37
38	1984	0.10	8-31-88	8-9	0.30	0.40	$⁴0.60	2.04	3.78	5.64	12-31-87	5.63		12121	Dc	$⁴0.11	d4.27	d4.36	0.01		0.02	3 Mo Mar	d0.01	Nil	38
39	....	None Since Public			....	Nil	....	Equity per shr $9.13			12-31-87	383.		15009	Sp	0.75	0.33	1.17	△d1.37		d7.93	6 Mo Mar	d0.35	d6.91	39
40◆	1974	Q0.07	7-1-88	6-9	0.21	0.28	0.24	94.8	206.	106.	12-31-87	147.		19938	Dc	3.24	1.08	0.29	2.40		2.72	16 Wk May	d0.10	0.22	40
41	1981	Q0.06	6-30-88	6-10	0.12	0.24	0.24	2.83	28.3	10.7	12-31-87	4.70		2388	Dc	0.33	d1.18	0.41	⁵⁶0.51		0.52	3 Mo Mar	0.02	0.03	41
42	1977	Q0.12½	9-30-88	8-26	0.31¼	0.50	0.25	258.	603.	320.	2-29-88	175.		33488	Dc	d0.30	d2.07	d2.49	*72.01	E3.00	2.28	9 Mo May	0.37	0.64	42
43	1984	Q0.12½	4-1-88	3-7	0.05	0.10	0.10	1.31	2.93	0.43	12-31-87	2.07		795	Je	0.45	*0.69	*0.65	0.58		0.96	9 Mo Mar	0.35	0.73	43
44	1973	0.05	2-27-87	2-9	....	Nil	0.05	0.53	13.2	4.03	2-29-88	7.28		670	Fb	1.10	0.96	0.55	0.62		0.62				44
45◆	1898	Q0.47	8-1-88	7-1	1.27	1.88	1.44	60.8	949.	1202	2-28-88	361.		p85131	My	2.49	d0.81	2.05	2.50	E3.30	3.01	3 Mo Feb	2.09	2.60	45

◆ **Stock Splits & Divs By Line Reference Index** ¹3-for-2,'84(wi'83):2-for-1,'87(wi'86). ²2-for-1,'85,'86. ⁷1-for-200 REVERSE,'86. ⁸1-for-10 REVERSE,'86. ¹⁹5-for-4,3-for-2,'84.
²⁰Adj to 2%,'86:3-for-1,'87. ²¹2-for-1,'86,'87. ²⁴3-for-2,'87,'88. ²⁷2-for-1,'84,'87. ²⁸2-for-1,'84,'87. ²⁹2-for-1,'84. ³³2-for-1,'87. ⁴⁰3-for-2,'85,'86. ⁴⁴Adj for 5%,'86. ⁴²2-for-1,'86.

Source: Standard & Poor's *Stock Guide*, July 1988. Standard & Poor's Corporation, 345 Hudson St., New York, NY 10014.

GLOSSARY

accounts payable: amounts that a company owes for goods, services, or supplies obtained on open-book accounts with other businesses

accounts receivable: debts incurred by customers of a business as the result of buying merchandise on time

accrued expenses: expenses that have been incurred for wages, salaries, and commissions and that have not been paid as of the date of the balance sheet

accumulated depreciation: the amount of annual depreciation accumulated over the years

accumulation account: a mutual fund account that initially begins with a small investment, with the investor having every intention of adding to it at later dates

accumulation privilege: a privilege granted by a mutual fund when it allows the graduated sales charges to apply not only to the initial purchase but also to any subsequent purchase by the same shareholder in which the aggregate investment becomes large enough to qualify for a quantity discount sales charge

acid test ratio: a ratio obtained by deducting inventories from current assets and dividing the remainder by current liabilities to indicate the real test of a corporation's ability to meet its current bills

aggressive growth funds: a type of mutual fund whose investment objective is to seek maximum capital gains

American depository receipts (ADRs): evidence of ownership in European corporations

amortization: the decrease in the value of a bond when it is bought at a premium

annual exclusion rule: the exemption of $10,000 a year from gift taxes

annual reports: financial statements that summarize business activities and provide other useful information about a company

annual statement of financial condition: a statement to be submitted to the SEC by every member of the NASD, which contains information that will not be kept confidential and must be made available to the public on demand

appraisal fee: a fee ordered by the lender, as part of closing costs, to determine the amount of a loan

articles of partnership: the contract entered into when a partnership is formed

asked price: the price at which a buyer can buy a stock

assets: items that a business owns

auction market: organized stock exchanges that provide central marketplaces where orders from all over the country to buy or sell securities can be executed in a matter of minutes

balance sheet: a listing of what is owned and what is owed by a company as of a specific date

balanced fund: a mutual fund that invests in common stocks, preferred stocks, and bonds of established companies and whose main objectives are safety of principal, modest income, and an increase in the value of the shares

bear market: a situation characterized by the stock market's abrupt downward trend over a period of time

bearer bond: *see* coupon bond

best efforts commitment: a commitment of an investment banker to sell an entire new issue of stocks and to withdraw the offer to sell if the entire issue is not sold

bid price: the price at which a seller can sell a stock

Big Board: another name for the New York Stock Exchange

blue-chip stock: stock of a company that is a leader in a major industry, has a proven record of earnings during good times and bad, has an unbroken dividend record over a period of years, and has definite prospects of being able to continue its stellar past performance

blue sky laws: state laws indicating that the blue sky will not be the limit when offering securities for sale

bond: an interest-bearing certificate of indebtedness issued by a corporation or a government

bond accumulation: the increase in value of a bond because it was bought at a discount

breakpoint: the point at which an investor is granted a quantity discount sales charge because of the amount of money invested

brokerage houses: commission houses whose members execute customers' orders to buy and sell securities on the floor of an exchange

bull market: a situation characterized by the stock market's continued upward trend for a period of time

buy-and-sell agreement: an agreement in which each partner agrees to sell his or her interest in the partnership and the other partner or partners agree to purchase such interest at the price and under the terms and conditions set forth

buying on margin: paying for only a part of the total price of stocks and borrowing the balance from one's broker or a bank

call: an option to buy a stock at a certain price within a specified date

callable bonds: bonds that may be redeemed at the option of their corporate issuer

callable preferred stocks: preferred stocks that are redeemable at a certain price at the option of the issuing corporation

capital asset: any property that is not used in the operation of a trade or business

capital gain: a profit from selling a capital asset that an investor bought, held for a certain period of time, and later sold

capital loss: a loss from selling a capital asset

capital stock: *see* capitalization

capital surplus: the amount that stockholders pay into the company that is over the purchase price of the common and preferred stocks

capitalization: the outstanding common and preferred stocks of a company

certificate of deposit (CD): an account in a depository institution that has a set maturity date

close corporation: a corporation whose stock is not available for purchase by the general public

closed-end fund: a mutual fund company that does not sell its own shares nor stand ready to redeem them and whose shares must be bought from someone who already owns them

combination privilege: a privilege allowed a shareholder to combine investments in all of the mutual funds managed by a company to determine whether he or she qualifies for a quantity discount sales charge

commission houses: *see* brokerage houses

conduit theory: if more than 90 percent of the income from a limited partnership or a mutual fund is distributed to the investors, the distributor is simply acting as a conduit of the income, and therefore it is taxed only on the investor's return

contractual plan: also known as penalty, front-end load, or prepaid charge method—a type of accumulation account that requires the mutual fund investor to sign a contract to invest a fixed number of dollars each month for a stated number of years and charges a front-end load

conventional real estate mortgage: a mortgage not insured by a government agency, whose fixed rate of interest is the going rate and whose term is usually 30 years

convertible bonds: bonds that may be converted at the option of the holder during a specified period of time into another type of security, usually common stock

convertible preferred stock: preferred stock that can be exchanged for the common stock of the same company under certain conditions

corporate bonds: bonds issued by private enterprises

corporation: an artificial being created by law and endowed with the rights, duties, and powers of a person

cost of goods sold: the direct expenses incurred in manufacturing something for sale

coupon bond: also known as a bearer bond—an unregistered bond to which coupons with interest dates are attached for each interest payment

Curb Exchange: former name of the American Stock Exchange

current assets: cash and other assets that a business can reasonably expect to convert to cash within the space of one year

current liabilities: obligations that are due and payable within one year

current ratio: a ratio obtained by dividing current assets by current liabilities to indicate whether a company has adequate assets with which to pay its current bills

current yield: bond interest that takes into consideration the bond's current market price

cyclical stocks: stocks of businesses that are adversely affected by a decline in general business activity

date of record: the date on which all stockholders whose names are registered on the books of the company are entitled to the dividend declared

debenture bonds: corporate bonds that are simply long-term notes and that are only as good as the credit rating of the company that offers them

defensive stocks: stocks of businesses whose products or services are consumable necessities and are always in demand

deflation: prolonged period of falling prices

demand deposit account: an account in a depository institution from which funds may be withdrawn on demand at any time

depository institutions: institutions that accept money from the public and pay interest on that deposit

depreciation: a decline in value caused by usage, passage of time, or obsolescence

discretionary account: an account for which an investor gives a stockbroker the authority to exercise judgment in buying and selling securities without prior consultation

diversified money-market funds: money-market funds that invest in all types of short-term debt obligations, including U.S. Treasury obligations

dividend return per share of common stock: a ratio obtained by dividing the dividend per share by the current market price of the share

dollar cost averaging: a method of buying shares of mutual funds or common stock by which a person invests the same number of dollars every month or every quarter and continues to invest regularly, regardless of fluctuations in price

Dow Jones industrial average (DJIA): the oldest, best-known, and most widely watched stock market average, which consists of 30 industrial stocks that are considered to be sufficiently representative of what the market is doing as a whole

due date: five business days after the trade date to buy or sell stocks

earnings per share (EPS): a ratio obtained by dividing the balance of the net income (after paying any preferred dividends) by the number of outstanding common shares

EE bonds: nonnegotiable government savings bonds that are bought at a 50 percent discount and mature at their face value

employee stock ownership plan (ESOP): a retirement plan for employees that invests solely in their company's stock

enabling declaration: a document that gives authority, through its bylaws, to the board of directors of a home owners' association to regulate and administer the affairs of a condominium project

equipment trust certificates: corporate bonds that come in serial form so that they mature at stated intervals, often issued by airlines and railroads

equity: ownership

equity real estate investment trust: a type of REIT that invests its customers' money in the ownership of large properties such as apartment houses, shopping centers, large tracts of vacant land, etc.

ex-dividend date: the date on which the stockholders of record will *not* receive the dividend declared

family privilege: a privilege that applies to the combined investments of an investor and his or her family members that are of sufficient quantity to qualify for a quantity discount sales charge

FHA-insured mortgage: a mortgage insured by the Federal Housing Administration, with which the lender deals

fiduciary: one who is empowered by law to invest for someone else

fill or kill order: a special kind of limit order that instructs the broker to cancel an order if the order to buy at a certain price cannot be executed

firm commitment basis: the commitment of an investment banker to buy an entire new issue from a corporation at a set price

first-in, first-out (FIFO): method of inventory evaluation under which the oldest items in the inventory are assumed to be the first ones sold

first-mortgage bond: a corporate bond that is backed up by a blanket mortgage on all of the corporation's fixed capital assets

fixed assets: assets that are relatively permanent in nature, such as buildings, equipment and machinery, and land

floor traders: NYSE members who assist the various commission houses in their transactions

401(k) plan: basically an employee contribution retirement plan in which contributions are limited to $7,000 a year, although the employer may also contribute

front-end load method: *see* contractual plan

fully registered bond: a bond whose owner's name and address are recorded on the books of the issuing corporation

general obligation bonds: municipal bonds that are backed up by the full credit and general taxing power of the state, city, town, or political subdivision that issues them

general partner: a partner who is active in the business and is fully responsible for its debts

good delivery: the delivery of securities such that a transfer agent will be able to transfer them to a new owner without additional legal requirements

good-till-canceled (GTC) order: an order instructing a broker to buy or sell a stock at a certain price until the order is canceled

gross national product (GNP):   the sum of all the goods and services sold in a country in one year

gross revenue: the gross income of a business that sells a service

gross sales: the gross income of a manufacturing company that sells products

growth and income fund: a mutual fund that invests mainly in blue-chip companies

growth fund: a mutual fund that invests in the common stock of the more established companies but whose primary objective is an increase in the value of the investment

growth stock: a company stock that has a better-than-average increase in its market price in a relatively short period of time

guaranteed bonds: corporate bonds that are guaranteed by a corporation other than the one that originally issued them

HH bonds: current income government bonds that can be acquired only by exchanging EE bonds for them and that are sold at their face value

home mortgage loan: a special type of loan granted for the sole purpose of purchasing residential property

impound accounts: prepaid items, such as taxes and insurance, that the mortgagee requires to be paid by the month as part of the closing costs

income bonds: bonds guaranteed only as to payment of principal at maturity, the interest on which is paid only when and if it is earned

income fund: a mutual fund that seeks a high current income primarily through a portfolio of fixed-income securities, including some high-dividend-paying common stocks

income statement: a summary of the income and expenses of a company for a specific period of time, usually one year

individual retirement account (IRA):   a voluntary personal pension account limited to a maximum annual contribution of $2,000 and denied to those who have a pension plan where they work or who exceed a certain adjusted gross income

inflation: loss of the purchasing power of dollars

information bulletin: a document that gives the buyer an overall, easy-to-understand view of a condominium project

interest expense: any interest that a business has to pay during the current year

inventories: raw materials, work in process, supplies, and finished goods ready for sale

investment banker: *see* investment banking institution

investment banking institution: the channel through which new issues are offered to the general public

involuntary conversion: conversion of a person's property taken by a government's right of eminent domain

jumbo certificate of deposit: a CD in the amount of $100,000 or more whose interest rate can be negotiated between the depositor and the institution

Keogh plan: a voluntary personal pension plan for the self-employed, limited to a maximum annual contribution of 15 percent of adjusted gross income

last-in, first-out (LIFO): method of inventory evaluation under which the most recently acquired items in the inventory are assumed to be the first ones sold

level charge account: *see* voluntary plan

leverage: another word for a loan on real estate; more particularly, a real estate loan that is used deliberately to increase profits when the property is sold

liabilities: what a business firm owes to others

limit order: an order specifying the price at which a stock is to be purchased

limited partner: a silent partner who is neither active in the business nor liable for its obligations

load: the front-end sales charge of a mutual fund

long-term liabilities: obligations of a business that are not due during the current year

lump-sum account: a single investment in a mutual fund company

market order: an order to a broker to obtain the best price when the order reaches the floor of the exchange

marketable debt: the federal government's debt, which consists of U.S. Treasury bills, Treasury certificates, Treasury notes, and Treasury bonds

mini-warehouse limited partnership: a partnership that purchases parcels of land and builds mini-warehouses on them

MIP order: an order to buy shares under the NYSE's monthly investment plan

money-market fund: a type of mutual fund that invests in short-term credit obligations that yield high interest and provide relative safety, and whose shares are issued at $1 and redeemed at $1

mortgage bonds: corporate bonds that are secured by a specific mortgage on some or all of a corporation's real property

mortgage deed: a document that pledges the building and the land as collateral for the mortgage payments

mortgage real estate investment trust: a type of REIT that invests exclusively in mortgages by loaning money to others who plan to build office buildings, large apartment houses, etc.

municipal bond fund: a mutual fund that invests in municipal bonds

municipal bonds: also called **municipals**—bonds issued by states, local governments, and authorities

municipals: *see* municipal bond fund

mutual fund: a company that makes investments on behalf of individuals and institutions with similar financial goals by pooling their financial resources

mutual fund application: a form on which a mutual fund shareholder indicates how she or he elects to receive the income dividends and/or capital gains distributions that may be paid by the fund

negotiated market: *see* over-the-counter (OTC) market

net income: the income realized when the profits at the end of the fiscal year exceed the losses

net profit: *see* net income

new issues: securities that are offered to the public for the first time

no-load funds: funds sold by companies that do not utilize a sales force of commission houses and broker/dealers

nominal yield: the interest stated on the face of a bond

nonqualifying dividends: dividends from foreign holdings of a mutual fund

odd-lot brokers: NYSE members serving investors who buy less than round lots of shares

odd-lot order: an order for less than 100 shares of stock

open account: *see* voluntary plan

open corporation: a corporation whose stock is available for purchase by the general public

open-end fund: a mutual fund that continuously and aggressively offers new shares to the investing public and stands ready to redeem those shares at their asset value at any time

operating expenses: mutual fund charges that include management fees, 12b-1 fees, and other expenses

origination fee: a fee usually charged by the lender, as part of closing costs, to cover the lender's expenses

other income: income from wages, salaries, commissions, self-employment, and pass-through entities such as S corporations, REITs, and mutual funds

over-the-counter (OTC) market: a large number of small broker/dealers who operate outside the organized stock exchanges and do not have established locations where business may be transacted

par value: the stated value on a stock certificate

participating preferred stockholders: stockholders that are allowed to share with the common stockholders in the distribution of profits

partly registered bond: a bond registered only as to principal, not as to interest

partnership: an association of two or more persons to carry on a business as co-owners for a profit

passbook accounts: regular savings accounts for which depositors are issued passbooks to show that they have made deposits

passive income: income from a business or partnership in which the investor does not materially participate in the conduct of that business

penalty method: *see* contractual plan

1 percent of the amount of a conventional real estate mortgage

portfolio income: gross income from dividends, interest, annuities, and royalties that are not derived in the ordinary course of a trade or business

post-tax profit margin: a ratio obtained by dividing net income by sales to indicate a company's profit per dollar of sales

stock that represents a limited ownership in a corporation

prepaid charge method: *see* contractual plan

present interest rule: a gift rule that states that the donee of a gift must have the right to its ownership benefits now

pretax profit margin: a ratio obtained by dividing income before taxes by sales to indicate whether a company is operating efficiently

price-earnings ratio: the ratio obtained by dividing the current market price of a stock by its earnings per share for the previous year

primary distribution: the distribution of securities that are being offered to the public for the first time

prime rate: the interest rate that commercial banks charge their best corporate customers and on which all other interest rates depend

principal underwriter: the organizer of an underwriting syndicate

private placement: the distribution of securities that are not offered to the public

but are offered directly to an institutional investor

private placement limited partnership: a partnership that invests in commercial income-producing property to provide a long-term profit for its partners

profit and loss statement: *see* income statement

promissory note: a note that states the total amount of a loan, the monthly payment required, the interest rate, and the due date

proprietorship: a business owned by one person

prospectus: a digest of the registration statement to be issued and given to a prospective purchaser before or at the time of the sale of securities

proxy statement: a form that when signed and mailed back to a corporation by a shareholder gives someone else the right to cast the shareholder's vote at the annual meeting

prudent man rule: a uniform state law that sets forth broad principles by which fiduciaries can invest money that has been entrusted to their care

put: an option to sell a stock at a certain price within a specified time

qualifying dividends: dividends from investments of mutual funds in domestic corporations

quantity discount sales charge: a sales charge that allows a person to invest a larger sum of money in mutual funds at less than the customary sales charge under certain conditions

quick assets: cash, accounts receivable, and marketable securities

quick ratio: *see* acid test ratio

real estate: land, including whatever is made a part of the land by nature or human beings

real estate investment trust (REIT): a trust that purchases and holds income-producing properties of all types and has its shares publicly traded

real estate limited partnership: a business firm that invests in commercial real estate by using the limited partnership as its legal vehicle

recording fees: fees charged by local authorities, as a part of closing costs, for recording documents such as the deed to a property and the mortgage

refunding operation: the process of calling bonds

registered traders: NYSE members who trade strictly for their own accounts

registrar: a bank whose duty it is to register stocks in the names of customers on the books of the company

registration statement: a statement that contains all the details about the new securities that a company offers for sale to the public

regular savings account: an account in a depository institution from which funds can be withdrawn upon a 30-day written notice, if so required by the institution

Regulation T: a rule governing the use of credit between a broker/dealer and a customer in the buying and selling of securities

Regulation U: a rule governing the amount of credit that a bank may extend to a customer who wishes to purchase stocks or bonds on margin

regulatory agreement: a document requiring that a condominium project meet the regulations specified in Section 234 of the National Housing Act

residential income property: any piece of residential property that is purchased for either income or profit

retained earnings: that portion of a company's net earnings that is not distributed to the stockholders in the form of dividends

revenue bonds: municipal bonds that are backed up by a specific revenue, such as from tunnels, turnpikes, and bridges that charge a toll for their use

right of eminent domain: a government's right to buy a person's property in order to build a highway or a school, for instance

round-lot order: the conventional trading unit of 100 shares of stock

sales literature: any communication in writing, on radio, or on television used by an issuer, an underwriter, or a dealer to induce the purchase of shares of an investment company

second mortgage: a high-risk loan that has second claim against a property if it should be foreclosed

secondary distribution: the distribution of a large block of securities that have already been issued and are being offered for redistribution to others

selling and administrative expenses: the expenses incurred to run a sales department, pay salespersons' commissions, and run an administrative department

selling group: a group of dealers who agree to sell a specified amount of a new issue but do not assume the same liability as the members of an underwriting syndicate

serial bonds: bonds that mature at different times and on successive dates, as specified by the serial numbers on the bonds

series of preferred stock: preferred stocks that are issued and originally sold on different dates

shared-appreciation mortgage: a mortgage stipulating that the lender is entitled to share in the profits, if any, when the real estate is sold

short sale: the selling of stock not owned

simplified employee pension (SEP) plan: a qualified small-company plan that permits an employer to contribute to the employees' IRA accounts in excess of the normal $2,000 limitation

single purpose money-market funds: money-market funds that invest only in U.S. Treasury obligations

sinking fund bond: a bond whose issuer is required to set aside, at regular intervals, a specific amount of money for the purpose of retiring all or part of the entire bond issue before or at maturity

special situation stock: a stock whose value is increased when something unusual happens, such as oil discovery on land owned

specialists: NYSE members whose job is to maintain a fair and orderly market in certain stocks assigned to them, sometimes risking their own capital to do so

statement of intention: a form letter stating that a mutual fund shareholder intends to invest a sufficient sum over a 13-month period in order to qualify for the quantity discount sales charge

stock dividends: a distribution of profits in the form of stock rather than cash

stock right: the preemptive right of existing stockholders to participate in new stock offerings of their corporation

stock split: the division of outstanding common stock into additional units, such as two for one or three for one

stock warrant: a certificate, usually issued along with a bond offering, that gives its holder the option to purchase common stock at a stated price, which is almost always at a lower price than the current market value of the stock

stockholders' equity: the stockholders' investment in a corporation

stop order: an order designed to limit losses or protect profits

Subchapter S corporation: a corporation that has all the advantages of operating in the corporate form but is treated more as a partnership for federal income tax purposes

subscription and purchase agreement: primarily a sales contract for the purchase of a condominium

systematic payout plan: *see* systematic withdrawal plan

systematic withdrawal plan: also known as systematic payout plan—a plan under which a shareholder deliberately spends a part of his or her capital in a mutual fund account by redeeming some shares every year

taxable gift: a gift made in any one calendar year in excess of the $10,000 annual exclusion

tax-sheltered annuity (TSA): a tax-deferred annuity offered by insurance companies, with a wide range of investment options and with a penalty for early withdrawal during the first ten years

the third market: trading in large blocks of listed stocks by institutional investors through broker/dealers who are not members of any of the stock exchanges

times-preferred-dividends-earned ratio: a ratio obtained by dividing net income by total preferred dividends

trade date: the date on which a transaction to buy or sell stocks takes place

trading flat: the quoting of a bond that is in default and therefore has no accrued interest

transaction expenses: the bulk of the sales charge of mutual funds

transfer agent: a bank that transfers registration of a stock from one customer to another when the ownership changes

Treasury bonds: federal interest-bearing obligations that are issued with maturities ranging from five to 30 years, purchased in either coupon or registered form and bought and sold through stockbrokers

Treasury notes: federal interest-bearing obligations that are issued for their face amount, with maturities ranging from one to seven years

truth-in-lending statement: a statement required by federal and state law and prepared by a lender, which, among other things, states the annual rate of interest being charged by the lender

12b-1 fee: a fee allowed by the Securities and Exchange Commission that pays for advertising charges and sales commissions paid to brokers and is deducted from the total assets of the fund

underwriting syndicate: a group of investment bankers who agree to underwrite a specific amount of a new issue

universal life policy: a high cash value policy developed by crediting the premium payments with a variable high market interest rate and by spreading the cost over the first ten years, with a penalty for early withdrawal

VA-guaranteed mortgage: a mortgage that is guaranteed by the Veterans Administration and extended to veterans only

value-added strategy: a principle stating that a real estate owner should add improvements to the property to justify raising rents

variable-rate mortgage: a mortgage that permits the lender to vary the interest rate of a loan during the term of the loan

voluntary plan: also known as a level charge account or an open account—a type of accumulation account that allows an investor to make subsequent purchases whenever he or she wants to do so

voting trust certificates: evidence that the common stockholders have placed their stock in the hands of a trustee, usually a bank, for a certain period of time because the corporation is in financial trouble

yield to maturity: bond interest that considers the nominal yield, market price, and time period during which the bond is held

INDEX